COLLINS P...

OFFICE
ORGANIZER

HarperCollins*Publishers*

HarperCollins*Publishers*
P.O. Box, Glasgow G4 0NB

Edited and typeset by Book Creation Services

First published 1995
Revised edition published 1998

Reprint 10 9 8 7 6 5 4 3 2 1 0

ISBN 0 00 472174 8

A catalogue record for this book is available from the British Library

Printed and bound in Great Britain by
Caledonian International Book Manufacturing Ltd, Glasgow G64

Contents

1
The Modern Business

2
Communicating on Paper

CONTENTS

7
Energetic Electronics
THE ELECTRONIC OFFICE

8
Buying and Selling
TRADING AND ACCOUNTING DOCUMENTS

9
Healthy, Safe and Secure   223
HEALTH AND SAFETY AT WORK

Introduction

The *Collins Office Handbook* is an easy-to-use reference book for the whole spectrum of those involved in office practice, from the post-room assistant, to the PA/secretary, and on into middle management, as well as those people working as sole traders, often at home. Those not permanently in work will also find the book useful because it gives advice on successful job-hunting and working as a temp.

The *Collins Office Handbook* combines information in quick-access formats such as tables, diagrams and A–Z listings of key terms, with more instructive passages that give advice and detailed information on such diverse subjects as letter-writing, employment law, company structure, finding staff, travelling abroad and effective work practices.

The book covers the basic skills, such as using the telephone and dealing with the mail, as well as the higher-level management skills such as effective interpersonal and written communications, producing reports and dealing with foreign clients and colleagues.

Special features include boxed information, drawing the user's attention to particularly useful tips, reminders and information, and Green Notes, ideas for those who are interested in keeping their office practice environmentally friendly.

Since almost all offices are now home to some kind of computer equipment, a whole chapter is devoted to office electronics, with an extended A–Z glossary defining the most common buzz words, information on the law as it relates to information systems and advice on how to plan a system and how to take care of it.

How to use this book

The *Collins Office Handbook* is packed with vital information. Efficiency being one of the watchwords of office working, this book has been carefully structured to help the user find the relevant information fast. However, if time permits, a random browse through its pages will also reveal a host of fascinating facts and useful tips.

The contents at the start of the book details the chapters, with their numbered sections and unnumbered sub-sections. Use it to locate the chapter most likely to deal with the subject needed.

The book is thoroughly cross-referenced throughout, so that the user can find extra information quickly. Cross-references appear in two forms; one refers to whole sections (e.g. '2.4 Memoranda' refers to the section of that name), and the other refers to sub-sections, and gives the page reference (e.g. 'Sole traders, p.3' refers to the sub-section to be found on that page). Many chapters contain Key Terms sections, which are A–Z listings of words connected with the subject of the chapter. Key Terms sections act as starting points for specific queries, either for quick definitions or to find cross-references to places where further information will be found.

Illustrations have reference numbers, which denote the section to which they refer. For example, illustration 2.3-1 is the first illustration to be included in section 2.3.

1
The Modern Business

1
The Modern Business

There are many different forms of business in the UK. Each is set up with the aim of making a profit (unless it is classed as a non-profit-making organization, of course) by providing either goods or services. Businesses can range from the single person who offers typing services to the multinational giants that have diversified into many different fields. All business activity is regulated by various laws, and all profits are taxable by the government.

It is usual to classify businesses into three broad categories:

- A business may belong to either the public or the private sector. Fundamentally, the distinction is in the ownership and control of the company. Companies in the private sector are owned and controlled by private individuals, whereas those in the public sector are in the control of the government.
- Companies may be classified according to what they do: they may be manufacturers (who produce goods), traders (who buy and sell goods) or service companies (who provide a service). Obviously, these classifications can become blurred, because many companies combine one or more of these functions.
- Companies may be classified according to who owns them and how this ownership is implemented. See 1.1.

Businesses can be constructed in a variety of ways, but most have a clear line of control from the shareholders through various levels of management, to the general workforce.

Understanding the way your company has been set up, and knowing about the chain of command, can help you fulfil your particular role more effectively, but it can also enable you to see what types of position you may aspire to in the future.

1.1 Business ownership in the UK

From the legal point of view, businesses are categorized according to their ownership. Each category of business is governed by specific legislation, and individual businesses are operated under the jurisdiction of the law. The major categories of ownership

2

are: sole traders; partnerships; limited liability companies; state-owned industries; and local authority organizations.

Sole traders

Sole traders are one-person bands. There are more sole traders than any other type of business in the UK. The individual is classed as being 'self-employed', and in the eyes of the law, the sole trader and his or her business are one and the same. In other words, their private affairs and their business affairs are not separated in the eyes of the law (or the Inland Revenue).

Sole traders have unlimited liability, which means that they are personally liable for all of the debts that they may incur.

They may employ various people from time to time – solicitors, accountants, bank managers, office staff, etc. – and on occasions sub-contract parts of their work to others. Sole traders often work from home. For advice on setting up an office at home, see 10.10, Working from home.

For information about keeping accounts and dealing with the Inland Revenue, see 8.6, Money matters for sole traders.

Partnerships

These are created when two or more people agree to go into partnership together with the aim of making a profit and sharing expenses. Common partnerships appear in the form of practices of GPs and dentists, where partners share the considerable expenses of setting up and staffing a surgery, and the benefit of larger lists of patients.

Partnerships can consist of up to 20 people. They may draw up a written agreement between them, or they may keep their partnership on a less-formal basis. Partnerships are governed by the Partnership Act 1890.

Like sole traders, partners have unlimited liability – if the company finds itself in debt, the partners must pay. Each individual is not only liable for his or her share of the debts, but also for the total debt of the business as a whole. So, if one of two partners fails to pay his or her portion of a debt, the other is liable for the whole. Again like sole traders, the private affairs of the partners are considered to be part of their business and they are not separated in the eyes of the law.

It is, however, possible to create a limited partnership, in which one partner takes unlimited responsibility for any debts, while all the other partners enjoy limited liability. In this case, the personal affairs of the limited liability partners are considered separate from the business of the partnership.

If one member of a partnership wishes to leave the business, then the partnership must be dissolved. At this point profits or debts are distributed among the partners as if the business were closing. In many cases, the partnership is almost immediately re-formed with the remaining partners. In the same way, if a partnership wishes to admit new members, the partnership is dissolved and reconstituted.

Limited liability companies

A company is created as a separate legal entity. That is, its affairs are completely separate from those of its owners. In limited liability companies, the owners put money into the company by buying shares. If the company runs into debt, then the owners stand to lose money up to a limit of the amount that they have invested. In this way, their liability is limited to the level of their investment. The money raised by selling shares is known as authorized share capital.

There are three different types of share, and each entitles a shareholder to certain rights: *preference shares* entitle a shareholder to claim a proportion of the profits before anyone else is paid; *voting shares* give a shareholder the right to vote on company policy at annual general meetings; and *ordinary shares* to claim dividends – a share of the annual profits (but not to vote). In this way, profits are divided up, and control of the company is assigned according to investment. New shares may be issued at any time so long as the shareholders have given their permission and the issue is carried out according to the regulations laid down in its Articles of Association (see below).

Companies are created in one of three ways: by Act of Parliament, by Royal Charter, and (the most-common method) by registration with the Registrar of Companies.

Registration involves lodging a number of documents with the Registrar of Companies, including the company's Memorandum of Association and Articles of Association.

Limited liability companies can be private (with Limited or Ltd after the company name), or public (with plc – public limited company – after the name). The question of whether a company is private or public is determined by the method by which shares are sold. If shares are sold only by agreement between the existing members of the company, then the company is private. Private limited companies must lodge a statement of accounts and some other information with the Registrar of Companies every year, but other information need not be made public in this way.

Public limited companies sell their shares to members of the general public. This may be done through the stock exchange (in which case the company is said to be 'quoted' or 'listed'), but this need not always be the case. Public companies are governed by a board of directors (see p.8). This board, headed by an elected chair, formulates policy on the shareholders' behalf and is responsible for seeing that the company is properly administered. The affairs of public companies are public.

Memorandum of Association

This document is drawn up when a company is formed, and lodged with the Registrar of Companies. It gives information about the external aspects of the company, including: the names of its directors; details of the share capital; the business the company intends to pursue.

Articles of Association

Also lodged with the Registrar of Companies, this document gives the company's internal regulations, e.g.: rules on how the board is to be elected; what kinds of shares are to be issued; rules on how the company is to be closed (known as 'winding up'); how the company is to go about borrowing money, keeping accounts, etc.

State-owned industries

It sometimes happens that the government decides to buy some or all of the companies in a certain industry, and to run them as one huge network. Such state industries in the UK include the Post Office and London Underground, and they are said to belong to the 'public sector'. The chair of such an industry is nominated by the government and the industry is subject to government control.

Co-operatives

These are set up with the aim of sharing profits, or saving money by buying in bulk. They may be formed by a group of individuals or a group of businesses. The major co-operatives in the UK are the Co-operative Wholesale Society (CWS) and its more familiar retailing fellows, the Retail Co-operative Societies. There are now also a number of workers' co-operatives.

Local authorities

These own and control businesses that supply utilities and services to the public in their region, much in the same way as state-owned industries. The 'board' is elected by the local population, and they in turn formulate policy and appoint paid people to run each 'business'. Like state-owned businesses, local authorities are said to belong to the 'public sector'.

Company legislation

Companies in the UK are governed by the following Acts of Parliament:

> Partnership Act, 1890
> Limited Partnerships Act, 1907
> Companies Act, 1981
> Companies (Beneficial Interests) Act, 1983

Copies of all of these Acts are available from HMSO (Her Majesty's Stationery Office). See Useful addresses, pp.115-116.

1.2 Company hierarchy

All companies are different in their structure and established hierarchy. This may depend upon what they have been created to produce, and also on the management style of their owners and managers. Indeed, some companies may not have any discernible hierarchy at all.

Illustration 1.2-1 shows a possible company hierarchy, suitable for a large company.

Shareholders

Shareholders are the owners of the company. The control they have over the company's affairs and operation depends on the kinds of shares and the number of shares they hold. The share-

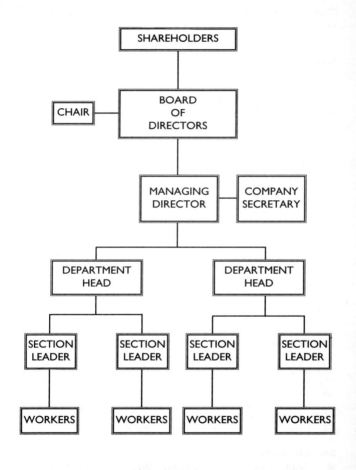

1.2-1 A typical company hierarchy.

holders meet every year at an annual general meeting (AGM). Here they elect a company chair and a board of directors, on the recommendation of the existing board.

Chair

The chair of a company may be full- or part-time. He or she is the person who presides over the board of directors, bringing, in general, a wide knowledge of the business world and company management. In many instances, the chair acts as a figurehead, speaking for the company at high-profile media events, for example.

Board of directors

The board of directors is a group of people who together discuss issues of policy and make high-level decisions. The board can be made up of a variety of people, not necessarily employed on a full-time basis by the company. The composition of the board, and those nominated to serve on it, is usually subject to the agreement of the shareholders.

Directors may be either 'non-executive' or 'executive'. Executive directors are usually full-time employees of the company, and they are most often high-ranking department heads (or 'vice-presidents'). They become members of the board simply by virtue of the post they hold, and so recruitment of such officers is a matter for board approval.

Non-executive directors are people who are asked to join the board in an advisory capacity. They may be business management specialists or experts in a field associated with the company's business. Alternatively, if a company receives considerable investment from another, it is often the case that a high-ranking person employed by the investing company is given a seat on the board of the company receiving investment.

Managing director

This is the person who is responsible for the day-to-day running of the company, and for ensuring that the decisions of the board are implemented. The managing director is almost always a member of the board, and as such, his or her appointment is often subject to the approval of the shareholders.

Company secretary

This is the person who is responsible for the company's running according to the law. He or she must ensure that the proper accounts are lodged, that meetings of the board and shareholders are called and run according to the Articles of Association (see p.5) and that the decisions of the shareholders and board are implemented. The company secretary has a professional qualification.

Department heads

Responsible for the working of their respective departments and for the interaction of the various departments. There may be many or a few separate departments, depending on the size of the company and its business. They could include: finance; personnel; sales and marketing; production; and research and development.

The position of department head may well bring with it the title of 'director' and a possibility of a seat on the board.

Section heads

If the departments are large enough, they may be split into sections, with the workers in each section reporting to a section head, who in turn reports to the head of department.

2
Communicating on Paper

2
Communicating on Paper

Since the earliest days of writing and paper-making, people have used the written word to communicate their commercial needs or describe their product. With the advent of long-distance trading across the length and breadth of continents, those involved in commerce have negotiated agreements and made many other arrangements on paper rather than by word of mouth.

Today, with an efficient transport system and sophisticated machinery for reproducing the written word, and, of course, the prevalence of literacy in many countries, it is no longer necessary to engage a scribe who can read and write, or a footsore messenger to carry letters and documents halfway across the known world.

The use of the written word has become paramount in business. This may seem an obvious point, but still, many people underestimate the necessity of learning to use words effectively and efficiently. Getting the ink onto the paper does not entail as much organization and relative expense as it once did, but even today, poorly written communications can cost time and money.

This section deals in detail with this basic skill, which is required of all office personnel, almost without exception. It begins by looking at some of the accepted rules of good English, and details some common errors, with advice on how to go about remedying them.

Letter-writing is the principal area in which the written word is used in business, and knowing how best to go about writing a formal business letter can go a long way towards proving (to some people) that you know what you are doing. The section on letter-writing includes the rules of composing, punctuating and laying out a formal letter.

There is a section on writing reports – a function in which several 'layers' of staff may become involved. It shows how to plan and organize an argument, how to use graphics and how to produce a well-composed, error-free document.

Finally, the section closes with a look at stationery and gives details of the information to be given on printed stationery, and the types and sizes of papers and paper products available.

First is a quick-access list of definitions of key terms to do with written English.

2.1 Key terms

Note: some words are highlighted in boldface. This means that you will find them defined in this list.

abbreviation
A shortened form of a word. Unlike a contraction (see below), an abbreviation does not always include the last letter of the original word. See also List of abbreviations, contractions and acronyms, pp.39–49.

accent
A mark, usually written above a letter to show how that letter should be said. The two most common accents occur in French: the acute accent – é, and the grave (pronounced graav) accent – à.

acronym
A word that has been made out of the initial letters of a title or phrase, for example, SERPS, UNICEF, NATO. See also List of abbreviations, contractions and acronyms, pp.39–49.

addressee
The person to whom a letter is addressed.

adjective
In grammar, an adjective is a word that describes an object or a person.

adverb
In grammar, an adverb is a word that describes an action.

article
In grammar, an article may be definite (e.g. 'the'), or it may be indefinite (e.g. 'a', 'an').

attention line
In a letter, a line written above the address, giving the name of the person for whose attention you are writing.

bc
Abbreviation of 'blind copies'. It is used at the bottom of the file copy of a letter to indicate that a copy has been made and sent to a third party without the knowledge of the addressee. See also Copies, p. 66.

boldface
Text enhancement possible with word-processing and computers. The letters that are in **boldface** appear to be much heavier than those that are in light (or

ordinary weight). In some dictionaries, as in this list, words highlighted in boldface indicate a cross-reference.

cc
Abbreviation, meaning 'copies' and used at the foot of a letter to indicate that copies have been made and sent to certain people other than the addressee. See also **bc**, and Copies, p. 66.

cedilla
A diacritical mark, often found in languages such as French and written under the letter c: ç. It shows that the letter is pronounced like an 's'. See also Common diacritical marks, p.55.

circumflex
A diacritical mark, often found in French for example, written over vowels: â, ê, î, ô, û. See also Common diacritical marks, p.55.

clause
In English grammar, a distinct part of a sentence, containing a verb. See also **definitive clause**; **subordinate clause**.

cliché
A phrase that is much used, and that has therefore become worn out and meaningless.

complimentary close
In a letter, the complimentary close is the form of words used to sign off. For example, Yours sincerely, or Yours faithfully. See Subscription, p.64.

confidential
The contents of a document marked confidential could be sensitive, and should only be disclosed to certain people. Some managers trust their administrative staff, and so allow them access to documents so-marked. See also **private**.

conjunction
In English grammar, a conjunction is a word that joins two parts of a sentence, e.g. 'and'.

continuation sheet
Second or further sheets of a letter. See also Continuation sheet, pp.66 and 95.

contraction
A word that has been shortened and still includes the first and last letters of the original word. For example, Mister = Mr, Mistress = Mrs. Contractions do not normally need a full stop at the end. See List of abbreviations, contractions and acronyms, p.39.

decoration
A medal or other state honour (e.g. a knighthood). In formal letters, decorations should be listed as a series of initials after a person's name. See Titles and forms of address, p.72–77.

definitive clause
A clause that defines the subject of a sentence. For example, in the sentence, 'the cat that sat on the mat was black', the subject is the cat, and the words that define the cat (the definitive clause) are 'that sat on the mat'.

designation
In a letter, the position of the writer, given below his or her typed name. See Designation, p.65.

diacritical mark
One of a number of marks used in some languages to show that the pronunciation of a letter is not as normal. Examples include accents and cedillas. There are no accents in standard English, but you may have to use them if you are writing to foreign countries, or when you are using words that have their basis in other languages. See Common diacritical marks, p.55.

enclosures
Any material other than the letter, which may be included in an envelope. The existence of enclosures is denoted by the use of the abbreviation 'Enc.' or 'Encs.' (the plural) at the foot of a letter. See Running order of a standard business letter, p.59.

enhancement
One of a number of ways in which to make letters or words stand out on the page. Familiar enhancements are: *italics*, **bold** and underlining.

footer
The margin at the bottom of the page, often used for footnotes or information that is the same for each page.

form letter
A standard letter that, with minor changes, can be used in a large number of similar situations; e.g., chasing payments or acknowledging receipt of something. See Form letters, p.66.

fully-blocked layout
A method of laying out a letter in which all lines start at the left-hand margin, and no indentation is used. See Layout, p.56.

grammar
The so-called 'science' of constructing sentences.

grave
When pronounced 'graav', a downward-slanting accent often found in languages such as French, e.g. à and è. See Common diacritical marks, p.55.

header
A margin at the top of a page, usually used for information that is the same from page to page (e.g. in a report, title, date, writer's name, etc.).

honour
A higher academic qualification or membership of a professional body. In formal letters, honours should be listed as abbreviations after the addressee's name. See Titles and forms of address, pp.72–77.

house style
Many companies have a set way of laying out and punctuating letters. Such a style is known as house style.

indented
Set a few spaces to the right of the left-hand margin. In most novels, for instance, the first lines of paragraphs are indented.

infinitive
The basic form of any **verb**: 'to say', 'to do', 'to run', 'to jump'. See Grammar , p.19, for notes on splitting the infinitive.

interjection
In English grammar, a word or phrase that is an exclamation, e.g. Stop! Interjections are always followed by exclamations marks (which should only be used for this purpose).

italics
Enhancement that makes the letters seem to slant forwards, *like this*.

justified text
A text layout in which all the lines are of the same length. This is done by varying the spaces between the words. See also **unjustified text**.

letterhead
Company information which appears on paper used for letter-writing. The word is also used to refer to the paper on which this information is printed.

logo
A design or symbol that represents a company. Logos (short for logotype) are normally commissioned from specialist designers, along with other items that together form the 'corporate identity'.

margin
Space left around the edges of a document. The left and right margins should be equal to each other if possible, unless one of them is to be used for notes or corrections, in which case it should, of course, be bigger.

memorandum
A short note to pass information between colleagues in the same company. See 2.4, Memoranda.

noun
In grammar, the name of a person or thing. In English, 'proper nouns' include the names of people, places and organizations, and so should normally have capital letters.

object
In a sentence, the word that denotes the person or thing to whom the verb is done. For example, in the sentence 'the cat chased the dog', the word 'dog' is the object of the verb 'chased'.

oblique stroke
A form of punctuation written /. It is often used to indicate two alternatives, (e.g. him/her), but in formal writing, the alternative should be spelled out ('him or her').

open punctuation
The style of punctuating a letter, which involves virtually no punctuation at all (except in the body of the letter, that is). See Punctuation of letters, p.59.

parenthesis
An aside, something put into the sentence as a kind of 'by the way'. A parenthesis may appear in brackets (sometimes called parentheses) and can work in much the same way as this sentence.

per procurationem (pp)
Sometimes the writer of a a letter may be unavailable to sign it. In such cases, the letter is often signed *per procurationem* (for and on behalf of), with the abbreviation 'pp' set against the signatory. See also Running order of a standard business letter, p.59.

plural
Two or more things. When the subject of a sentence is plural, the verb should be plural as well.

private
A private letter should only be opened by the addressee, because it is personal. In contrast, a letter that is confidential may well be opened by a secretary who has her manager's confidence.

pronoun
A word that can be put into a sentence as a substitute for a noun, such as 'he', 'she' and 'it'.

salutation
The opening phrase of a letter, usually, 'Dear Sir' or some variation of it. See the table on pp.72–77 for the various forms of salutation for people of different rank.

semi-blocked layout
A method of laying out a letter in which some indentations are used, e.g. at the start of paragraphs and for the complimentary close, etc. See Layout, p.56.

signatory
The typed name of the person signing a formal letter, usually placed after the signature. See Signatory, p.64.

signature
The handwritten form of a person's name.

singular
Only one. In sentences where the **subject** is singular, the **verb** should be singular as well. See Grammar, p.19.

standard punctuation
In a letter, full punctuation. See Punctuation, pp.21–26.

subject
In grammar, the subject of a sentence is the person or thing that is performing the action. For example, in the sentence, 'the cat chased the dog', the cat (unusually, perhaps) is the creature doing the chasing, and so 'cat' is the subject of the sentence. See also **object**.

subordinate clause
The part of a sentence that adds something to the information being given, but that is not crucial to its meaning. Subordinate clauses are often introduced with a comma and the word 'which'. For example, 'My briefcase, which is usually very heavy, is blue in colour'. The first meaning of the sentence is 'My briefcase is blue'. By taking away the subordinate clause, no vital information has been lost to make the sentence nonsensical.

subscription
An alternative term for **complimentary close**.

tilde
A diacritical mark, often found in Spanish, e.g. ñ. See also Common diacritical marks, p.55.

topping-and-tailing
In letter-writing, the practice of handwriting the salutation and complimentary close, to add a personal touch. See Topping and tailing, p.65.

umlaut
A diacritical mark, often found in German and Dutch, e.g. ä, ö, ü. See also Common diacritical marks, p.55.

unjustified text
In typesetting, a style of layout in which the lines are not all of the same length. The spaces between the words are constant, leading to a 'ragged' right-hand margin. See also **justified text**.

verb
In grammar, an active word such as chased, sat, eat, play or talk.

2.2 Written English

One of the most important skills for any office worker or business person is written English. Even if English is your first language, and you are capable of speaking it perfectly well, it does not follow that your formal written English is the same.

Good writing skills are important for two major reasons:

● Showing that you have a basic command of written English will lead, rightly or wrongly, to your clients and outside colleagues believing that you and your company are competent and professional.
● Being capable of delivering your message in an efficient manner avoids (potentially costly) confusion and saves time and trouble for everyone.

The following section looks at common errors in English grammar, punctuation and spelling, and provides instant reference for common abbreviations, foreign words and diacritical marks and accents.

Grammar

Good grammar and the use of plain English ensure that confusions do not arise.

Avoid splitting the infinitive

'To play', 'to write', 'to type', 'to see', 'to hold', 'to work': these are all infinitives. If you add a word between the two parts of the infinitive (usually an adverb), you are splitting it: 'to boldly go', 'to easily see', 'to quickly write'. Avoid splitting the infinitive wherever you can; rearrange the sentence if you have to: 'to go boldly', 'to see easily', 'to write quickly'.

Do not end a sentence with a preposition

A preposition is a word indicating position – on, up, in, to, from, with, etc. Avoid allowing this word to hang off the end of a sentence. 'Whom should I speak to?' is fine in spoken English, but in formal English, use 'To whom should I speak?'.

Neither is paired with nor, either with or

Imagine that you have a decision to make between two alternatives, and they are equally good. You would say, 'Take either one or the other'. But if neither fits the bill, you would say, 'Neither A nor B is right'.

The number of the verb equals the number of the subject

Always check that the verb makes sense with the subject of the sentence (i.e. the person doing the verb). If the subject is singular, so should be the verb. If it is plural, the verb should be too:

> Mr Jackson and his wife (they) are going to the annual dinner. (Plural subject, plural verb.)

Use the right pronoun

A pronoun is a word that stands in place of a noun (he, she, him, her, I, etc.). Make sure that you use the right type of pronoun.
For example:

Mrs Perkins and I (not 'me') are going out for lunch.

He carried the box. The person who carried the box was he (not 'him').

We (not 'us') earlybirds are productive in the mornings.

A subordinate clause must refer to the subject of the sentence.

A subordinate clause is a group of words that adds extra information to the sentence. The information that it adds, however, is not essential to the sentence, and could quite easily be removed without any change of sense. In the sentence below, the subordinate clause (the words before the comma at the start of the sentence) could be taken away without changing the sense of the sentence.

Walking the last stretch to work, she saw a man with a large dog.

It is the woman who is the subject of the sentence, and the subordinate clause refers to her, not to the man. If it is the man who is doing the walking to work, the sentence must be turned around in the following way:

She saw a man with a large dog walking the last stretch to work.

Punctuation

Punctuation is used to separate words into groups in order to make their meaning absolutely clear.

Full stop – .

Used to mark the end of a sentence.It is also used to show a shortened word where the abbreviation does not include the last letter of the original.

> etc. (full stop) = **etc**etera
> Mr (no full stop) = **M**iste**r**
> Dr (no full stop) = **D**octo**r**
> & Co. (full stop) = **and Co**mpany

See the List of contractions and abbreviations on p.39 for full details.

In the UK and the USA (where it is called a period), the full stop is also used to indicate a decimal point (e.g., 10.6). In some European countries, the decimal point is indicated with a comma.

Comma – ,

Used to separate one part of a sentence (a clause) from another.

> We are in agreement on most points, but there are a number of minor changes we would like to propose.

If the clause can be removed from the sentence without changing its main meaning, use two commas in a similar way to brackets, one before and one after the clause:

> Mr Jackson, our new marketing manager, will also be attending the meeting on Tuesday.

The clause separated by commas must relate to the subject of the sentence, in this case, Mr Jackson. Otherwise, brackets should be used (see below).

Commas are also used to separate the items in a list:

You will need to bring with you a notebook, a pen, the file and a copy of the agenda.

In English there is no comma before the word 'and' in a list. However, US punctuation often adds one in this position (this is called the 'serial comma').

Semi-colon – ;
Used to mark a pause that is not quite as long as a full stop. The two parts of a sentence separated by a semi-colon are normally linked in some way:

The reception area is run by our receptionist during office hours; the security guard takes over at 5.30pm.

It is also used to separate items in a list where a comma is not adequate (for example, when the items are complex enough to include commas of their own). When using a semi-colon for a list, it is normal to add a colon at the start:

Letters can be laid out in a number of ways: fully blocked, in which all the lines except the letterhead begin at the left-hand margin; semi-blocked, in which the first lines of paragraphs are indented; and indented, in which the recipient's address, all the paragraphs and the close are all indented.

Colon – :
Used in two ways: to mark the start of a list (as above, and in this sentence); and to separate two parts of a sentence where the second part is an illustration of the first part (as if you had written i.e.).

Apostrophe – '
Used to indicate the possessive:

This is Jennifer's desk.

Note: This desk is hers (no apostrophe). The same goes for 'his', 'theirs', 'its', 'ours' and 'yours', although one's does take an apostrophe.

When making a possessive from a noun that already has an 's' at the end (or sounds as if it does) you will need to decide whether to add an apostrophe and an 's', or whether simply to add an apostrophe. If the noun has only one syllable, add apostrophe 's'. If the noun has two or more syllables, only add an apostrophe:

Mr Jones's correspondence has been put in his in-tray.

The office is close to St James's Park.

Mrs Harris' correspondence has already been taken to the mail-room.

There are some exceptions to this rule. They include biblical and Greek names (Archimedes' principle, for example), and phrases containing the word 'sake' ('for heavens' sake', 'for conscience' sake', etc.). If you are unsure what to do with the apostrophe, try turning the sentence around to avoid the problem altogether:

Isis' Temple = the Temple of Isis

for appearance' sake = for the sake of appearance

The apostrophe is also used to show that one or more letters have been omitted from a word:

isn't = is not	couldn't = could not
aren't = are not	can't = cannot
wouldn't = would not	shouldn't = should not
mustn't = must not	it's = it is

This use of the apostrophe is conversational, and it should be avoided in formal writing.

Inverted commas – '...' or "..."
Single inverted commas are used to show that a word or phrase is being used to mean something slightly different to the usual

meaning, and to indicate new coinages or slang words. Use inverted commas where you might otherwise use 'so-called'.

He erects his cardboard 'tent' every night on The Strand.

More and more advertisers are following the American lead and including 'knocking copy' in their advertising.

Inverted commas are also used to show that the spoken or written word is being quoted.

She said, 'Working with such an efficient organization has been a pleasure and an education'.

The quotation in the above example is only one part of the sentence, and so the full stop should be placed outside (not inside) the quotation marks. In the example below, the quotation is the whole sentence, and therefore the full stop is placed inside the quotation marks:

'Working with such an efficient organization has been a pleasure and an education.'

If you need to indicate a quote within a quote, use single inverted commas followed by double inverted commas (quotation marks). Make sure that each pair of marks is 'closed' in the correct place:

She said, 'I have always wondered who coined the phrase "the little gnomes of Zurich".'

Note in this instance, the position of the full stop.

Exclamation mark – !
Used in place of a full point to mark a sharp command or an exclamation (both known as interjections). Many people now use the exclamation mark to add excitement to a simple statement, or to punctuate a joke, but this should be avoided – as Oscar Wilde is said to have commented, using an exclamation mark in this context is tantamount to laughing at your own joke.

Question mark (also called a query) – ?
Used in place of a full point at the end of a question.

Brackets (also called parentheses) – (...) or [...]
Round brackets are used to add abbreviations, extra information, definitions or illustrative material, for example:

British Broadcasting Corporation (BBC)

London Weekend Television (LWT)

The meeting at our office (which you will find located on the first floor of the Speedwell Building) will be attended by the managing director.

Use round brackets also to indicate numbers or letters used to enumerate entries on a list:

We will need to (a) survey the market, (b) analyse our costs and (c) set a price.

Square brackets are used to indicate a parenthesis within a parenthesis, in the same way as double inverted commas are used to show a quote within a quote. There are specialized uses of square brackets in some fields (e.g. law and mathematical sciences).
When using brackets, always check that they have been closed in the right place.

Dash: — or –
An informal method of indicating part of a sentence in parenthesis, in a similar way to a pair of commas or brackets. It is said to be equivalent to a pause that is a little longer than a comma and a little shorter than a semi-colon. Try to avoid this in formal English. A dash should have a single space on either side of it. Most computers distinguish between dashes and hyphens (see below), the dash being the same width as the letter 'm' (called an em dash) or the letter 'n' (called an en dash). A hyphen is slightly smaller than an en dash.

Hyphen: -
Used to show that a word has been 'broken' at the end of a line, and to separate suffixes from proper nouns where the word would otherwise be unclear:

recreation = leisure, play	re-creation = to create again
recover = to get well	re-cover = to cover again
reform = to improve	re-form = to form anew

The *Collins Gem Spelling and Word Division* is a very useful pocket reference for checking hyphenation and word breaks.

Capital letters

Capitals are used to identify the start of every sentence, and in several other instances: at the start of proper nouns (names of people, places, organizations, etc.); for the titles of things (books, plays, magazines, newspapers, etc.); in some abbreviations (always in acronyms, see pp.39–49); for the word 'I'; for important words connected with religion – God (when referring to the one God, but not when referring to another god, the Church (meaning the movement, not the building which is a church), the Bible, the Qur'an, Allah, Shiva, etc.

Spelling

However well-qualified or experienced people may be, many are let down by their spelling. Poor spelling gives a bad impression – rightly or wrongly, people believe that if a person cannot spell, he or she cannot be good at the job or is too slapdash to be trustworthy. Sometimes this prejudice extends from the individual to besmirch the whole company.

Most computer word-processing programs include a spell-check system which can be used to check documents for errors. However, such systems are not infallible, and relying on them can lead to howling errors (especially where you may have spelled a 'real' word, but with the wrong meaning, e.g. wear and where). Also, bear in mind that some spell-checks are programmed with American-English. Regardless of the technology you have at your fingertips, learning to eradicate spelling errors from your written English is well worthwhile.

LIST OF COMMONLY MISSPELLED WORDS

Spelling errors fall into three categories: confusions, in which one word is confused with another (perhaps because it sounds the same, e.g. there and their); misuses; and straight misspellings. The following list gives some words that are commonly misspelled in their correct form:

absorb, absorption
acknowledge, acknowledgement
accept = to receive
   except = to make an exception
accidentally
accommodate/accommodation
achieve, achievement
acquaintance
acquire, acquisition
address, addressing, addressee
adequate
adverse = bad
   averse = does not like
advertise, advertisement
aeroplane (airplane is US spelling)
affect (verb) to influence
   effect = (noun) result
agree, agreeing, agreeable
aggression
allot, allotted, allotment
allowed = permitted
   aloud = capable of being heard
all right (not 'alright')
aloud (see allowed)
alternately = one after the other
   alternative = another option
amateur
among
analyse, analysis (singular), analyses (plural)
anonymous
anti = against
   ante = before, as in antenatal

anxious, anxiety
apparent
appear, appearance
appropriate
arctic
argue, arguing, argument
assure (see insure)
atmosphere
attach, attached
awful, awfully
averse (see adverse)
bachelor
beautiful, beautifully
believe
benefit, benefited
breathe
business = a firm
    busyness = being busy
busy
canvas = cloth
    canvass = to survey opinion, seek votes
careful, carefully
cereal (see serial)
character, characteristically
colour
commit, committed, committee, commitment
comparative, comparatively
complete, completely
complement = something that completes
    compliment = to praise
conceive, conceivable
conscientious
conscious
contemporary = happening at the same time
    modern = happening now
council = group of people who organize things (councillor)
    counsel = advice (counsellor)

curriculum vitae (singular)
  curricula vitae (plural)
damage, damaged, damaging
decease (see disease)
deceive, deceit
decide, decided, decision
defence, defensive
definite, definitely
dependent = influenced by
  dependant = a person who depends on someone/something
descend, descendant
desert = arid place
  dessert = pudding
desperate, desperately
dessert (see desert)
detach, detached
deteriorate
develop, developed, development
device = a machine
  devise = to plan
diamond
diary, diaries
diesel
diner = a person who eats dinner
  dinner = a meal
disappear, disappeared, disappearance
disappoint, disappointment
disaster, disastrous
discipline
disease = illness
  decease = die
dissatisfied
disservice
dissuade
doubt
draft = plan, first try
  draught = mouthful, breeze
draught (see draft)

draw = make a picture
    drawer = part of a cupboard
drawer (see draw)
dual = double
    duel = fight
due, duly
duel (see dual)
effect (see affect)
eight, eighth
elicit = to draw out
    illicit = illegal, secret
eligible (see illegible)
embarrass, embarrassment
emigrant = someone leaving the country
    immigrant = someone coming into the country
eminent = famous
    imminent = immediate
    immanent = inherent
enquire = to ask
    inquire = to investigate
ensure (see insure)
except (see accept)
excite, exciting, excitement
exercise
exhibition
exhilarating
expense, expensive, expensively
faint = to be weak, to lose consciousness
    feint = distracting movement, faint lines
faithful, faithfully
February
finish, finished, finishing
foreign
forty
forward = in front
    foreword = preface
fourteen
fuel, fuelling

fulfil, fulfilled, fulfilment
grief, grievous, grievance
guarantee, guaranteed, guaranteeing
guide, guidance
half, halves
happen, happened
height
hear = e.g. to hear a sound
   here = opposite of there
heir = beneficiary of a will
hole (see whole)
honest, honestly
humour, humorous
hygiene
identical, identically
illegal, illegally
illegible = cannot be read
   eligible = fit to be chosen
illicit (see elicit)
illiterate, illiteracy
immanent (see eminent)
immediate, immediately
immense, immensely
immigrant (see emigrant)
imminent (see eminent)
inadequate
incidentally
independent
indispensable
inoculate
inquire (see enquire)
install, instalment
insure = to protect against
   assure = to give assurance
   ensure = to make sure
irregular, irregularity
it's = it is
   its = belonging to it

jeopardy
knew = was aware of
   new = novel, fresh
know = to be aware of
   no = negative
knowledge, knowledgeable
label, labelled
language
lead (see led)
leant (see loan)
led = past tense of to lead
   lead = present tense
leisure
lend (see loan)
lent (see loan)
liaise, liaison
library
like = to enjoy
   such as = for example
likelihood
livelihood
loan = a payment
   lend = to make a payment
   lent = made a payment
   leant = past tense of to lean
loose (see lose)
lose = to misplace
   loose = untied, not fitted
maintain, maintenance
manage, manager, management
manoeuvre
marry, marrying, marriage, married
maybe = perhaps
   may be = (it) may happen
messenger
meter = machine for measuring
   metre = 100 centimetres
minute = very small, 60 seconds

miscellaneous
necessary
new (see knew)
no (see know)
occur, occurred, occurring, occurrence
of = belonging to
   off = away from
parliament, parliamentary
passed = passed by
   past = before
past (see passed)
partial = biased
   part = a section
peace = opposite of war
   piece = a section
peculiar, peculiarly
permit, permitted, permission, permissable
personal = private
   personnel = staff
phenomenon (singular), phenomena (plural)
physical, physically
piano, pianos
picture = drawing
   pitcher = jug
piece (see peace)
pitcher (see picture)
pleasant, pleasure
possess, possession
potato, potatoes
practice = (noun) custom
   practise = (verb) to rehearse
precede = to go before
   proceed = to move on
predecessor
   pre-decease (die before)
prepare, preparation
previous
primary, primarily

principle = rule
   principal = chief
proceed, procedure
profession, professional, professionally
pronunciation
public, publicly
pursue, pursuing, pursuit
quality
rain = precipitation
   rein = lead for a horse
   reign = to rule
real, really
receive, receipt
recommend
reconnaissance
refer, referring, reference
regret, regretted
rein (see rain)
reign (see rain)
relevant
retrieve
review = look over again
   revue = cabaret show
revue (see review)
rhythm
ridicule, ridiculous
right = correct, opposite to left
   rite = ritual
   write = to make words
roof, roofs, roofing
route = means of getting somewhere
   rout = retreat
routine
said
satisfied, dissatisfied
scarce, scarcity, scarcely
science, scientific, scientifically
scissors

seam (see seem)
secret, secrecy
secretary
seem = appearance
   seam = line of stitching
sentence
separate, separation
serial = story told in parts
   cereal = foodstuff e.g. wheat
service, servicing, serviceable
severe, severely
shelf, shelves
similar, similarity, similarly
sincere, sincerely, sincerity
skill, skilful, skilfully
so = as a result, like that
   sew = stitch
solicitor
special, specially
speech
stationery = (envelopes, etc.)
   stationary = not moving
statistics, statistically
storey (see story)
story = tale
   storey = floor of a building
straight, straighten
succeed, success, successful, successfully
such as (see like)
sudden, suddenness
supersede (not supercede)
supervise, supervisor
surprise
syllabus
tariff
technique, technical, technically
temperature
temporary, temporarily

their (see there)
there = opposite of here
    their = belonging to them
    they're = they are
    there's = there is
    theirs (belonging to them)
through = the way between
    thorough = in depth
tire (see tyre)
to = towards, or e.g. to do
    too = excessive
    two = 1 + 1
tobacco
tomato, tomatoes
tomorrow
traffic
truth, truly, truthfully
twelve, twelfth
two (see to)
typical
tyre = rubber cushion on a wheel
    tire = become fatigued
underrate
unnatural
unnecessary
until
usual, usually
vaccinate
valuable
various, variety
vehicle
view
visit, visited, visitor
waist (see waste)
waive = not claim
    wave = sea swell
waste = misuse, rubbish
    waist = middle
...ve (see waive)
... (see where)

weather = rain, sunshine, etc.
   whether = if
Wednesday
weigh, weight
welcome
where = in what place
   wear = e.g. to wear clothes, to wear out
whether (see weather)
whole = complete
   hole = cavity
whose = belonging to whom
   who's = who is
wise, wisely, wisdom
withhold
woman, women
write (see right)
yield
your = belonging to you
   you're = you are

Six ways to improve your spelling

- Read as much as you can.
- When you have time, slow down your reading speed, say the words under your breath, looking at how they are spelled.
- Make a list of words you frequently misspell, put the list somewhere prominent and read through it as often as possible.
- Ask a friend to give you exercises in dictation (or read from a book onto a tape recorder). Check what you have done, write down and learn the correct spellings of the words you have got wrong.
- Always read through documents you have written, even if they have already been checked by computer. Ensure that your word-processing software is set in the correct 'language'; i.e., American English or UK English, depending on your needs.
- Always check words of which you are unsure in a dictionary, or you may like to invest in a spelling dictionary (there are several good ones on the market).

Using a thesaurus

The words 'thesaurus' means 'treasury', and *Roget's Thesaurus* is by far the best known of such treasure-troves. A thesaurus is a book of words, grouped together with their synonyms and accessed through an index. Using a thesaurus is simple, and it is invaluable in finding that word on the tip of your tongue, or providing you with an alternative for an over-used workhorse of a word that seems to crop up in every one of your sentences.

● Think of the word for which you need a synonym.
● Look up that word in the index at the back of the thesaurus. You will find a list of different meanings for the word you are looking to replace, and it is up to you to decide which meaning you want.
● When you have decided on a particular meaning, you will see a reference. The reference is not a page number, but a section number, followed by a part of speech (noun, verb, adjective, etc.).
● Find the paragraph that relates to your reference in the front half of the book, and it should give you some synonyms from which to choose.

For example, look up the word 'book'. The index shows two meanings: book and account. The meaning of account is chosen, and the reference given is 808vb, showing that the reference will lead to a list of verbs meaning roughly the same as 'to account'. 808vb leads to a section at the start of the book, headed 'Accounts', and giving nouns and adjectives as well as verbs, so there is plenty to choose from.

Most word-processing software has a thesaurus utility, which can be helpful when composing on-screen. These can, however, be slightly unreliable, particularly if you are unsure of the meanings of all the words, so ensure that you check any possible synonyms in a dictionary before replacing a word.

ABBREVIATING UNITS OF MEASUREMENT

Most units of measurement are abbreviated, but even if there is more than one (say, centimetre), they are never made plural (2 cm, not 2 cms).

LIST OF COMMON ABBREVIATIONS

Abbreviations are words that have been shortened. They are usually indicated with a full stop at the end. Contractions are words that have been shortened and that include the first and last letters of the original. Contractions do not normally need a full stop. Initials are sometimes used as abbreviations, especially for the names of organizations and academic qualifications. Such initials sometimes have full stops, and sometimes not. However, modern usage is leaning towards leaving out full stops. Where the initials spell a word, it is called an acronym, and the letters never take full stops.

For abbreviations of the names of UK counties, see p.78. For the abbreviations of the names of US states and their ZIP codes, see p.79.

AA = Alcoholics Anonymous, Automobile Association
a/c = account
ACAS = The Advisory, Conciliation and Arbitration Service
ACT = Advance Corporation Tax
AD = *anno Domini* (after Christ)
ad lib = *ad libitum* (at leisure)
ADP = automatic data processing
ad val. = *ad valorem* (according to value)
AG = Aktiengesellschaft (German public company)
AGM = annual general meeting
AH = *anno Hegirae* (the Muslim era, similar to the Christian AD)
AI = artificial intelligence
a.k.a. or AKA = also known as
a.m. or am = *ante meridiem* ('before noon')
AOB = any other business
a/p = accounts payable
appx = appendix
APR = annual percentage rate
ASA = Advertising Standards Authority
assoc. = association/associate(d)
a.v. or A/V = *ad valorem* (according to value)
av. = average
Ave. = avenue
b. = born (birthdate)
BA = Bachelor of Arts

BAA = British Airports Authority
bal. = balance
BBC = British Broadcasting Corporation
BC = before Christ
bc = blind copies
BCL = Bachelor of Civil Law
b/d = brought down
BD = Bachelor of Divinity
b.e. or BE = bill of exchange
B/F or b/f = brought forward
bk = bank or book
bkcy = bankruptcy
bkpt = bankrupt
B/L, b/l or b.l. = bill of lading
BL = Bachelor of Law/Letters
BM = Bachelor of Medicine (Oxford)
BMA = British Medical Association
BMus = Bachelor of Music
b.o. = back order; branch office; buyer's option
B/O = brought over
BOTB = British Overseas Trade Board
B/P or bp = bills payable
BPhil = Bachelor of Philosophy
B/R or br = bills receivable
b rec = bills receivable
BRS = British Road Services
bs = balance sheet, bill of sale (also B/S or b/s)
BSc = Bachelor of Science
BSI = British Standards Institution
BST = British Summer Time
BTG = British Technology Group
C = Celsius
c. = *circa* (roughly this date)
C/A = capital account; credit account; current account
CA = chartered accountant
CAB = Citizens' Advice Bureau
CACM = Central American Common Market

CADCAM = computer-aided design, computer-aided manufacture
CADMAT = computer-aided design, manufacture and test
C & D = collection and delivery
C & F = cost and freight
cap = capital
CAP = Common Agricultural Policy
CARICOM = Caribbean Community and Common Market
CB = cash book
CBD = cash before delivery
CBI = Confederation of British Industry
cc = copies
CC = county council
CCT = Common Customs Tariff
CCTV = closed circuit television
C/D = certificate of deposit
cd = carried down
cd fwd = carried forward
CEO = chief executive officer
c/f = carried forward
cf = carried forward
cf. = *confer* (compare)
CGT = capital gains tax
chq = cheque
cif = cost, insurance and freight
cifi = cost, insurance, freight and interest
CIM = computer-integrated manufacture
Cllr = Councillor
cm = centimetre
C/N = cover note, consignment note, credit note
c/o = cash order, care of, carried over
Co. = company
COD = cash on delivery
COH = cash on hand
COI = Central Office of Information
COM = computer output on microfilm
COMECOM = Council for Mutual Economic Assistance
comm = commission
Comr = Commissioner

contd = continued
COREPER = Committee of Permanent Representatives
Corpn = corporation
cpd = compound
cps = characters per second
CPU = central processing unit
cr = credit
CRE = Commission for Racial Equality
CRS = Co-operative Retail Society
CSO = Central Statistical Office
CT = corporation tax, credit transfer
cum = cumulative
cum div = with dividend
cum pref = cummulative preference shares
CV = curriculum vitae
CWO = cash with order
CWS = Co-operative Wholesale Society
cwt = hundredweight
d. = died (death date)
DCL = Doctor of Civil Law
dd = direct debit
DD = Doctor of Divinity
deb = debenture
def = deferred
DES = Department of Education and Science
disc = discount
div = dividend
DM = Deutschmark
D/N = debit note
do = ditto, the same as previously
DOE = Department of the Environment
dos = disk operating system
DP = data processing
DPhil = Doctor of Philosophy (Oxford)
dr = debtor
Dr = doctor
dsp = *decessit sine prole* ('died without issue')
DTI = Department of Trade and Industry

DTP = desktop publishing
E & OE = errors and omissions excepted
EC = European Community
ECGD = Export Credit Guarantee Department
ECOWAS = Economic Community of West African States
ECS = *échantillons commerciaux* ('commercial samples')
ECU = European Currency Unit
EDP = electronic data processing
EEC = European Economic Community
e.g. = *exempli gratia* ('for example')
EFT = electronic funds transfer
EFTA = European Free Trade Association
EFTPOS = electronic funds transfer at point of sale
EGM = extraordinary general meeting
enc(s) = enclosure(s)
EPOS = electronic point of sale
ERDF = European Regional Development Fund
ERM = (European) Exchange Rate Mechanism
ESOPS = Employee Share Ownership Plans
et al = *et alia* ('and others')
etc. = *et cetera* ('and so on')
et seq = *et sequens* ('and following') ·
EU = European Union
ex div = without dividend
ex off = *ex officio* ('by virtue of office')
F = fahrenheit
fac = facsimile
fas = free alongside ship
fax = facsimile
FCA = Fellow of the Institute of Chartered Accountants
ff = following
ffy = faithfully
fig. = figure (reference to an illustration)
fl. = flourished (date when a person was working)
fob = free on board
foc = free of carriage
FOREX = foreign exchange
FPS = Fellow of the Pharmaceutical Society
Fr = franc

FRCP = Fellow of the Royal College of Physicians
FRCS = Fellow of the Royal College of Surgeons
FRIBA = Fellow of the Royal Institute of British Architects
FT = Financial Times
ft = feet (length)
GDP = gross domestic product
GIGO = garbage in, garbage out
gm = gramme (weight)
GmbH = *Gesellschaft mit beschrankter Haftung* (German limited company)
GMT = Greenwich Mean Time
GNP = gross national product
GP = general practitioner
gsm = grams per square metre
HC = House of Commons
HL = House of Lords
HMC = Her Majesty's Customs
HMSO = Her Majesty's Stationery Office
HO = Home Office
Ho. = house
HP = hire purchase
HRH = His/Her Royal Highness
hrs = hours
ibid. = *ibidem* ('in the same place')
IBM = International Business Machines
i.e. = *id est* ('that is')
IMF = International Monetary Fund
Inc = incorporated
incl = including
info = information
inst = of this month
int = interest
int al = *inter alia* ('among others')
IT = information technology
ital = italic
JP = Justice of the Peace
Kb = kilobyte
kg = kilogram (weight)
km = kilometres (length)

l = litre (volume)
LAFTA = Latin American Free Trade Association
lb = pounds (weight)
L/C = letter of credit
l.c. = lower case letters
LGS = Loan Guarantee Scheme
Ltd = limited
m = metres (length)
MA = Master of Arts
MAFF = Ministry of Agriculture, Fisheries and Food
max = maximum
MB = Bachelor of Medicine
Mb = megabyte
MBA = Master of Business Administration
MBChB = Bachelor of Medicine and Chirurgery
MBE = Member of the Order of the British Empire
MC = master of ceremonies
MCom = Master of Commerce
MD = managing director
MD = Doctor of Medicine (from Latin *Medicinae Doctor*)
memo = memorandum
MEP = Member of the European Parliament
mfg = manufacturing
mfr = manufacturer
mg = milligram (weight)
Mgr = Monseigneur
mgr = manager
MICR = magnetic ink character recognition
min = minute
misc = miscellaneous
MLitt = Master of Letters
mm = millimetre (length)
MMC = Monopolies and Mergers Commission
MOD = Ministry of Defence
MORI = Market and Opinion Research International
MP = Member of Parliament
mpg = miles per gallon
mph = miles per hour

Mr = Mister
MRCP = Member of the Royal College of Physicians
MRCVS = Member of the Royal College of Veterinary Surgeons
Mrs = Mistress
Ms = woman whose status is not known/given
MS = manuscript
msc = moved, seconded and carried
MSc = Master of Science
mtg = meeting
N/A = not applicable, no advice
NATO = North Atlantic Treaty Organization
NB = *nota bene* ('take note')
NCR = no carbon required
nd = not date
necy = necessary
NGO = non-governmental organization
NHS = National Health Service
NI = National Insurance
NIC = Newly Industrialized Country
NIS = not in stock
NL = no liability (Australian limited company)
np = new paragraph
NPO = non-profit-making organization
NV = *Naamloze Venootschap* (Dutch Plc equivalent)
o/a = on account
ob = *obiit* ('deceased')
O/D = overdraft, on demand
OFGAS = Office of Gas Supply
OFT = Office of Fair Trading
OFTEL = Office of Telecommunications
OGM = ordinary general meeting
OHP = overhead projector
o/o/o = out of order
oos = out of stock
OPEC = Organization of Petroleum Exporting Countries
OR = Official Receiver
o/s = outstanding

OTE = on-target earnings
oz = ounces (weight)
p. = page (pages = pp.)
p.a. = per annum ('every year')
PA = personal assistant
P&L = profit and loss
p&p = postage and packing
para = paragraph
PAYE = pay as you earn
PC = Privy Councillor
PC = personal computer
Pc = Police Constable
pcm = per calendar month
pd = paid
p/d = post dated
pft = profit
PhD = Doctor of Philosophy
PIN = personal identification number
Plc = public limited company
PPI = printed postage impression
PO = postal order, or post office
pqe = post qualification experience
p.m. or pm = *post meridiem* ('after noon')
pp. = pages
pp = *per procurationem* ('for and on behalf of')
prelim = preliminary
Prof. = professor
pro tem = *pro tempore* ('for the time being')
PS = postscript (plural is PPS)
Pta = peseta
PTO = please turn over
QANTAS = Queensland and Northern Territory Aerial Services Ltd
    (Australian airline)
QB = Queen's Bench
QC = Queen's Counsel
QED = *quod erat demonstrandum* ('which was to be proved')
QUANGO = quasi-autonomous non-governmental organization
qv = *quod vide* ('which see', 'refer to')

qy = query
RAM = random access memory
R&D = research and development
re = with reference to
rcd = received
R/D = refer to drawer
ref = refer to
reqn = requisition
Rev = Reverend
RIP = rest in peace
ROM = read only memory
RPI = Retail Price Index
RSVP = *répondez s'il vous plaît*
Rt Hon = Right Honourable
SA = *société anonyme*
sae = stamped addressed envelope
SAYE = save as you earn
sec = second (unit of time)
S/N = shipping note
SO = standing order
SPQR = small profits, quick returns
Sq. = square (unit of measurement)
SRL = *société responsibilité limité*
St = saint, street
STD = subscriber trunk dialling
std = standard
stet = let stand (leave uncorrected)
tba = to be advised
tbc = to be confirmed
to = turn over
TOPS = Training Opportunities
tsvp = *tournez s'il vous plaît* ('turn over')
TUC = Trades Union Congress
TWI = training within industry
UAE = United Arab Emirates
UK = United Kingdom
u.c. = upper case letters (capitals)
ult = *ultimo* ('last')

UNO = United Nations Organization
USA = United States of America
v = *versus* ('against')
VAT = value added tax
VDU = visual display unit
viz = namely
vs = versus
waf = with all faults
WEDA = Women's Enterprise Development Agency
WHO = World Health Organization
WP = word processing
wpm = words per minute
x-cp = ex (without) coupon
x-div = ex (without) dividend
x-i = ex (without) interest
x-r = ex (without) rights
yd = yard (length)
yf = yours faithfully
ys = yours sincerely

Foreign words and phrases

The English language has for centuries been influenced by foreign languages, such as Greek, Latin and French. Some of these words are still used (or misused) in everyday writing and speaking, and many have important technical meanings, especially in the fields of law and finance. Unless you are using such words in such a technical context, it is better to find English equivalents. This avoids confusion and reduces the possibility of your using the wrong phrase in error.

LIST OF FOREIGN WORDS AND PHRASES

The following list gives some foreign words and phrases you may come across, along with the language they come from, their meanings, and common abbreviations. Unless foreign words and phrases have been accepted as part of the English language (e.g. café), they are usually indicated with *italics*, as here. Check with the *Collins English Dictionary*, which should tell you whether or not to use italics.

Origins: L = Latin F = French Gk = Greek Sp = Spanish

ab extra (L) = from the outside
ab initio (L) = from the start
addendum (L) = something to be added
à deux (F) = for two
ad hoc (L) = for a special purpose
ad infinitum (L) = without end
ad initium (L) (abbr. *ad init.*) = at the start
ad interim (L) = for the meantime
ad libitum (L) (abbr. ad lib) = to the desired extent, improvised
ad nauseam (L) = to a disgusting extent
ad rem (L) = to the point
ad valorem (L) (abbr. ad val.) = in proportion to the value of the goods
aficionado (Sp) = an enthusiast
a fortiori (L) = for similar but more convincing reasons
agent provocateur (F) = person who lures people to commit an offence
aide-mémoire (F) = reminder
à la (F) = in the style of
à la mode (F) = in fashion

---

amour-propre (F) = self-respect
a posteriori (L) = reasoning inductively from effect to cause
a priori (L) = reasoning deductively from cause to effect
au fait (F) = conversant
au fond (F) = at bottom
avant-garde (F) = radical, daring
beau geste (F) = magnanimous display
beau monde (F) = the world of fashion
belles-lettres (F) = literary writing
bête noire (F) = personal pet hate
bis (L) (in references to other sources) = found in two places
bona fide (L) = genuine
bonhomie (F) = good natured, exuberant friendliness
bon mot (F) = witticism
bon vivant (F) = a person who enjoys luxuries, especially food
carte blanche (F) = free hand, power to decide
cause célèbre (F) = a legal battle that excites popular interest
caveat (L) = beware
caveat emptor (L) = buyer beware
ceteris paribus (L) = all other things being equal
chef-d'oeuvre (F) = master work
circa (L) (abbr. c.).) = approximately
comme il faut (F) = as it should be
contretemps (F) = embarrassing or unlucky incident
coup d'état (F) = violent uprising or change of government
coup de grâce (F) = the fatal blow
coup de main (F) = sudden attack
cui bono (L) = who profits by this?
curriculum vitae (L) = account of one's career
debacle (F) = a disastrous defeat or downfall
de facto (L) = in fact
Dei gratia (L) = by the grace of God
de jure (L) = according to law, by right
de novo (L) = anew, once more
Deo volente (L) = God willing
de rigueur (L) = required by etiquette
détente (F) = relaxing of previously strained diplomatic relations
de trop (F) = superfluous, unwanted

distingué (F) = distinguished
distrait (F) = inattentive
double entendre (F) = phrase capable of two interpretations
douceur (F) = bribe
dramatis personae (F) = characters in a play, the people involved
éclat (F) = brilliant or conspicuous success
élan (F) = style and vigour
élite (F) = the best
émigré (F) = emigrant, refugee
en bloc (F) = in one lump
enfant terrible (F) = someone who behaves unconventionally
en masse (F) = as a whole; all together
en rapport (F) = in sympathy with
en route (F) = on the way to
entente cordiale (F) = an understanding (esp. between two nations)
entourage (F) = a group of attendants or retainers
entrepreneur (F) = innovator or organizer
ergo (L) = therefore, hence
erratum (L) = error, mistake
et alia (L) (abbr. et al.) = and others
ex gratia (L) = given as a favour or gratuitously
ex officio (L) = by virtue of one's office or position
ex parte (L) = on behalf of one side
ex post facto (L) = acting after the fact, retrospectively
fait accompli (F) = a thing already accomplished
faux pas (F) = false step, indiscretion
force majeur (F) = irresistible force
gratis (F) = free of charge
haute couture (F) = high fashion
hoi polloi (Gk) = the masses
ibidem (L) (abbr. ibid. or ib.) = in the same place (reference source)
idem (L) = the same (in references, the same author, or the same book, etc.)
id est (L) (abbr. i.e.) = that is
imprimis (L) = in the first place
in absentia (L) = in his/her absence
in camera (L) (legal) = in private, not in open court
in extremis (L) = in extreme circumstances

in flagrante delicto (L) = in the act of committing an offence
infra (L) = further on (in the book)
in memoriam (L) = in memory of
in situ (L) = in the natural, appropriate place
inter alia (L) = among other things
in toto (L) = entirely
ipse dixit (L) = arbitrary, unsupported assertion
ipso facto (L) = by that very fact or act
laissez faire (F) = freedom from interference (esp. from regulation)
lapsus linguae (L) = slip of the tongue
loco citato (L) (abbr. loc. cit. or lc) = in the place already cited above
métier (F) = a profession or trade; a person's speciality
modus operandi (L) = method of working
modus vivendi (L) = practical compromise
mot juste (F) = the right word for the context
mutatis mutandis (L) = the necessary changes having been made
née (F) = born, indicates a woman's maiden name
nolens volens (L) = whether willing or not
nom de plume (F) = pen name
non compos mentis (L) = of unsound mind; incapable of managing one's
    affairs
non sequiteur (L) (abbr. non seq.) = an argument that does not follow in
    a logical sequence
opere citato (L) (abbr. *op. cit.*) = in the work just quoted
outré (F) = outrageous
pace (L) = with due respect to
par excellence (F) = beyond comparison
pari passu (L) = with equal speed
passé (F) = outmoded
passim (L) = throughout
per annum (L) = every year
per capita (L) = for each person
per diem (L) = every day
per procurationem (L) (abbr. *per pro.* or pp) = for and on behalf of
per se (L) = of itself, intrinsically
persona grata (L) = acceptable person
persona non grata (L) = unacceptable person
pièce de résistance (F) = the most important part

post (L) = following
poste restante (F) = place in post office where letters are kept until
    collected
postmortem (L) = after death
prima facie (L) = at first sight
pro forma (L) = performed in a standard or set manner (usually
    describes
    a type of invoice)
pro rata (L) = in proportion
qua (L) = in the capacity of
quantum sufficit (L) (abbr. qs) = as much as is sufficient
quid pro quo (L) = tit for tat
quod erat demonstrandum (L) (abbr. QED) = which was the thing to be
    proved
quod vide (L) (abbr. qv) = which see (in reference works, refers to an
    article on this subject)
raison d'être (F) = reason for existing
rapprochement (F) = return to good relations, esp. between nations
scilicet (L) = that is to say
secundo (L) = secondly
sic (L) = spelled, written in this way
sine die (L) = indefinitely
sine mascula prole (L) (abbr. smp) = without male children
sine prole (L) = without children (abbr. sp)
sine qua non (L) = indispensable qualification
status quo (L) = unchanged state of affairs
sub finem (L) (abbr. s.f.) = near the end
sub judice (L) = under consideration (by the courts)
subpoena (L) = demand that a person appear in court
sub rosa (L) = in secret
sub voce (L) (abbr. *s.v.*) = under the word
sui generis (L) = unique
supra (L) = above (especially referring to earlier parts of a book)
tempore (L) (abbr. temp.) = in the time of
ter in die (L) (abbr. *t.i.d.*) = three times a day
terra incognita (L) = unknown territory
tour de force (L) = show of great skill or strength
ultimo (L) (abbr. ult.) = on the last

ultra vires (L) = beyond the legal power
vale (L) = goodbye
verbatim (L) = word for word
vide (L) (abbr. v.) = see, refer to
videlicet (L) = namely
vis-à-vis (F) = one thing in comparison with another
vox populi (L) (abbr. vox pop) = voice of the people

Common diacritical marks

Diacritical marks are those used in writing to change the pronunciation of a letter. There are no diacritical marks in standard English (words such as café come from French). However, you may find that you will need to use them when writing abroad.

The following list gives the most commonly-used diacritical marks, their names and shows how, if possible, you can avoid having to use them.

MARK	LETTERS	AVOIDANCE
acute accent	á, é, í, ó, ú	In French (only) capital letters do not have to have accents
grave accent	à, è, ì, ò, ù	No avoidance possible
cedilla	ç	No avoidance possible
umlaut (diaresis)	ä, ë, ï, ö, ü	In German only, an umlaut can be avoided by putting an 'e' after the accented letter (e.g. *über* = *ueber*)
circumflex	â, ê, î, ô, û	No avoidance possible
tilde	ã, ñ, õ	No avoidance possible

2.3 Letters and letter-writing

Letter-writing is one of the central skills in office administration. A well-presented letter will show the outside world that you and your company are professional, capable and on the ball. On the other hand, a badly laid-out letter that is full of grammatical and spelling errors, and takes an age to get to the point is irritating and time-consuming to deal with and, above all, bad public relations.

Even small companies send out numbers of letters every day, and so letter-writing can form a large part of the daily routine.

Because this is so often the case, it is a good idea to establish the rules of good letter-writing at the outset, and to practise them until they become second nature. In this way, you will use your time efficiently and effectively.

Most companies have their own way of doing things. They have a 'house style' for layout and punctuation, and an efficient referencing system, often related to their own method of filing documents. This chapter gives some of the possibilities, and the 'rules' for each standard format, but if you are new in a company, look back in the filing to find out which style has been used as the house style.

Layout

There are two forms of layout commonly used for letters:

- Semi-blocked, in which the first lines of paragraphs, the subscription and signatory (see 2.1 for definitions of these) are all indented, and the reference and date are placed on the same line;
- Fully blocked, in which each item of preliminary information is placed on a separate line and the paragraphs, subscription and signatory all begin at the left-hand edge of the page. Illustrations 2.3-1 and 2.3-2 show semi-blocked and fully blocked layouts.

These days, fully-blocked is the most commonly-used layout, but check back in the company filing to find out what style your company prefers to use.

Reference   Date

Addressee Name
and Address

Salutation

                    Subject Heading

    Body of letter ▨▨▨▨▨▨▨▨▨▨▨▨▨▨▨▨▨▨▨
▨▨▨▨▨▨▨▨▨▨▨▨▨▨▨▨▨▨▨▨▨▨▨▨▨▨▨▨▨
▨▨▨▨▨▨▨▨▨▨▨▨▨▨▨▨▨▨▨

    Second paragraph ▨▨▨▨▨▨▨▨▨▨▨▨▨▨▨▨
▨▨▨▨▨▨▨▨▨▨▨▨▨▨▨▨▨▨▨▨▨▨▨▨▨▨▨▨▨
▨▨▨▨▨▨▨▨▨▨▨▨▨▨▨▨▨▨▨▨▨▨▨▨▨▨▨▨▨
▨▨▨▨▨▨▨▨▨▨▨▨▨▨▨▨▨▨▨

    Third paragraph ▨▨▨▨▨▨▨▨▨▨▨▨▨▨▨▨▨
▨▨▨▨▨▨▨▨▨▨▨▨▨▨▨▨▨▨▨▨▨▨▨▨▨▨▨▨▨
▨▨▨▨▨▨▨▨▨▨▨▨▨▨▨▨▨▨▨

                    Subscription

                    Signatory
                    Position or Company Name

Enclosures

2.3-1 A letter laid out in the semi-blocked style.

Reference

Date

Addressee Name
and Address

Salutation

Subject Heading

Body of letter

Second paragraph

Third paragraph

Subscription

Signatory
Position or Company Name

Enclosures

2.3-2 A letter laid out in the fully-blocked style.

It is desirable that your layout and punctuation are consistent, not only when using continuation sheets, but also from letter to letter. Check with your company's files to find out what their preferred layout and punctuation styles are, and stick to them.

Punctuation of letters

As with layout, there are two commonly used forms of punctuation for letters.

The first, called *standard punctuation*, makes use of normal punctuation for written English, including commas at the end of address lines, full stops after abbreviations, etc. (see illustration 2.3-3). Standard punctuation is most commonly used with semi-blocked layout (see 2.3-1).

The second, called *open punctuation*, is much quicker for a keyboard operator to execute, because it involves no punctuation at all (except, of course, in the body of the letter), and is consequently more frequently used. See illustration 2.3-4.

Running order of a standard business letter

The standard running order of a business letter is as follows:

Letterhead
This is your company's details. The letterhead is normally designed and pre-printed. However, if no letterhead is available, type the required information either at the left-hand edge, centred or at the right-hand edge, depending on your company's usual style. (For the information that should be given on a letterhead, see Letterhead, p.93)

Letter reference
This is often made up of two sets of initials: those of the person writing the letter and those of the person typing the letter, separated by an oblique stroke. Sometimes the first set of initials is written in capital letters, while the typist's initials appear in lower-case (small) letters. If your office is using a numerical or alpha-numerical filing system (see 3.1 Filing), you may also need to include the filing reference number.

Ref. AL/cd   16th June, 1998

Mr. J. Fielding,
A3 Electricals Ltd,
124 Craven Road,
HOXTON
HT1 0NB

Dear Mr. Fielding,

              Subject Heading

    First paragraph ▬▬▬▬▬▬▬▬▬▬▬▬▬▬▬▬▬
▬▬▬▬▬▬▬▬▬▬▬▬▬▬▬▬▬▬▬▬▬▬▬▬▬▬▬▬▬▬
▬▬▬▬▬▬▬▬▬▬▬▬▬▬▬▬▬▬▬▬▬▬▬▬▬▬▬▬▬▬
▬▬▬▬▬▬▬▬▬▬▬▬▬

    Second paragraph ▬▬▬▬▬▬▬▬▬▬▬▬▬▬▬▬
▬▬▬▬▬▬▬▬▬▬▬▬▬▬▬▬▬▬▬▬▬▬▬▬▬▬▬▬▬▬
▬▬▬▬▬▬▬▬▬▬▬▬▬▬▬▬▬▬▬▬▬▬▬▬▬▬▬▬▬▬
▬▬▬▬▬▬▬▬▬▬▬

            Yours sincerely,

            Alan Long
            Marketing Manager

Enc.
c.c. Joan Greystone

2.3-3 A letter showing standard punctuation.

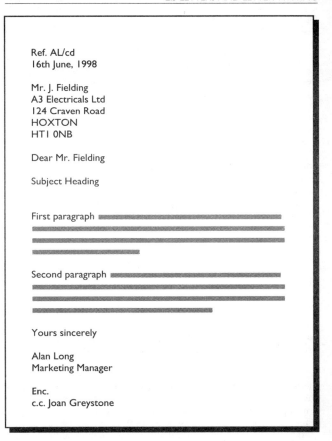

2.3-4 A letter with open punctuation and fully-blocked layout.

Date

The standard way to write the date in English is in figures and words (not 15.6.95, for instance), in the order in which you would say it: date, month, year.

In the USA and Europe, when dates are written as figures, the day and the month are swapped. So, in the UK, 6.4.95 means 6th April 1995, whereas in Europe and the USA, it means 4th June 1995. To avoid confusion when writing abroad, always write the date in figures and words.

Private/Confidential

If you need to indicate that the letter is only to be read by the addressee (and not by the person who opens the mail), then give this indication after the date. Private means personal. Confidential means sensitive. The difference is that letters marked 'private' should only be opened by the addressee. Letters and other documents marked 'confidential' will have their circulation confined to relevant members of staff only.

If the mode of postage is unusual – e.g. recorded delivery, special delivery, registered post, e-mail, facsimile transmission (see 5.2 Postal services), or by hand – the method of postage is indicated at this stage.

Addressee's name and address

If writing to a particular person in a company, write their name and title, followed by the company name, full address, and postcode, as it will appear on the envelope. Full details on running order for addresses are given in Addressing envelopes, p.68.

If previous correspondence indicates that all letters should be addressed to the company, omit the person's name from the top of the address, but add the words 'For the Attention of...' after the postcode. If, however, you are planning to use a window envelope (see Addressing envelopes, p.68), write the attention line at the start of the address as normal.

If you are writing to a company that is a partnership, you will find that the 'company' name appears as a string of names: e.g. Sturrock, White, Hempel & Co. In this case, it is usual to add the plural for mister in the address: Messrs Sturrock, White, Hempel & Co. When using this type of address, the salutation (see below) should be 'Dear Sirs'.

Salutation

All letters should open with a salutation: 'Dear ...' If you are writing to a particular person, use that person's courtesy title and surname (e.g. 'Dear Mr Laing'). If you are on very good terms with the addressee (perhaps you are close colleagues or old friends), it is permissible to use a Christian name only ('Dear Charles').

Some companies use a salutation without the courtesy title ('Dear Charles Laing'). This can be useful when you do not know whether the person to whom you are writing is a man or a woman, but it has an impersonal feel about it that could be undesirable. If in doubt, call the addressee's company and find out. If the addressee turns out to be a woman, find out whether she is Miss or Mrs, or if she prefers to use Ms.

If you are not writing to a named person, use the salutation, 'Dear Sir', or, when addressing a partnership, use the plural, 'Dear Sirs'.

Subject heading

This is a title that indicates the subject of the letter for quick reference. The subject may be given as a project title, or reference to an account, but whatever way you head your letter, find a way to sum up the subject accurately in two or three words.

Body of the letter

Whatever your letter is about, aim for clarity and brevity. Do not make your correspondent read three pages before finding out what it is you want or are offering.

The first paragraph should refer to previous correspondence or contact (a letter, a telephone call or a meeting, perhaps) and sum up why you are writing. The next paragraphs give further information, and the final paragraph should state what action you are expecting or what action you are yourself taking. For example:

Subject heading:	Project X
First paragraph:	Thank you for your letter of nth date, requesting information on project X, which is enclosed.
Second paragraph:	As you will see, we offer x, y and z ....

Third paragraph: If, after you have looked through the enclosed information, you have any further queries, please call me and I will do my best to answer them.

See Letter-writing tips, p.67, for further hints on how to compose a business letter.

Subscription (also called 'complimentary close')

This is the standard method of closing a letter, before the sender signs his or her name. Which form of subscription you use depends on the salutation at the start of the letter. If you opened with 'Dear Sir(s)', you should close with 'Yours faithfully' (capital letter for 'Yours', and lower case for 'faithfully'). If you opened with the name of a person, and you have never met that person, or the relationship is formal in any other way, close with 'Yours sincerely'.

If the sender and addressee are close friends or colleagues of long standing, it may be permissible to use a more familiar subscription, such as 'Best regards' or 'Kind regards', but you should make sure that the level of familiarity with which you close is the same as that with which you have opened. For example, it would be incongruous to open with 'Dear Charles' and close with 'Yours sincerely', or to open with 'Dear Charles Laing' and close with 'Kind regards'.

The relationship between the writer and the addressee should be reflected in the salutation and the complimentary close. When composing letters, therefore, make sure that you balance these three elements.

Signature and signatory

Next comes the sender's signature, which is usually made up of initials and surname. Some people sign with their full Christian name followed by the surname, but this is incorrect (except in American usage, in which the Christian name is given, followed by the middle initial and the surname).

If the letter is less formal (i.e. the salutation and subscription indicate a closer-than-normal relationship between the correspondents), it may simply be signed with a Christian name.

In some instances, it happens that a sender is not available to sign a letter once it has been typed, and that the letter cannot wait for the signature. In this case, it is permissible for another person to sign the letter *per procurationem* ('for and on behalf of'). If this is the case, the abbreviation 'pp' should be written or typed before the signatory.

The signatory is a typed version of the sender's name. Here it is useful to give his or her full name. If the sender is a woman, it is also informative to give the preferred courtesy title in brackets after the name (see Forms of address, p.70, for details). Equally, if the Christian name may give rise to confusion as to whether the sender is a man or a woman (e.g., if the name is Frances or Leslie), it may be useful to the addressee to indicate this. This is the only case where a man gives his courtesy title in a signatory.

Remember to leave enough space for the sender to sign between the subscription and the signatory. Six or eight lines is usually enough.

Topping-and-tailing

Some company executives like to add a personal touch to some of their correspondence by handwriting the salutation and the subscription as well as their signature. This is sometimes known as 'topping-and-tailing'. If this is required, type out the information up to the salutation as normal. Leave space for the salutation to be handwritten, and continue with the subject heading. At the end of the letter, leave space for the subscription and signature to be written in, but remember to type the sender's name in the usual place.

Designation

The designation (the position in the company of the sender) is typed on the line below the signatory, and should give an accurate job title. If a job title is not appropriate, the designation may be simply the name of the company. This kind of information is useful to the addressee when he or she wants to contact the sender either by telephone or by letter, and so to avoid confusion and waste of time on all sides, make the designation accurate and informative.

Enclosures

If you are sending other material with the letter, (not including continuation sheets) indicate this after the designation, so that the addressee can check that all the material is present on arrival. If you are including only one extra sheet, type the abbreviation 'Enc'. If there are two or more sheets, add the plural 's' – 'Encs'. Some companies also add the number of enclosures (e.g. 'Encs 4') just to make sure.

Copies

If you are planning to send a copy of the letter to someone other than the addressee and the sender, indicate this using the abbreviation 'cc'. For example, cc Mrs J. Fellowes. The names of recipients of further copies can be added in a list.

   If you are asked to send copies of the letter to people without the addressee knowing, do not indicate this on the top (outgoing) copy of the letter, but do remember to indicate it on the file copy, using the initials bc (blind copies), underneath the 'copies' line.

Continuation sheets

Your letter may run to two or more pages. If this is the case, indicate the existence of a continuation sheet with a catchword, such as 'over', 'PTO' or 'continued' (or any abbreviation of it). Place the catchword at the right-hand margin at the bottom of the page.

   The continuation sheet usually has no letterhead, or an abbreviated letterhead giving the company name only. On the left-hand side of each continuation sheet, give the addressee's name and company, along with the date of the letter. On the right-hand side, give the number of the page.

Form letters

Some companies find that they send many letters with substantially the same wording. In these cases, it is a time-saver to produce a form letter (or standard letter) which includes the majority of the information necessary, but has gaps for the variables (names and addresses, for instance).

   When you have typed the form letter, make a good number of photocopies, using a machine that produces copies of the highest possible quality. You may have to have the photocopies made by a bureau if your photocopier is not up to scratch. Remember to keep the master in a safe place, where it will not get crumpled. When your stocks of the letter are running low, use the master (and *not* a photocopy) to make more copies.

If you are amending form letters with a typewriter, ensure that the typeface on the form letter closely matches that of the additional information that you will be typing in. If a close match cannot be made, choose a typeface that is completely different.

If you are using a word processing program on a computer, the process is made much easier. Simply keep a copy of the form letter on disk or on your hard drive, and amend it appropriately, printing out a hard copy whenever you need to. In this way, you do not need to keep a stock of photocopied forms, and the resulting letter will be of much higher quality.

With a computer it is also possible to produce large numbers of 'personalized' form letters without amending each one individually. The process involves identifying each variable on the form letter and then writing a file that gives the information for each 'gap' in turn. The computer does the rest. This procedure is known as mail-merging. (See 7.1 for further details.)

Letter-writing tips

● Keep your letters short and to the point.
● Use a subject heading, but make sure that it accurately reflects the subject of the letter.
● Make sure that your letter starts with a statement of intent and ends with a request or promise of action.
● Never use words that you do not understand or do not know how to spell. If you are unsure, look it up in a dictionary. (See p.27 for a list of common errors.)
● Avoid using too many adjectives or adverbs. You will be able to do this if you choose the correct nouns and verbs.
● Avoid flowery language.
● Don't use words and phrases that could be ambiguous. If there is any chance of a misunderstanding arising, find an alternative way of saying it.
● Always be cordial and polite. Never be abusive, even if you are writing a letter of complaint.
● All parts of a letter are designed to give important

67

information. If your letters give accurate information, you will increase efficiency all round. For example, the addressee will know how to contact the sender, and you will know where to find your file copy in a hurry.

● Think out your letter before you start to compose it. Make notes if this helps to organize the information in a logical order.

● If you can amend a standard or similar letter to say what you need to say, do so. It will save you time.

● If you have difficulty finding the right words and phrases for your letters, consider investing in a book of sample letters.

Outgoing letters are silent emissaries on behalf of your company, and the recipient will form a favourable or unfavourable impression of your company depending on the state of your correspondence. Make sure, therefore, that all correspondence is error-free, cordial and consistent.

Addressing envelopes

In order for the Post Office to do its job efficiently and get your post to the right place at the right time, it is necessary to ensure that you give the correct information on the envelope.

The Post Office requests that you give the following address information, with each item on a separate line:

● Addressee's name
● Addressee's company name in full
● Building number (or name) and street name
● Name of locality, or for rural areas, the village or hamlet
● Name of postal town in CAPITAL LETTERS
● Name of the county or its standard abbreviation (see p.78 for a list of standard county abbreviations).
● Postcode in CAPITAL LETTERS on a separate line, and with no punctuation.

If the address is unusually long, and you find yourself short of space, put the town and county on the same line. If you need even more space, move the postcode up to the county line, but leave, say, six spaces between the county and the postcode so that postal workers and their automated systems can locate and assess it instantly.

The address should be positioned in the lower part of the front of the envelope, to the right-hand side, leaving space for postage above it. If you are using window envelopes, then this position will be slightly different.

If you need to add an attention line (see Key terms, p.13), type it two lines above the address.

Unless you are addressing an unusually large package or parcel, you need only leave single-line spaces between the lines of the address.

Special instructions to the Post Office (Air Mail, Special Delivery, etc.) should be printed in the top left-hand corner of the front of the envelope.

It is also advisable to write the sender's name and address either on the back of the envelope or on the front, in the top left-hand corner (above the postal instructions, if there are any). This helps the Post Office to return undelivered mail without having to open the envelope. Further details on postal facilities

OFFICE
MANAGEMENT CONSULTANTS

6th Floor
329 Brook Street
LONDON W26 1BZ

Mr J Fielding
A3 Electricals Ltd
124 Craven Road
HOXTON
HT1 0NB

2.3-5 Envelope addressed using the open punctuation style.

Remember to cross-check that the address written on the envelope corresponds to the address written at the head of the letter, and that the punctuation and layout style also correspond to those of the enclosed letter.

and
special instructions can be found in section 5 (pp.134–142), and
in the Post Office's annual publication, *The Post Office Guide.*

Forms of address

Some people consider the rules regarding customary forms of
address outmoded or 'politically incorrect'. Whatever your personal feelings, when it comes to producing correspondence on
behalf of your employer, it is as well to know and use the correct
forms, as a matter of good manners, if nothing else.

Titles

Every person should be addressed with a title. Those with special
titles include members of the aristocracy and the peerage
(barons, earls, counts, etc.), clerics (bishops, priests, etc.), those
holding office (such as mayors and city councillors), members of
the armed forces (colonel, major, brigadier, etc.) and diplomats
(such as ambassadors).

People who do not have such titles ('ordinary' people), are
addressed as Mr, Mrs, Miss or Ms, depending on their sex and
marital status. An alternative to 'Mr' is to use the courtesy title
'Esq.' (Esquire). If your company prefers to use this, give the initial or full Christian name and the surname followed by 'Esq.':
e.g. Charles Laing Esq. Any honours and decorations (see below)
always come after this courtesy title.

Miss, Mrs or Ms?

The use of the title 'Ms' is becoming increasingly popular among
women of all ages. Many believe that women use it simply as a
feminist statement that their marital status is unimportant to
their business standing. However, this is not always the case. A
large number of women are now opting to retain their maiden
name in their professional lives after they are married. This is
often a good idea because it avoids the confusion that may arise
out of a sudden name change. In these cases, it would be ridiculous to call a woman Mrs with her maiden name.

Whatever a woman chooses to call herself, and for whatever
reason, it is polite to respect her wishes and use the title she has
chosen for herself. If you are unsure what this may be, call her
company and find out.

Salutations and subscriptions

Each title has its own special salutation and subscription, and it is just as important to get these right as it is to use the correct title. In some very formal correspondence, you should also use the customary form of reference. For example, in the body of a letter to the Queen, one would refer to her as 'Your Majesty', rather than as 'you'. The table on p.72–77 gives each title, along with the appropriate salutation, subscription and form of reference (where applicable).

Honours and decorations

Honours are the letters that people are entitled to list after their names to indicate that they have a degree or that they are a member of a professional body. Some of these honours also mean that such people can take a title, such as Doctor or Professor.

Some people do not list their honours. If you are responding to a letter, follow the style they themselves use. If you are writing to somebody for the first time, it is probably best to use the full form.

When a person has more than one honour in the same discipline, you need only list the higher honour. However, if the honours are from different disciplines, you need to list the highest honour in each field, with a space between each set of initials. As a general rule, list the least prestigious honours first and work up.

Decorations are similar sets of initials denoting that a person has been decorated. They may have received a medal (say the Victoria Cross, VC) or they have been made a member of an order (e.g. Order of the British Empire, OBE). Again, some of these decorations carry with them titles (e.g. DBE refers to a Dame) and corresponding salutations.

The table on p.72–77 lists the various types of honour and decoration in the order in which they should be placed in abbreviated form after a person's name.

If you are dealing with foreign clients or colleagues, you will need to know the correct form of address, even if you are writing to them in English. The most common forms are given in Addressing a letter abroad, p.305.

Titles and forms of address

The following table lists the appropriate forms of address, with salutations, subscriptions and forms of reference

The Queen
Address: The Queen's Most Excellent Majesty
Salutation: Madam, or May it please Your Majesty
Refer to as: Your Majesty
Subscription: I have the honour to remain Your Majesty's
                  faithful subject
Note: In most circumstances, it is more usual to write, not to the Queen herself, but to her Private Secretary. In this case, the form is as follows:
Address: The Private Secretary to Her Majesty the Queen
Salutation: Dear Sir, Madam
Subscription: Yours faithfully

Royal Prince
Address: His Royal Highness Prince (Christian name) or,
                  if a duke, His Royal Highness the Duke of
                  (place)
Salutation: Your Royal Highness
Refer to as: Sir
Subscription: I have the honour to remain Your Royal
                  Highness's most dutiful subject
Note: As for the Queen, it is more usual to write to a Private Secretary. In this case, follow the instructions above.

Royal Princess
Address: Her Royal Highness the Princess (Christian
                  name or place) or, if a duchess, Her Royal
                  Highness the Duchess of (place)
Salutation: Your Royal Highness
Refer to as: Madam
Subscription: I have the honour to remain Your Royal
                  Highness's dutiful and obedient subject

Royal Duke
Address: His Royal Highness, The Duke of (place)
Salutation: Your Royal Highness

Refer to as:	Sir
Subscription:	I have the honour to remain Your Royal Highness's dutiful servant

Royal Duchess

Address:	Her Royal Highness, The Duchess of (place)
Salutation:	Your Royal Highness
Refer to as:	Madam
Subscription:	I have the honour to remain Your Royal Highness's dutiful and obedient servant

Duke

Address:	His Grace the Duke of (place)
Salutation:	My Lord Duke
Refer to as:	Your Grace
Subscription:	I have the honour to be Your Grace's most obedient servant

Duchess

Address:	Her Grace the Duchess of (place)
Salutation:	Madam
Refer to as:	Your Grace
Subscription:	I have the honour to be Your Grace's most obedient servant

Earl

Address:	The Earl of (place)
Salutation:	Dear Lord (place)
Subscription:	I am, Sir, your obedient servant

Countess

Address:	The Countess of (place)
Salutation:	Dear Lady (place)
Subscription:	I am, Madam, your obedient servant

Baron

Address:	The Lord (place)
Salutation:	Dear Lord (place)
Subscription:	I am, Sir, Your obedient servant

Baron's wife
Address: The Lady (place)
Salutation: Dear Lady (place)
Subscription: I am, Madam, Your obedient servant

Knight
Address: Sir (Christian name + surname) KCB
Salutation: Dear Sir (Christian name)
Subscription: I am, Sir, Your obedient servant

Knight's wife
Address: Lady (husband's surname)
Salutation: Dear Lady (husband's surname)
Subscription: I am, Madam, Your obedient servant

Prime Minister
Address: according to rank (i.e. if he or she is also a knight, baron, dame, member of the clergy, use the address that is appropriate for that rank).

Privy Councillor
Address: The Rt. Hon. (name or title).Salutation and subscription according to rank.

Member of Parliament
Address: according to rank, but add the initials MP after the name.

Secretary of State
Address: HM Principal Secretary of State for (Department)
Salutation: Sir/Madam
Subscription: I am, Sir (Madam), Your obedient servant

Ambassador (British)
Address: His Excellency HBM's Ambassador and Plenipotentiary
Salutation: My Lord (+ other according to rank)
Refer to as: Your Excellency
Subscription: I am (+ other according to rank) Your obedient servant

Consul-General
Address:	(Name) Esq., HBM's Consul-General, Consul, Vice-Consul, etc
Salutation:	Sir
Subscription:	I am, Sir, Your Obedient Servant

High Court Judge
Address:	The Hon. Mr (Mrs) Justice (surname)
Salutation:	Dear Judge (surname)
Subscription:	Yours sincerely

Circuit Judge
Address:	His Honour Judge (surname)
Salutation:	Dear Sir/Madam
Subscription:	Yours sincerely

Archbishop
Address:	The Most Reverend and Rt. Hon. the Lord Archbishop of (place)
Salutation:	Dear Archbishop
Subscription:	Yours sincerely

Bishop
Address:	The Right Reverend the Bishop of (place)
Salutation:	Dear Bishop
Subscription:	Yours sincerely

Vicar
Address:	The Reverend (Christian name + surname)
Salutation:	Dear Mr (surname)
Subscription:	Yours sincerely

Rabbi
Address:	Rabbi (first name and surname)
Salutation:	Dear Rabbi (surname)
Subscription:	Yours sincerely

Minister
Address: The Reverend (first name and surname)
Salutation: Dear Mr (surname)
Subscription: Yours sincerely

The Pope
Address: His Holiness the Pope
Salutation: Your Holiness

Cardinal
Address: His Eminence the Cardinal (place)
Salutation: Your Eminence

Priest
Address: The Reverend (Christian name + surname)
Salutation: Dear Father (surname)
Subscription: Yours sincerely

Lord Mayor/Lady Mayor
Address: The Right Worshipful the Lord (Lady) Mayor
Salutation: My Lord (Lady) Mayor
Subscription: Yours sincerely

Lady Mayoress
Address: The Lady Mayoress of (place)
Salutation: My Lady Mayoress
Subscription: Yours sincerely

Councillor
Address: Councillor Mr (Mrs) (surname)
Salutation: Dear Councillor
Subscription: Yours sincerely

A table showing order of precedence in honours and decorations

1. Bt (baronet) and Esq. (esquire)
2. Decorations and orders
3. The following appointments:
   Privy Councillor (PC)
   Aide de Camp to HM the Queen (ADC)
   Honorary Physician to HM the Queen (QHP)
   Honorary Surgeon to HM the Queen (QHS)
   Honorary Dental Surgeon to HM the Queen (QHDS)
   Honorary Nursing Sister to HM the Queen (QHNS)
   Honorary Chaplain to HM the Queen (QHC)
4. Educational degrees
5. Medical qualifications; religious orders
6. Memberships and Fellowships of learned societies and
   professional bodies
7. The following appointments:
   Queen's Council (QC)
   Justice of the Peace (JP)
   Deputy Lieutenant (DL)
   Member of Parliament (MP)
8. Membership of HM armed forces

For abbreviations not listed here, see List of abbreviations, p.39.

GREEN NOTE: PAPERCLIPS
*Environment-consciousness in the office goes all the way
down to the innocuous paperclip. Most paperclips are
wonderfully green – in that they are reusable, and most
people reuse them as a matter of course. However,
coloured paperclips are not green because they are coated
with a plastic that is not biodegradable.
Avoid buying them if you can.*

List of abbreviations of UK counties

The following is a list of the abbreviations of UK county names preferred by the Post Office. For counties in Northern Ireland, the word County may be abbreviated to Co.; the Scottish regions and counties should preferably not be abbreviated.

COUNTY	ABBREVIATION
Bedfordshire	Beds
Berkshire	Berks
Buckinghamshire	Bucks
Cambridgeshire	Cambs
County Durham	Co. Durham
East Sussex	E. Sussex
Gloucestershire	Glos
Hampshire	Hants
Hertfordshire	Herts
Lancashire	Lancs
Leicestershire	Leics
Lincolnshire	Lincs
Mid Glamorgan	M. Glam
Northamptonshire	Northants
Northumberland	Northd
North Humberside	N. Humberside
North Yorkshire	N. Yorkshire
Nottinghamshire	Notts
Oxfordshire	Oxon
Shropshire	Salop
South Glamorgan	S. Glam
South Humberside	S. Humberside
South Yorkshire	S. Yorkshire
Staffordshire	Staffs
Warwickshire	Warks
West Glamorgan	W. Glam
West Midlands	W. Mids
West Sussex	W. Sussex
West Yorkshire	W. Yorkshire
Wiltshire	Wilts
Worcestershire	Worcs

US states, their abbreviations and ZIP codes

US states are abbreviated in two ways. First, in written addresses, there is a standard abbreviation, usually with a full stop. Second is the postal code (known in the USA as the ZIP – zoning improvement plan – code), made up of two letters, followed by five figures. For example, NY 10016 refers to central New York.

STATE	ABBREVIATION	ZIP CODE
Alabama	Ala.	AL
Alaska	Ak.	AK
Arizona	Ariz.	AZ
Arkansas	Ark.	AR
California	Calif.	CA
Colorado	Colo.	CO
Connecticut	Conn.	CT
Delaware	Del.	DE
Florida	Fla.	FL
Georgia	Ga.	GA
Hawaii	Hi	HI
Idaho	Ida.	ID
Illinois	Ill.	IL
Indiana	Ind.	IN
Iowa	Ia.	IA
Kansas	Kans.	KA
Kentucky	Ken./KY	KY
Louisiana	La.	LA
Maine	Me.	ME
Maryland	Md.	MD
Massachusetts	Mass.	MA
Michigan	Mich.	MI
Minnesota	Minn.	MN
Mississippi	Miss.	MS
Missouri	Mo.	MO
Montana	Mont.	MT
Nebraska	Nebr./Neb.	NE
Nevada	Nev.	NV
New Hampshire	N.H.	NH
New Jersey	N.J.	NJ

79

STATE	ABBREVIATION	ZIP CODE
New Mexico	N.M./N. Mex.	NM
New York	N.Y.	NY
North Carolina	N.C.	NC
North Dakota	N.D./N. Dak.	ND
Ohio	O.	OH
Oklahoma	Okla.	OK
Oregon	Ore./Oreg.	OR
Pennsylvania	Pa./Penn.	PA
Rhode Island	R.I.	RI
South Carolina	S.C.	SC
South Dakota	S.D.	SD
Tennessee	Tenn.	TN
Texas	Tex.	TX
Utah	Ut.	UT
Vermont	Vt.	VT
Virginia	Va.	VA
Washington	Wash.	WA
West Virginia	W. Va.	WV
Wisconsin	Wis.	WI
Wyoming	Wyo.	WY

Letters checklist

Before committing letters to the post, make the following routine checks:

- If you are typing a letter for someone else, check back spellings and other details before you start – never take a chance on getting it wrong.
- Always read through for spelling errors – don't leave it up to your computer spell-check facility. While you are doing this, make sure that you have got the date and any other information right. If in doubt, check back with the sender.
- Check that the addressee's name and address is the same on the letter as on the envelope. Make sure that you have included the post code.
- If the letter is marked 'Personal', 'Private' or 'Confidential', ensure that the envelope has also been marked in the same way.
- Check that the letter has been signed by the appropriate person.
- Make sure that any continuation sheets are present, and that they are in the correct order.
- Check that the relevant enclosures are present, and in the correct order.
- Check that the right number of copies have been made and are waiting to be filed and/or distributed.

2.4 Memoranda

A memorandum is a short letter or note sent to a particular in-house member of staff or circulated to groups of people. Although increasingly, with the advent of information technology, many companies send internal messages by means of 'electronic mail' (e-mail). Memoranda are not normally sent out of house.

Some companies provide memoranda pads ready-printed (see Memo pad, p.97), but if this is not the case, ensure that memoranda contain the following information as a matter of form: sender's name and department (possibly also an extension number); addressee's name and department; date; subject. It may save time to produce a memorandum form on a word-processor with space for each of these items.

Memoranda are not normally signed, but if they contain financial information it may be usual for the sender to add initials as confirmation.

Memoranda are not normally used for confidential information. If they are, they should be placed in a sealed envelope and marked 'Confidential'.

If any other information is attached to the memo, this should be indicated with the abbreviation 'Enc(s)' as for a normal letter.

Always keep and file copies of all memoranda, as with other forms of correspondence.

Be cautious about sending sensitive or confidential information via e-mail, since the contents could be read by anyone with access to the recipient's computer. You can purchase special software to protect your mail. With many e-mail programs you can also mark them as being 'confidential' or 'personal', and request a receipt on delivery of the message. The benefit of e-mail is that you can send messages quickly, straight from your computer, and you can send the same message to a number of recipients, usually at the push of a button.

2.5 Producing reports

All managers will at some time or another, be asked to produce a report of some sort. It may be a report of the discussion that took place at a meeting, or a review of working practices, equipment, current stock levels or staff performance.

Because of the introduction of personal computers, word processors and DTP equipment, some members of staff now write and produce their own reports. Other companies prefer to have the work divided between the writer of the report and a secretary or WP operator. This section gives hints on how to write a readable and effective report, and how to produce a finished document.

The aim with reports is to be accurate, concise and brief.

Contents

Whatever their contents, reports should (unless entirely inappropriate) contain: a heading; a reason for the report; the argument; conclusion and recommendations.

Heading

This must include: the writer's name and department; the name and department of the addressee (that is, the person who requested the report, if appropriate); date of report; reference number if applicable; title (to be as concise as possible); the word 'Confidential' if applicable.

Reason for the report

The first paragraph or two should state why it is necessary for the report to be compiled, and what the object of the exercise is. For example, you have been asked to look into the pros and cons of establishing a crèche on the premises. The reason for the report would, therefore, be to prove that it would be possible to establish a crèche and that it would be beneficial to employers and employees alike. Begin by saying this.

Argument

Organize the evidence in a logical manner, dividing it into related points. Discuss each point separately. Back up each point with proof, such as statistics, graphics, examples, etc.

Conclusion/recommendation

State the conclusion that you have reached or the recommendation that you would like to make, and repeat the points of the argument that led you to it.

Making notes

You will find it much easier to write a report if you have a clear idea in your mind of the line of argument you want to take before you put pen to paper. So begin by making a note of all the evidence you have amassed, and decide on a line of argument. Group together the evidence under various headings and gradually the argument of your report will start to take shape.

Try to give yourself enough time to mull over your notes. Even if you leave them overnight before starting to write your report, you will find that when you come to writing, you will have remembered a few things you forgot to list in your initial notes, and the outline has become clear in your mind.

Hints for good writing

- Aim to be accurate, concise and brief.
- Never use words you don't understand.
- Keep jargon to a minimum, but use technical words accurately.
- Consider the people who are going to read the report. If they are not experts, you may have to define your terms or use everyday alternatives so that they understand what you are talking about. You may even need to provide a glossary of technical terms.
- Say what you want to say in as few words as possible. For example, if you mean 'now', don't say 'at this time'.
- Avoid using too many adjectives and adverbs. If you have chosen the right nouns and verbs, you shouldn't need them.
- Avoid using clichés – phrases that are worn out from use, and which consequently mean nothing.
- Reports on meetings should be written in the third person: 'It was decided', 'A proposal was put forward'. Individual reports can be written using the first person: 'I looked into the cost of ...'

See section 2.2, Written English, for further advice on grammar, spelling and punctuation.

The art of persuasion

You may find yourself needing to write a report that persuades somebody to take a specific course of action. The golden rule is to find out what the priorities of your reader are, and then write the report from that point of view.

The priorities of most managers, for example, involve saving money, increasing efficiency and improving product quality. If you can show how implementation of your proposal will result in one or more of these priorities being met, you have a good chance of your recommendations being taken up. Show that you understand the drawbacks of the present system: how much it costs; how much time is wasted; how it leads to a high turnover of staff. Then go on to explain your proposal. Prove (with numbers if possible), how your proposals could bring benefits to the company in the priority areas, leading to money saved, efficiency increased or quality improved, or ideally all three.

When you have finished writing, ask yourself four questions:

- Have I included all the information that may be needed for the reader to make a decision?
- Have I covered all the possible options and made a convincing case for the alternative that I am recommending?
- Have I explained my proposal adequately and proved that it is better than the other alternatives?
- Have I successfully put myself in the reader's shoes, and presented the problem and the solutions with his or her priorities in mind?

Graphics

When you have drafted the report, you should be able to say whether or not you want to include graphics (illustrations such as pie charts, graphs, etc.). If you need to use someone else to produce these graphics, discuss them with that person before you start to lay out the report. This will give the artist time to do their work at the same time as you are doing yours.

There are several simple types of graphics that you can put to very good effect. Choose the ones that are best suited to your purpose.

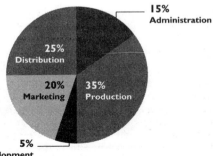

2.5-1 Pie chart.

Pie chart

The familiar 'cake' image can be used to represent a percentage share in something. For example, the chart could represent the operating budget of the company, and each segment relates to each department's share of the budget.

Illustration 2.5-1 is a pie chart showing the division of a company's budget into various operating areas: production, administration, distribution, marketing and R&D. Notice how the slices of the pie are roughly equivalent to the percentages they represent. Labels are written horizontally for ease of reading and leader lines (pointing from the outside labels to the appropriate segment) are horizontal and vertical lines, rather than diagonals.

Bar graph

Used to show statistics or figures, usually fluctuating over a period of time. The bars are drawn to length according to the level they represent. A bar graph could be used to represent increasing sales over a period of time. Illustration 2.5-2 is a simple bar graph showing fluctuating values (perhaps they are sales or costs) over a period of time.

In bar graphs, time is usually given along the horizontal axis, and the other value is given along the vertical axis. Unlike this

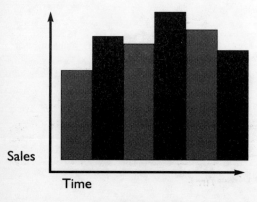

2.5-2 Bar graph.

one, many bar graphs show real values (written in numbers) along both axes.

Line graph

Such a graph can be used to show fluctuations or trends over a period of time. Line graphs can also be used to compare different elements, for example, number of people attending the cinema against the number of people watching television and the number of people attending the theatre. If you are comparing different trends, you may need to use a key to make the graph clear.

Illustration 2.5-3 shows a line graph that compares three different trends over the same time period. As with the bar graph (2.5-2), the horizontal axis is used to show time, and the vertical axis to show magnitude. The lines are distinguished either by colour, or by using a different dot-dash sequence. This example also has a key, which is used to explain what each line represents.

Flow chart

Shows the different stages of a process. The stages are represented by boxes, and arrows are used to show links between the stages. See illustration 1.2-1.

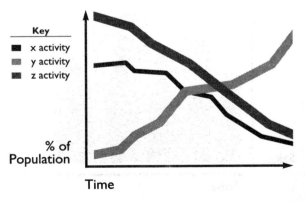

Key

■ x activity
■ y activity
■ z activity

% of Population

Time

2.5-3 Line graph.

Using icons

All graphics can be made more interesting by incorporating icons into them. Illustration 2.5-4 is a bar graph showing the sales of a company's product (in this case, wine) in which the bars have been turned into icons representing wine bottles. The bigger the volume of sales the taller the bottles.Other simple icons can be used in a similar way to make your graphics look more interesting.

Most wordprocessing programs for your computer will allow you to create icons and graphics on-screen, and you can normally save commonly used graphics in a 'clipboard' or file on your hard disk. There are also a number of design programs which will allow you to merge text and graphics, and move them around to create a satisfactory design.

Reproduction and binding

At this stage, you should think about how you are going to make copies of the document, and how you are going to bind it. Check supplies of materials or call to confirm prices on out-of-house reproduction and binding. If you are using a computer, you can print collated copies as required, or supply a disk to a company who can reproduce and bind the required number of copies.

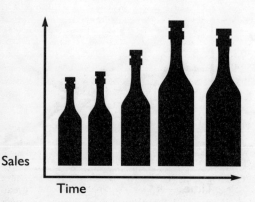

Sales

Time

2.5-4 A bar graph that makes use of icons.

Layout

Before starting to type, consider how the report should be laid out. If you are producing a report written by someone else, discuss this with him or her. Above all, the layout should be clear, so that it helps the reader to understand the various stages of the argument. Here are some options to consider.

Paragraph numbering or headings?

Complex reports should be divided into paragraphs and sub-paragraphs, either by using a system of headings or numbers. Headings can be typed in all capitals, bold, underlined or upper and lower case, depending on the status of the paragraph or section to which they refer. If you use this type of layout, make sure that the hierarchy of headings is consistent.

Alternatively, you could label each paragraph and sub-paragraph with a two- or three-digit numbering system. This book has a two-digit numbering system. This method is often much clearer than using headings. One added advantage of this style is that it allows you to refer back or forward to specific paragraphs by number. It may also reduce the need for page numbering.

You may also wish to use bullet points to distinguish between key parts of your argument or message. Most computers will automatically bullet or number your paragraphs, and indent them appropriately.

Paragraph indents

Decide whether you want to indent each paragraph (as in a semi-blocked letter – see Layout, p.56), or whether they would look better full out to the left-hand margin.

Justified or unjustified?

Some electronic typewriters and all computers allow you to decide whether or not you would like to justify the text. Justified text starts at the left-hand margin and finishes at the right-hand margin, so that all the lines are of the same length. Because this involves varying the spacing between the words in the line, there may be some unsightly lines where the spaces are too great. Therefore, some words are 'broken' (and carried on to the next line using a hyphen). So you might decide on unjustified text:

the line starts at the left-hand margin and finishes within a few characters of the right-hand margin. In this way the spaces between the words are all the same, and words are not broken at the ends of lines.

Position of page numbers
If your document is likely to be more than a couple of pages long, it is a good idea to number each page, so that if the sheets come loose from their binding, they can be replaced in the correct order. Page numbers should be positioned either in the top right-hand corner or centred at the foot of the page. If you are using a computer, you can normally choose page numbering as a document option.

Footnotes
Footnotes serve two functions. First, they are used to indicate an aside, that would unduly complicate the report if placed in the body of the text. Second, they are used to show that there is a reference to a book or journal, and the details of the source of the reference are given in the footnote. (See the paragraph on bibliographies, below, for the publication information that is normally given.)

Footnotes are indicated in the text with a superscript number (like this [1]) and the relevant information is placed either at the foot of each page, at the end of each chapter, or at the end of the document.

Footnotes should start at [1] and be numbered in numerical order right to the end of the document. If, however, you have decided to divide the report into chapters, and you want to list footnotes at the end of each chapter, start numbering at one again at the beginning of each chapter.

You may choose to use a symbol, such as an asterisk (*) to indicate a single footnote, or a double asterisk (**) when there are two.

Bibliographies
Some reports offer lists of publications, either full information of the publications referred to in the footnotes, or further reading. Type lists of books or journal and magazine articles in alphabetical order by the authors' surnames.

If you are citing a book, give the following information in this order: author's surname and initials; title of the book in *italics* or <u>underlined</u>; publisher; date of publication.

If you are citing an article from a magazine or journal, give the following information in this order: author's surname and initials; 'title of article in single inverted commas'; title of journal in *italics* or <u>underlined</u>; publisher if appropriate; volume number and/or date of publication.

Numbering graphics

If the writer has used any kind of graphic, from tables to pie charts or graphs, decide on a method of numbering. Perhaps you might use *Fig. 1, Fig. 2, Fig. 3*, and so on. If you and your colleagues consider this too old-fashioned, you may wish to give the paragraph numbers to which the graphics relate, followed by an illustration number: 1.2-1, for example.

You may also need to make decisions on:

- type size
- type font
- use of bullet points
- spacing between the lines

If there are two or more writers collaborating on a report, it may be a good idea to circulate a list of these decisions, so that the text that comes back for typing is consistent.

Checking the first draft

The first draft of the report should be as close as possible to finished. Print out a draft copy and ask the writer to make any changes he or she requires.

Pay attention to:

- Consistency in headings or numbering.
- Accuracy of information in graphics, tables, footnotes, etc.
- Spelling, punctuation and grammar.
- Overall order of the argument.
- Length: is the report too long?

*If your company produces a large number of documents
for distribution to clients or to the general public, it might
be a good idea to use the services of a professional proofreader.
Many proofreaders have technical backgrounds, and are adept at
pointing out errors and suggesting other ways of doing things.
Proofreaders usually charge an hourly rate based on the complexity
of the piece to be proofread. Contact the Society of Freelance Editors
and Proofreaders, who publish an annual directory of members,
giving each member's technical qualifications and experience.*

*The Society of Freelance Editors and Proofreaders (SFEP)
Mermaid House
1 Mermaid Court
London SE1 1HR
Tel: 0171 403 5141*

Correction and production

Now all you have to do is to make the corrections that have been
asked for (including, perhaps a proofreader's corrections) and
print out a master copy. Avoid making further changes that have
not been requested – you may be at risk of introducing new
errors. It may be a good idea to ask someone else to give the final
version one last look for spelling errors (but not the originator of
the text, or they may be tempted to make yet more changes).

Don't lose the first draft of the document – you never know
when you may be asked to reinstate sections previously dropped.
Send the master for reproduction and binding. When the copies
are returned, remember to file the master copy (unbound) as a
record, but also in case you need to make more copies.

When using a computer, make sure that you back up all
copies, and label each version accordingly – with the final document, or 'master copy' labelled 'edited' or 'final' on your hard
disk. You may like to keep final documents in a separate file from
unedited or draft documents, to avoid later confusion.

*You will find that if you have a large number of copies to
circulate, it is probably cheaper to make photocopies than
to print off copies from your computer's printer.*

2.6 Company stationery

Almost all companies have their stationery designed and printed,
then supplied on order from the printer. In fact, the design of
the company's stationery is often the first thing that people think
about when they are on the verge of going into business.

The full complement of stationery includes: letterhead on A4
and possibly also on A5 and ¾A4; continuation sheets; printed
envelopes; printed address labels; business cards for various
members of staff; compliment slips; printed invoices and orders;
printed memo books; facsimile front sheets.

Letterhead

Usually on A4 paper (210 x 297 mm), the letterhead includes the
name and address of the company, sometimes with a brief
description of what the company does (especially if it is a sole
trader or partnership), telephone number(s), fax number(s) and
telex number(s), web sites and e-mail addresses. It should also
include statutory information, such as the company's VAT registration number (if the company uses printed invoices, this need
not appear on the letterhead), its registered office and its registration number.

This information can be placed in one of a number of positions: at the top and centred; at the top right-hand corner; at the
foot of the page. Alternatively, it can be split up so that the statutory information is placed at the foot of the page, and the contact information at the head.

Some companies also use a logo (a designed symbol) and this
is prominently placed on letterheads. With CAD (computer-
aided design) logos and company information can appear virtually anywhere on the page, such as running along the sides. Your
letterhead is the first impression many of your clients may have
of your company, so it is important that your logo reflects your
image, and that your company details are easy to read.

Some companies also print the letterhead on A5 (148 x 210 mm, half the size of A4), used for very short letters, such as acknowl-edgements. A size known as ⅔A4 (210 x 198 mm) is also popular (some banks send out bank statements in this format, for instance).

You may be able to produce a letter template on your comput-er, with your company logo and details in place. This allows you to create documents on headed paper, and send them off elec-tronically, or print them with the logo and company information in place. Letter templates allow you to 'design' your document on-screen, and if you have a good printer you may be able to dis-pense with pre-printed letterhead altogether.

GREEN NOTE: RECYCLING OFFICE PAPER

Recycling paper is important for a number of reasons:

● *It reduces demand for paper made from new (or 'virgin') wood-pulp and therefore the need to plant new forests of single species trees, which destroy precious ecosystems.*
● *It reduces the amount of energy used to process new wood-pulp.*
● *It reduces the amount of material filling up landfill sites.*

Not all paper can be recycled, and so any recycling system in your office must first of all enable staff to sort paper. Provide staff with two separate bins (one for recycling paper and one for other rubbish), and give them a list of the papers they should recycle. The most valuable papers for recycling are:

● *computer printout paper*
● *white papers: photocopying paper, office stationery and printed papers.*

Mix these papers with papers that are less easily recycled (such as envelopes with gum, newspapers, glossy magazines and brochures), and the aggregate will be low-grade, and the value of the higher-grade papers will be lost.

*For further advice on how to set up and operate a
successful recycling programme in your office, contact
Friends of the Earth, who publish a booklet entitled:*
Paper Chase, A Guide to Waste Paper Collections.

*Friends of the Earth
26–28 Underwood Street
LONDON
N1 7JQ
Tel: (0171) 490-1555*

Continuation sheets

Many companies do not print continuation sheets, but use plain paper of the same weight and colour as the letterhead. Printed continuation sheets could include a shortened form of the address, possibly giving only the company name or the logo. Obviously, they should be printed to complement the size of the letterhead in use. If you use a computer, your program will automatically insert a page break in a pre-set position, and run on to a second, or 'continuation' sheet automatically.

Envelopes

Again, many companies use plain envelopes, but if you are printing them, position the company name and address at the top left-hand corner or on the back flap. It is not necessary to give the telephone number or other information.

Compliment slips

Used when sending out items that do not require a full letter; perhaps a printed information sheet or brochure. Again, make sure that it includes all the name, address, telephone, telex, e-mail, web-site and fax information, in the same position as on the letterhead. It should also include the words 'With Compliments', centrally placed, but leaving space for the sender to add a signature or a short message if necessary.

Compliments slips should be printed on A7 (74 x 105 mm).

Address labels

Like printed envelopes, address labels need only include the name and address of the company.

GREEN NOTE

It is now possible to get good quality paper that has not been treated with chemicals that harm the environment, or that has some recycled elements. Find out whether your company's paper is 'green'. If not, research suppliers of recycled or environmentally-friendly papers – their product is probably the same price as for ordinary papers. However, Beware! Some low-grade recycled papers can jam photocopiers and sensitive printers, so take advice before converting to green paper products.

Business cards

Normally printed on card, the same colour as the company's letterhead. Size varies, but for ease of use should probably be no larger than a credit card.

They should show: company name, address and logo; telephone number, including the holder's extension number; any other telephone numbers that might be useful (a sales representative's mobile telephone, for example); fax, e-mail, web site and telex numbers; the holder's name and title (or department), usually centred in prominent type.

Facsimile front sheet

For use when sending faxes. Information as letterhead, but without the statutory information. The words 'Facsimile Transmission' in a prominent position, followed by a format that enables the user to give the sender's name and extension number, the addressee's name and company, the date, and space for a short message. There should also be space to give a contact number if the transmission is not successful, e.g.: 'If you encounter problems with this transmission, please contact (name and extension number)'.

Invoices and orders

Should include all the information on the letterhead, including the statutory information and the VAT registration number. Space should be allocated for the details of the invoice or order to be filled in, including details of the goods, price, VAT, terms of business (often drafted by a solicitor and printed on the reverse of an invoice, quotation, estimate or order), delivery information, etc.

Memo pad

Because memos are normally only used internally, the information given need only show the company's logo or name. The exception is that some companies are spread over more than one site, and in this case, memo books should give relevant site information.

E-mails

If you are sending an e-mail (electronic mail) outside the company, you may wish to produce a document on headed paper on your computer, and then send attach the letter file to your message. This allows the recipient to print out your letter so that it appears in a more formal context (which can be important if it needs to be circulated). If you are simply sending a message by e-mail, include your company name, your position, and the address and telephone number on which you can be reached, after your name.

Paper quality

Paper is normally specified by name or by weight. The paper most often used for company letterheads, compliment slips, etc. is called 'bond', and its weight is either 70 g/m^2 or the better quality 110 g/m^2.

The weight refers to the weight in grams of one square metre of the paper (grams per square metre, abbreviated as g/m^2 or sometimes as gsm.

Other paper weights are as listed overleaf:

NAME	WEIGHT	USES
Bond	70 or 110 g/m²	Letterhead and top copies
Bank	40-45 g/m²	Carbon or file copies
Airmail	25-30 g/m²	Airmail letters
Duplicating	60-70 g/m²	Photocopies

Paper sizes

The metric system of paper sizes uses a prefix, A, followed by a number. Beginning with A0, each successive size is half the size of the one before (the one exception being ⅔A4). In the following list, the first dimension given refers to the top edge:

NAME	SIZE
A0	841 × 1189 mm
A1	594 × 841 mm
A2	420 × 594 mm
A3	297 × 420 mm
A4	210 × 297 mm
⅔A4	210 × 198 mm
A5	148 × 210 mm
A6	105 × 148 mm
A7	74 × 105 mm

GREEN NOTE

It is not possible at the moment to recycle envelopes with windows, even as low-grade waste. Therefore stick to normal white envelopes (preferably using green papers), re-use them if possible, and recycle them when they are finished with.

Envelope sizes

The convention when describing the size of an envelope is to give the side with the flap as the second figure. Envelopes designed to be used with metric papers are given a prefix – C.

NAME	SIZE	PAPER USED
C3	324 x 458 mm	A3 unfolded
C4	229 x 324 mm	A4 unfolded
C5	162 x 229 mm	A5 unfolded, A4 folded once
C6*	114 x 162 mm	A6 unfolded, A5 folded once, A4 folded twice
C5/6*	110 x 220 mm	A4 folded twice into three, A5 folded once or ⅔A4 folded once

* These sizes are preferred by the Post Office.

3
Information Systems
DOCUMENT STORAGE AND INFORMATION RETRIEVAL

3
Information Systems

DOCUMENT STORAGE AND
INFORMATION RETRIEVAL

Section 2 dealt with three forms of written communication: letters, memoranda and reports. This section covers the filing and storage of such documents so that they can be used as a reliable source of information about the activities of your company. It then goes on to look at other sources of information available to UK companies.

At the end of this section is a list of useful addresses for information on a very wide range of subjects related to doing business in the UK. Other addresses are given throughout this book, and can be found using the index.

3.1 Filing
There are two major criteria for a good filing system:
- It should protect documents from damage.
- It should enable easy access to information by *anyone*, not just the person who created the system.

Choosing an appropriate filing system
You may have inherited a filing system from your predecessor, or you may need to start a new filing system. If the latter is the case, you will need to consider: a suitable method of storage and a suitable method of classification of the documents stored. There are many different storage systems on the market: from the familiar cabinets containing hanging files, to box files and lever arch files, right through to microfilming documents using a central computer storage and retrieval system.

Points to consider:
- What amount of documents do you want to store?
- Are they confidential and therefore need a lock and key?

- Are they important legal documents and therefore need a fireproof safe?
- What is the nature of your business, and into what kinds of categories do the documents that your office handle fall?

The method of classification depends on the type of information you need to store. Whichever method you choose (and several are outlined below), be logical in your choice and consistent in your implementation of the system. Some offices require two separate systems (for example, one for suppliers and one for clients), but more than two systems may well become so confusing as to be useless. If you decide to change the filing system, do it all at once, not in bits and pieces.

Alphabetical order

Many filing systems (especially those containing correspondence) are arranged in alphabetical order with individual documents filed in reverse chronological order (that is, the most recent correspondence at the front) in each file. The following are some rules for alphabetical ordering:

- File in A–Z order. E.g.,

  Brown & Co.
  Cape & Co.
  Dale Ltd

- Nothing comes before something. E.g.,

  Brown, E.J.
  Browne, D.T.
  Brownlow, G.B.

- Names containing numbers should be filed as if they were spelled out. E.g.,

  123 Decorators Ltd = One Two Three
  21st Century Electronics = Twenty-first

Alternatively, file these documents in a separate section at the front end of your filing system (before the letter 'A').

- Where there are two names, file under the first and cross-reference under the second. E.g., Smith, Jones & Co. should be filed under Smith and cross-referenced under Jones
- Where the names are double-barrelled or hyphenated, file under the first name.
- If the name has a prefix, such as Le, La, Les, etc., treat the prefix as part of the name.
- If the name starts with Mac, Mc, etc., file as Mac.
- If the name starts with an abbreviation, file as if the abbreviation were spelled in full. E.g. St Michael Institute = Saint Michael Institute
- If the name starts with an article ('a', 'an', 'the'), ignore the article.

Geographical listing

Geographical order takes into account an area, and then lists places within that area in alphabetical order. E.g.,

London:
  Battersea
  Chelsea
  Clapham
  Kensington
  St John's Wood
  Seven Sisters
  Walthamstow
or:
England:
  Bristol
  Coventry
  Liverpool
  Manchester
or:
 Scotland:
  Aberdeen

Edinburgh
Glasgow
or:
Western Europe:
  Austria
    Salzburg
    Vienna
  France
    Bordeaux
    Lille
    Lyons
    Marseilles
    Paris
  Netherlands
    Amsterdam
    Haarlem
    Utrecht

Terminal digit system

This is a numerical system in which the reference number is read backwards from right to left. Where there are three pairs of two digits, the right-hand pair refers to a drawer, the centre pair refers to a file position in that drawer, and the left-hand pair refers to a document within that file. E.g., document 24 31 06 is the 24th document of file 31, to be found in drawer 06.

If there are two sets of three-digit numbers, the second set refers to the location, while the first set refers to the number of the document in the file.

The advantage of the terminal digit system is that every document is individually numbered and can be located at a precise position within the system. It may, however, be more time-consuming to implement, in that each document must be given the correct reference number.

Other numerical systems

There are several other numerical systems currently in use for more complex filing, including the Dewey Decimal system, which is used for filing books in libraries. They also include alpha-numerical systems, in which a document is allocated a letter and a number. For example, a document relating to a company called Hodgkins Removals Ltd could be filed under H/26. The letter refers to the file, and the number is that of the document, and gives its position in the file.

Indexing

Because all filing systems should be accessible to everyone, it is a good idea to make an index of the system. Keep the index up to date, and store it where other people can easily consult it.

Removing files from the system

If you are in charge of a filing system, never allow people to take away files without telling you. Set up a 'loan' system so that you can easily keep track of where the files are.

Put a marker card at the location of the borrowed file, with information on it telling you who has the file and when it is to be returned. A reminder to yourself could be kept in a Bring forward file (see below), so that you can chase files when they become overdue.

Day files

A day file is a separate file that contains copies of your outgoing correspondence and other documents originated by you in date order. This enables you to find documents that have not yet been filed, or anything that may have gone astray, for instance if a document was not received. Simply take an extra copy of every document you produce (preferably on different-coloured, lightweight paper) and drop it into the front of the file. Bind the documents together in reverse date order (they should already be sorted) when the file is full.

Never remove single documents from a file – they could easily become lost. Instead, take the whole file and photocopy the single document you require.

Bring forward files

A useful system for ordering documents that need to be attended to on a particular day. Use a concertina file, and label each pouch with a number referring to a date of the month, up to 31. As items come up, place them in the pouch for the day when you should attend to them. File any documents that refer to dates beyond the capacity of the file in the main filing system and make a note in your diary.

Once you have attended to a day's documents, you can use that pouch for the same day in the following month.

File security and safety

Confidential files and documents should be kept under lock and key in a separate filing cabinet. The originals of legal and other valuable documents should be kept in a fireproof cabinet or safe, or at another secure location.

Research files

It may be that you, your manager or department have a certain specialist field, and that you need to keep an eye on the press for developments. In this case, it is useful to keep a research file for clippings. Divide the clippings by subject area and file each subject area separately. Remember to note on the clipping the name and date of the publication.

Dead files

From time to time, it will be necessary to weed out old files and dispose of them, or move them to an archive, so that you have enough space to continue filing properly. Some documents must be kept for a certain period of time. Check before you destroy anything. Sensitive documents should be shredded.

Instead of destroying files, it may be useful to rent warehouse space for archive filing. It is possible to rent secure storage space to which you can gain access during office hours. The warehouse filing system should be just as organized as the office system, and remember to keep an index of the archive in the office.

Hints for good filing

- Create a filing system that is logical and accessible to all.
- Index the system and keep the index up to date.
- Keep in control of 'wandering files'. Ensure that borrowing forms are filled out and that files are returned promptly.
- Ensure that the method of filing is appropriate to the material being filed.
- Don't use paperclips to hold documents together, replace them with staples.
- Ensure that documents are flat, not creased, when filed and that they do not protrude over the edge of hanging files.
- Keep up to date with the filing. File every day if you can. If not, keep a day file (see above).
- Never file anything until it has been dealt with (see Bring forward file, above).
- While filing documents, glance over them to check that they have been dealt with. If not, draw this to the attention of the relevant person.
- If filing facsimiles, remember that they deteriorate very quickly, so make a back-up photocopy.
- Always label files, giving the full title and opening date.
- When files are full, add the closing date to the label.

For hints on electronic filing see 7.4, Hints for easy-access electronic filing.

3.2 Keeping an address file

Note down and file the names and contact information for every person that you meet in a business context; from the person who gave you a good price on bulk photocopying, to the name of your most important client (and his or her PA).

Address files are kept in a variety of forms – in pocket-sized, loose-leaf binders, rotary card indexes, or even on computer database.

Whatever the format, ensure that the file is kept up to date, and that it is legible (so that other people can use it). Ease of access is important, so make sure that whatever system you use, you can get at it quickly. If you are keeping hard files (card indexes or address books), type the information onto sticky address labels, rather than hand-writing them. Include the following information:

- name
- job title and company
- full address
- telephone number
- fax number
- notes

Notes are useful to remind you of the circumstances of chance contacts, and of the reason for your last communication. An address file that includes notes (such as 'cheap photocopying', 'international distribution') becomes invaluable when staff change and your successor needs to take the reins.

The rules for correct filing should be followed when filing names and addresses. Cross-referencing between individuals' names and their company names is particularly important.

If you type the address labels using a word processor it would be a simple matter to produce an extra card index or a portable address book in a short space of time if required, say for a new member of staff.

Computer database systems can carry large amounts of information, and can be programmed to print out only the relevant address details onto sticky labels for the hard file. A word processor or database system also enables you to keep security copies, should an address file be lost or damaged. You might also be able to use the same listings for circulars or function invitations.

Many computer software programs also come with 'address' files, which can be accessed quickly by keyword or number, and used to dial a fax from your computer, or to add addresses to letters, documents and labels.

Make a habit of collecting business cards. You may find it useful to make the relevant notes on the back of the card on the spot, for transfer to the index later.

It is best not to do this in front of the contact, however. This applies most particularly if your contact is from the Far East. In these regions, business cards are considered an extension of the person, and writing on the business card demonstrates that you have little respect either for person or persona. (See also 12.6, Business etiquette abroad.)

Note for the self-employed

If you work from home, it is very easy to mix up your business and your personal life. However, it is a good idea to keep two address books – one for business and one for personal contacts. If you use a computer, keep separate desktop files for 'work' and 'personal'.

Home addresses

Unless the contact works from home, home addresses and telephone numbers that have been given to you should be used with discretion, and they should not generally be circulated.

Never give out the home telephone numbers of members of staff. Instead, take a message and call the staff member yourself with the caller's contact number.

3.3 Sources of information

It is a great advantage to know where to find information. Market surveys, addresses and details of competitors and possible clients, details of training courses; a wealth of information is now available to the modern business, either through electronic databases such as Ceefax, Prestel and Oracle, through a specialist library, or on the Internet.

Standard reference books

Collins English Dictionary
A basic requirement for all offices is a concise, single-volume dictionary, large enough to provide you with the correct spellings and definitions of all the words you want to look up. The *Collins Concise English Dictionary* is particularly recommended because it is up-to-date and contains a wide range of information.

Roget's Thesaurus
A 'treasury' of synonyms to help improve your word-power. See Using a thesaurus, p.38.

Telephone Directories
The Business Directory is regional, and lists all businesses in your area. *The Yellow Pages* gives a useful classified list. Both are available free from British Telecom, and you can order copies of directories for other parts of the country – also free of charge. Your local authority may also distribute a directory of useful business addresses in your area.

The Royal Mail Guide
Published by the Post Office, and updated monthly, this is the definitive guide to Post Office services. For a copy of the Royal Mail Guide, send payment to the address below. Check your local Post Office customer services department for further information.

> Royal Mail Letters
> Royal Mail Guide
> Freepost KE8421
> 76 Turnmill Street
> LONDON
> EC1B 1ES

Whitaker's Almanack
A useful annual directory. Includes a list of institutions and associations (who can be contacted in the search for specialist information). Lists members of the peerage, politicians, etc. Also gives up-to-date information on other countries around the world, including population statistics.

The World's Best Business Hotels
Published by Bloomsbury, this directory lists some 500 hotels in 80 countries, with details of facilities for business travellers.

Key British Enterprises
Dun & Bradstreet's directory of more than 20 000 British companies.

Kompass Register
Gives details of companies both in the UK and abroad.

Who's Who
Biographies of prominent people.

Who Owns Whom
Gives up-to-date details of company 'parentage'.

Libraries

The British Library
The British Library is one of Britain's copyright libraries. That is, a copy of all books published in the UK is automatically sent to the British Library to establish copyright. The library is divided into sections by subject. The following list gives telephone numbers for some of its departments:

- Main switchboard (0171) 636-1544
- Biotechnology Information (0171) 412-7293
- Business Information (0171) 412-7454
- Japanese Information Service (0171) 412-7924
- Newspaper Library (0171) 412-7353
- Patents (0171) 412-7919
- Science and Information Service (0171) 412-7494
  (0171) 412-7288
- Science and Technology (0171) 412-7477

Local libraries
These can provide a wealth of self-help books as well as leaflets on a wide range of employee-related matters. There is usually a reference section that includes dictionaries and directories. All

local libraries are part of the inter-library loan scheme, through which it is possible to order books (provided you know the title, author and publisher) that are not held at the library. Some local libraries also hold indexes of periodicals giving details of articles, and some have copies of past newspapers and magazines on microfilm.

University and college libraries
These resources are often open to outside users. A local university or college may charge a small fee to outside users, or you may simply need to produce a letter from your employer explaining why you need to use the service and for how long.

Other libraries
Many government departments run libraries that are open to members of the public (as long as you have a good reason for using them). It is best to call before you visit to check opening times and gain permission to use the library. Such libraries include: Department of Trade and Industry (London); Employment Department (London and Sheffield); ACAS (London); the Scottish Office (Edinburgh); the Welsh Office (Cardiff); Confederation of British Industry (London).

Some foreign embassies (such as the US Embassy, Grosvenor Square, London) also run libraries to provide information in an effort to improve exports to this country.

Librarians
Make a friend of the librarian in any library you use regularly. You will find that he or she is a mine of information, and can save you a huge amount of time finding the right reference source.

Other sources of information
There are now a number of companies specializing in providing information for business users. Government departments also produce a mountain of leaflets, booklets and handbooks on legislation, codes of practice, employment advice, etc. Here are some suggestions.

Prestel
Computer information system operated by British Telecom. It uses the telephone lines to send hundreds of thousands of pages of on-line information. This service also enables you to transact business by computer.

Oracle
On-line information service offered by the BBC, and accessed through a television.

Ceefax
The ITV equivalent of Oracle. Both Oracle and Ceefax are classified as 'teletext' services.

The Internet
The Internet is a worldwide network of computers, holding vast quantities of data that you can access directly from your computer. Access to the Internet is channelled through the high-speed links provided by commercial organizations known as service providers. Technically, anyone with a PC and modem can telephone a service provider and access the Internet. You will need to purchase software to use and start exploring 'the Net' (see p.188). When you are on the Internet you can access any of the huge amount of electronic data that is stored on the computers that make up the Internet.

The Information Bureau
Formerly the Telegraph Information Service, the Information Bureau can supply the answers to almost any question, either instantly over the telephone or, after a telephoned request, by fax the same day. A fee is charged for each enquiry.

> The Information Bureau
> 51 Battersea Business Centre
> 103 Lavender Hill
> LONDON
> SW11 5QL
> Tel: (0171) 924-4414

Registrar of Companies

Central registry of all companies registered in the UK and
Northern Ireland. Operates a company search service and can
provide microfilm copies of documents held, for a small fee. For
full details of services, contact:

> The Registrar of Companies (Search Room)
> Companies House
> 55–71 City Road
> LONDON
> EC1Y 1BB
> Tel: (0171) 253-9393

There are regional registries in Cardiff, Leeds, Birmingham,
Manchester, Glasgow (for companies registered in Scotland) and
Belfast (for those registered in Northern Ireland).

Her Majesty's Stationery Office (HMSO)

Publishes a wide variety of documents, booklets and leaflets,
including codes of practice and legislation (and the Highway
Code). A telephone ordering service is available, and you can pay
by credit card. A free list of almost all HMSO's publications can
be obtained from:

> The Stationery Office
> Publicity, Room 2D
> St Crispins
> Duke Street
> NORWICH
> NR3 1PD
> Tel: (01603) 622211

Central Statistical Office

Information related to government statistics.

> Office for National Statistics
> 1 Drummond Gate
> LONDON
> SW1V 2QQ
> Tel: (0171) 233-9233

Extel

A subscription service widely used in business, and often available in specialist libraries. Information is supplied in an updata-

ble card index for UK companies, giving details of directors, nature of business, etc.

Extel Financial Ltd
Fitzroy House
13–17 Epworth Street
LONDON
EC2A 4DL
Tel: (0171) 251-3333

Department of Trade and Industry
Among other things, the DTI publishes an annual list of publications produced by several government departments, including the DTI itself, the Monopolies and Mergers Commission and the Department of Energy. It is available free of charge.

Department of Trade and
   Industry
Library and Information
   Centre
1–19 Victoria Street
LONDON
SW1H 0ET
Tel: (0171) 215-5000
Fax: (0171) 215-5665

Chambers of Commerce
Each district in the UK has a Chamber of Commerce, which could provide useful advice and information on local business matters.

Useful addresses

British-American Chamber of Commerce
19 Stratford Place
London W1N 9AF
Tel: (0171) 491-3361

Commission for Racial Equality
Elliott House
10-12 Allington Street
London SW1E 5EH
Tel: (0171) 828-7022
or
Alpha Tower (11th Floor)
Suffolk Street
Queensway
Birmingham B1 1TT
Tel: (0121) 632-4544
or
Maybrook House (5th Floor)
40 Blackfriars Street
Manchester M3 2EG
Tel: (0161) 831-7782
or
100 Princes Street
Edinburgh EH2 3AA
Tel: (0131) 226-5186

Confederation of British Industry
Centre Point
New Oxford Street
London WC1A 1DU
Tel: (0171) 379-7400

**Equal Opportunities
   Commission**
Overseas House
Quay Street
Manchester M3 3HN
Tel: (0161) 833-9244
or
Caerwys House
Windsor Lane
Cardiff CF1 1LB
Tel: (01222) 343552
or
Stock Exchange House
7 Nelson Mandela Place
Glasgow G2 1QW
Tel: (0141) 248-5833

**Health and Safety Executive
   (HSE)**
Information Centre
Broad Lane
Sheffield S3 7HQ
Infoline:: (0541) 545500
Fax: (0114) 2892333
HSE Books: (01787) 881165

**Her Majesty's Stationery
   Office (HMSO)**
PO Box 276
London SW8 5DT
Enquiries tel: (0171) 873-0011

Institute of Directors
116 Pall Mall
London SW1Y 5ED
Tel: (0171) 839-1233

**Institute of Personnel
   Management**
IPD House
Camp Road
London SW19 4UX
Tel: (0181) 971-9000

**Department of Educational
   Employment**
Head Office
Moorfoot
Sheffield
Tel: (0114) 2753275

Office of Fair Trading
Field House
15–25 Breams Buildings
London EC4A 1PR
Tel: (0171) 211- 8000

**Office of
   Telecommunications
   (OFTEL)**
Export House
50 Ludgate Hill
London EC4M 7JJ
Tel: (0171) 634-8700

Trades Union Congress
Great Russell Street
London WC1B 3LS
Tel: (071) 636-4030

4

Across the Wires

TELEPHONE SKILLS AND SERVICES

4
Across the Wires
TELEPHONE SKILLS AND SERVICES

Since the invention of the telephone, telecommunications, both inland and abroad, have increased in complexity and capability in leaps and bounds. Aided by satellite, you can communicate by word of mouth or in writing across the world at a moment's notice and you can pay for your calls by credit card or have them billed to your office number wherever you are in the world.

4.1 Using the telephone

The telephone is a mixed blessing. While it puts you in contact with people all over the world at the touch of a few buttons, it can also bring unwanted interruptions at the most awkward times. This is most especially true of small companies, where it is often the case that everybody is responsible for answering calls.

If your company does not already have a receptionist, telephonist or secretary/PA who is detailed to handle all incoming calls, arrange for somebody to do this. They can then screen calls and put them through if you are not too busy, or they can deal with queries without interrupting you. If the person the caller is trying to reach is tied up with something, try to avoid giving a response to the effect of 'She's too busy to talk to you', which is offensive. 'She's not available just now. Can I take a message?' is much more helpful.

Because we don't pay for telephone calls on an as-you-use basis, it is easy to forget that telephone bills very quickly add up. Learning to use the telephone economically, therefore, is essential. If you find that your bills are becoming astronomical, it might be useful to have them itemized, so that the bill shows each number dialled for calls over a certain value threshold. This will tell you where your company is spending most of its telephone budget (and it may help you catch out those employees who are using the company phones to call long-distance for personal purposes).

Answering the telephone

When you answer the telephone, you are the caller's first contact with your company. Be clear, pleasant and helpful, and you will give them a good impression from the word go.

- Always keep a notebook handy, to note down callers' names and take any messages.
- Answer the phone promptly, within four rings if possible.
- Give your company's name or telephone number (find out what is preferred). Ask how you can help, then listen to the caller's request.
- Take the caller's name. Write it down if this helps you to remember. Some managers also like to know which company the caller is from and what it is they are calling about.
- Tell the caller if you would like them to hold on while you dial an extension or find the relevant person.
- Keep the caller informed as to what you are doing. Perhaps you cannot get an answer at one extension, and you want to try another – tell the caller so, and apologize for keeping them waiting.
- If the extension is busy, ask the caller whether he or she wants to hold, call back later or leave a message.
- If the caller wants to hold, don't let him or her hold on too long without getting back. Every time you go back to the caller, give him or her the opportunity to terminate the call or to opt to leave a message.
- If you are asked to take a message, write it down and make sure that it arrives with the appropriate person promptly. Ask the caller to spell out details of which you are unsure.
- Be attentive, polite and helpful – you never know who is calling.

This procedure also applies to those using switchboards.

If you are responding to a call on your extension, give your name or the name of your department when you pick up the phone, rather than simply saying 'hello'.

If you are responding to an extension at someone else's desk, give the name of that person – 'Roger's phone...', so that the caller knows immediately that you are not the person they are looking for.

Making outgoing calls

Time spent talking on the telephone is expensive, especially at peak times, so it is useful to know how to find the person you need to talk to with the minimum amount of fuss, and then how to get your message across.

Telephone rates

Different rates are charged for calls at different times of day, and these vary according to the telephone company with which your business has its lines. Find out when the cheapest calls can be made, and try to make most of your out-going calls during this time.

Plan your telephone timetable for the day if you can. Schedule calls that are long-distance or will take time for early morning, afternoon or early evening. Try to keep morning calls to local or very quick calls. Avoid making personal calls, especially at peak rate.

STD (Subscriber Trunk Dialling) codes

All telephones are connected to an exchange, which covers a particular geographical area. When dialling inside your local area, you need only dial the number you require. However, if dialling outside the area, you will first need to dial an STD code number to connect yourself to the exchange you require. STD codes are listed by geographical area in British Telecom's *The Code Book*, and in the front of *The Phone Book*. The STD system allows you to dial any number without having to be connected by the operator. The STD codes for a selection of UK towns and cities is given in section 4.11.

IDD (International Direct Dialling)

If you are dialling a number abroad, you will need to make use of the IDD system by dialling a series of codes before the number you are trying to contact: an international code, a country code, a local code and then the number. For example, if you are trying to reach a number in Manhattan, New York, dial the international code (**00**) + the country code for the USA (**1**) + the local code for Manhattan (**212**) + the number you require.

A list of selected country codes is given on pp.306–308, and city codes for major European cities on pp.311–322.

Each dialling area is charged at a different rate, depending on its distance from the caller. If you find that your company makes large numbers of long-distance calls, you may find that a Mercury option (a mechanism whereby you can switch to the Mercury system when making long-distance calls) will save money. There are a variety of competitive telephone systems now available, and you should investigate the options if you find that your company is spending a great deal of money on telephone bills.

International call charges also vary depending on the time of day, and the charge periods are not necessarily the same as for the UK. Check with the international operator, or in *The Phone Book*, in BT's handbook for businesses, or in the guide book for the telephone system your company uses.

Some countries are currently not included in the IDD system, and you will therefore need to make the connection through the international operator by dialling 155.

Before you start

Make a note of the person you want to speak to, and the substance of the conversation. This may be a list of questions or a list of the information you want to give. Make sure that you have all the information you will need (including the telephone number) in front of you before you dial.

Getting through

Dial carefully – misdialled numbers cost money and irritate people. If you do dial a wrong number, apologize before you hang up.

When you are through to the right number, ask for the person you would like to talk to (and give that person's extension number, if they have one).

Speak directly into the mouthpiece of the phone, so that you can be heard clearly. If necessary, reduce the background noise at your end to help the person at the other end hear you.

If you write with your right hand, hold the telephone receiver in your left, so that you have a free hand to take notes with if necessary.

If you are asked for your name, give your full name and the company you are calling from. When you are connected to the right person, announce yourself, again using your full name and giving your company.

Explain as quickly as you can what it is you want and ask for a specific response or action. 'I'm looking for a new photocopier and I wondered if you might send me information about the XX model' is better than 'I need a new photocopier'.

If you are calling on behalf of someone else, explain who you are and why you are calling: 'My name is Andrew Jennings. I'm calling on behalf of Julie Sheasby of Sheasby and Associates, to confirm that she will be able to meet you on Tuesday.'

If you need to give information, ask that the person at the other end repeats the message so that you are certain that they have got it right. Spell out any difficult words (people's names and addresses, for instance), and double-check figures. Do the same if you are receiving information.

If you fail to reach the person you need, leave a message for them with your name, company name, telephone and extension number, and ask that they call you back.

Remember, that if you are cut off during a call, the original caller should try to reconnect.

Who do I speak to?

Sometimes, you may be unsure who is the best person to answer the query you have. This is where your telephone talents will really be stretched. Depending on the clarity with which you explain your needs and the skill of the telephonist, this could be a matter of a quick transfer to the right person or the start of a lengthy (and expensive) wild goose chase.

You will need to explain to the telephonist what it is you require in as few words as possible, and then ask him or her to put you through to the relevant department. You may alternatively consider what kind of department might be able to answer your question: customer services, perhaps, or public relations. Ask the telephonist whether the company has this department and ask to be put through.

When you are put through to a department, let them know that you are unsure that you have reached the right person. 'I wonder if you might be able to help me...' or 'I wonder if I have been put through to the right department...' Phrases such as these alert your contact to the fact that you are unsure, and if you explain your query properly, they will either answer it or tell you which department you require.

When you get through to the right department and you have your question answered, it is a good idea to take the name of the person you spoke to, and the name of the department. File this information (perhaps in a card index or contact book, see 3.2, Keeping an address file) and when it comes to a similar question, you will already have the source of the answer to hand.

GREEN NOTE

The chemicals used to 'sanitize' office telephones may contain disinfectants that could be dangerous to your health if you inhale them in large quantities. A cloth dipped in clean water is by far the best solution.

4.2 Using answerphones

There are several types of answerphone generally available. One type is capable of answering a call and playing a recorded message. This is useful when needing to give standard information, perhaps if there is no-one at the office. It is possible to record any message, then set the machine. When a caller is connected, the machine will ring a couple of times, and then the tape recording is played. It might give a time when the office is open or staffed, or it may give standard information in response to enquiries that staff are too busy to answer in person.

Another type which is now more widely used allows the user to record an outgoing message and for the caller to register a tape-recorded message in response. These machines often come with a telephone handset built in, along with a wide range of other facilities:

● *Call collecting*: a facility whereby the owner of the machine may call it from another location to hear the messages that have been left. The messages are accessed by way of a small electronic 'bleeper', which gives the answerphone a security code, or through a spoken message. Some machines give you the option to hear your messages more than once, so that you can get down details you did not catch the first time. However, others 'wipe'

the messages when they have been collected, so make sure that
you have a pen and paper handy, and that you are in a quiet
place when you call in. If you have picked up a message that is
not for you but for one of your colleagues, remember to call the
machine and re-record the substance of that message.

● *Call screening:* some machines enable you to listen to calls as
they are recorded, through a small loudspeaker, and some also
enable you to reach the person in the process of leaving the message by picking up the handset. A useful facility to have if you are
too busy to answer all but the most urgent calls immediately.

Answerphones connect directly to the telephone network
through the normal telephone sockets fitted by a telephone company. Machines that do not have built-in handsets will require an
adaptor that will allow you to connect the answerphone and your
telephone to the system via the same socket. Those that have
handsets only have one plug, and so do not require an adaptor.
You will also need a power socket close by.

Some companies have an automated system whereby the caller
can use their telephone to access lines within the building by
pressing numbers in response to a series of instructions (see
Voice Mail (below). In this system, you can normally press a
number, or hold on, for operator assistance.

Voice Mail

Voice mail is a communication system that changes spoken telephone messages into digital form, then converts the digital
signals back to sound when the receiver logs on to the system to
'pick up' his or her 'mail'. The system has far more memory than
conventional telephone answering machines. It can also handle
many incoming calls simultaneously.

A voice-mail system consists mainly of software, which runs on
a personal computer (PC) connected to a company's phone
system; it can be added to any type of centralized phone system.
Automated software answers the phone and allows the caller to
use touch-tone identification to be connected to the appropriate
person or department. If no one answers the call, software
enables the caller to leave a message.

A variety of optional features are available with most voice-
mail systems. One such feature is automated call rerouting,

which automatically transfers incoming calls to people at remote locations. Fax-on-demand, allowing a caller to key in a facsimile-machine number, can be integrated with voice mail.

Leaving a message

When you are connected to an answerphone or voice-mail system, listen carefully to the instructions. You should already know what it is you want to say, but make sure that you give the following information: your name (and company), the day and time of your call, the name of the person you are trying to contact, and a message. If the message is short (perhaps you want to confirm a meeting or check that an order is being delivered) then by all means leave it on the tape. If your message is more complex it would be a good idea either to ask the other person to call back or to say that you will do so.

Spell out any words or figures that might be difficult to hear over the tape.

Never leave confidential or personal information on an answerphone tape. There is no guarantee that the message will be picked up confidentially.

4.3 Relaying messages

Use a message pad or form, and fill in the following information:
● name of caller
● caller's company
● caller's telephone number and extension
● your name
● date, day and time of the call
● name of person to whom the call was made
● message

Check all spellings and numbers, and read the message back to the caller to check that you have not misunderstood anything.

Always write messages down (it's easy to forget or misremember), and take them to the recipient (or the relevant in-tray or bulletin board) immediately, before you forget. Take responsibility for ensuring that the message gets to the right person. Do not pass it on to someone else.

4.4 Conference calls

It is possible to set up a conference call involving up to 60 (and sometimes more) 'delegates' at one time, both inland and abroad. Call the your telephone company for details of charges and procedures.

4.5 Sending facsimiles

The so-called fax machine transmits visual information from one location to another by turning it into digital impulses and passing them to the receiving machine at the other end of the telephone line. It can be used to transmit artwork (currently in black and white only), letters or other written information very quickly, to locations all over the world. All faxes are capable of both transmitting and receiving documents.

There are several makes of fax machine on the market. Some have a built-in handset, and so can be used as both phone and fax. This is most useful when you only have one telephone line. Some also have built-in answerphones and a facility for recording and listing details of all transmissions, incoming and outgoing.

If a number is engaged, some fax machines will redial the number at intervals until the machines connect. This may be handy when you are too busy to keep dialling until you get through. However, if you notice that the machine is redialling, check that you have the right number – you may be calling an ordinary telephone and causing a nuisance to the person who keeps having to pick up at the other end.

To ensure that your fax gets to the right person, use a fax front sheet (see Facsimile front sheet, p.96) and give all the addressee information.

Many computers are able to send faxes through a modem, which allows you to work directly from your software program, without having to print out and send a document manually. If you use this facility, make sure you keep a copy of all documents sent – in an 'out file' or something similar.

4.6 Sending telexes

The telex system uses a teleprinter to send messages at speed via the telephone lines to other telex users. Like the fax, the system can be used regardless of whether there is an operator present at the receiving end. Messages are keyed into the telex machine, and printed out at the other end. If your office does not have its own telex machine, it is possible to send telexes through one of many bureaux, including British Telecom. Consult the *Yellow Pages* for details of local telex bureaux.

If your fax machine prints on ordinary fax paper, the message will not be permanent. For this reason they are not admissable as documentary evidence in a court of law. You can now get 'plain paper' faxes which avoid this problem.
- *Always photocopy faxes and file the photocopy along with the fax.*
- *You may want to send the top copy of the fax to the addressee by post the same day. This makes doubly sure that the addressee receives the information and that he or she has a permanent copy for their records.*

4.7 ISDN Lines

An Integrated Services Digital Network (ISDN) is a high-speed digital network that can carry voice, data, and video signals simultaneously on the same telephone line. Standard telephone lines carry data at speeds up to 28,800 bits per second (bps); an ISDN line provides speeds up to 128,000 bps.

Many companies now have ISDN lines, which allow you to send information electronically, in much the same way as you would send an e-mail (see pp.97 and 128–129), but the information transfer is much faster. You can use ISDN lines to send complex files with pictures and layouts direct to a printer, for example.

ISDN lines provide the fastest link to the Internet, but you will need to purchase a special telephone connection, and you will only be able to use it if your service provider also has an ISDN link. When sending information by ISDN, follow the same procedure as for e-mails.

4.8 Sending an e-mail

Your company will need to be set up to send and receive e-mails (electronic mail), but once you are 'on-line' the facilities available to you are virtually limitless. See page 00 for details of getting onto and using the Internet.

E-mail, refers to messages that are transmitted from computer to computer over ordinary telephone lines under the direction of an intermediate service. This service is a 'host' computer that receives messages, holds them, and sends them to their destination. It is not necessary for the sender and receiver of a message to be connected simultaneously. A user of e-mail needs a computer, a telephone line, and an e-mail service, as well as a modem (unless you are on a network).

There are many ways of sending and receiving e-mails, but the basic procedure is much the same. In an e-mail program, which will be supplied by your service provider, you type your message, keying in the address exactly as it appears. An e-mail address has two parts: the user name and a domain name, separated by an @ symbol. The number of domains in a name depends upon how many branches are required to sort it. Each address is unique and must be used exactly as given. If you add spaces, or change upper to lower case, or the reverse, the address will be invalid and your message will not be sent. Your 'user name' is any name that you choose (as long as it has not been registered by another subscriber) and may include the company's details; for example, csmith.simpsons. Your host name is the name of the Internet service provider, which is the company that supplies you with Internet access and is responsible for sending and receiving messages to and from each user. There are never spaces between full stops or adjacent letters in an e-mail address, so take care not to add any. The last section of the domain name identifies your service provider's type of organization, and this may vary between countries. The word 'com' normally means 'commercial company', as does 'co.'. A two-letter country code may form the last part of the domain name of a service provider based outside the US; for example, co.uk.

When your address has been completed, you will be asked for a 'reference', which is basically a title for the message you wish to send. You may have the option of requesting a receipt, which you will receive when the person to whom you are sending the e-mail retrieves it from his or her mailbox. It is also possible to give a message special priority, and some cases to ensure that it remains confidential. You may send the same message to a number of recipients by clicking the appropriate category.

You will also be able to attach a file, which can be a letter or any other document – including photographs, designed work, artwork, and in many cases sound and video – and this will be downloaded by the recipient's computer when he or she receives your e-mail message.

Once you have addressed and sent your e-mail it is encoded by a modem and sent down the telephone line as an analogue message. The message arrives at your provider's server, and if the address is valid, it will send it through the Internet to the recipient's provider, where it is distributed to his or her individual mailbox. Once your message reaches the 'host', it will remain there until the recipient next connects to the Internet. Finally, the recipient's modem and computer decode the data and your e-mail message can be read as a text file. Files that you have attached to your message will be read as they appeared on your computer, and remain untouched.

4.9 Useful numbers for telephone services

Operator	100
Emergency services	999
International operator	155
Directory enquiries	192
International directory	153
Fault reports (business lines)	154
Speaking clock	123 (0171/0181 numbers)
Conference calls	0800-282-429
Calling a ship at sea	0800-378389

Most telephone companies offer a wide range of services, including: reverse charge calls; credit card calls; wake-up calls; message service; faxes, calls and telegrams to ships at sea; advice of duration and charge payable on international calls; freefone calls; telemessages and telegrams; information lines; call screening and transfer.

Information on calling subscribers in other countries and on making calls to the UK from abroad can be found on p.306.

4.10 Malicious calls

It is an offence to make obscene or threatening calls. If you receive a malicious call, do not argue with the caller, and try not to betray your emotion. BT recommends that, instead, you place the handset beside the telephone for a few minutes and then hang up. If the calls are persistent, unplug your telephone.

Never give your name or address to any caller unless you are certain that you know who they are.

British Telecom operates an advice line for those receiving persistent malicious calls. Dial 0800-666700. It is also possible to have your calls screened by the operator and only people named by you put through.

4.11 STD codes for selected UK towns and cities

AREA	STD CODE	AREA	STD CODE
Aberdeen	01224	Ipswich	01473
Bath	01225	Kings Lynn	01553
Belfast	01232	Leeds	0113
Birmingham	0121	Leicester	0116
Brighton	01273	Lincoln	01522
Bristol	0117	Liverpool	0151
Canterbury	01227	London	0171 (inner)
Cambridge	01223		0181 (outer)
Cardiff	01222	Manchester	0161
Coventry	01203	Milton Keynes	01908
Dover	01304	Newcastle	0191
Dundee	01382	Nottingham	0115
Durham	0191	Oxford	01865
Edinburgh	0131	Plymouth	01752
Exeter	01392	Portsmouth	01705
Gatwick	01293	Reading	0118
Glasgow	0141	Salisbury	01722
Gloucester	01452	Southampton	01703

Halifax	01422	Swansea	01792
Hertford	01992	Swindon	01793
Huddersfield	01484	Telford	01952
Hull	01482	Winchester	01962
Inverness	01463	York	01904

If you are calling from within the local area of the town or city listed (i.e. if your phone number has the same dialling code), you will not need to dial the area code. If you are calling from nearby, you may find that there is a local dialling code. Check regional editions of *The Phone Book* for details.

5
Getting it There
POSTAL AND COURIER SERVICES

5
Getting it There
POSTAL AND COURIER SERVICES

Who deals with the mechanics of the post is entirely dependent upon whether your company is big enough to employ post-room workers. Even if there is a post-room, it often falls to secretarial and administrative staff to open the mail and present it to the relevant person, and to ensure that outgoing mail is correctly typed, marked and packaged. This section gives advice on dealing with the post and other items for despatch.

5.1 Postal routine

Despite the advent of electronic mail systems, the demise of the paper postal system as we know it is still a long way off. When dealing with incoming mail, the key is speed. When despatching items, the key is accuracy.

People who deal with the mail do so every day, and so it is worthwhile setting up a routine and sticking to it to make sure that the job is done quickly and that nothing is missed or misplaced.

Incoming items

- When you receive the mail, deal with it immediately.
- Open each letter/package, starting with ordinary letters and date-stamp them (check you are using the correct date).
- Never open mail marked 'Private' and addressed to somebody else. Find out whether your manager would like you to open letters marked 'Confidential'. Date-stamp unopened letters on the front of the envelope.
- As you open each letter, scan it for details of enclosures. Check that the enclosures are present, and staple them to the covering letter. If there is anything missing (especially remittances of any kind), write this information at the bottom of the letter. Check that remittances tally with the information given in the letter.

● Check letters also for details of the sender's address. If these are not written on the letter, but on the envelope, staple the envelope to the back of the letter for future reference.
● Sort the mail according to addressee and make sure that it is distributed.
● Your company may require that you list remittances or registered mail. Remember to do so.

Some secretaries and personal assistants pile the mail in sequence according to its importance, starting with confidential and personal letters on top, moving down to routine letters, with circulars and newspapers at the bottom of the pile.

Other items may appear throughout the day, such as those sent by courier. It is most important that these are dealt with immediately.

If you receive faxes or e-mails on behalf of your company, make sure they are either manually distributed to the correct person, or electronically dispatched from your computer (if you are on a network). Faxes and e-mails may indicate that the message is a priority and it is important that you deal with it as such. Always keep a file of in-coming e-mails, in the event that the message does not reach its destination in-house, or it is unintentionally wiped.

Outgoing mail
● Find out what the despatch deadline is, and make sure that you are in time to catch the post.
● See Letters checklist, p.81.
● Make sure that the postage is correct and that parcels are packaged correctly. The *Royal Mail Guide* gives details (see 5.2 Postal services).
● Sort items of outgoing mail intothe appropriate categories: first-class letters, second-class letters, guaranteed delivery and other special items.
● For letters, turn the envelopes so that they are all facing the same way and bind them with an elastic band.
● Ensure that all mail is ready for despatch at the right time, with the necessary documentation and instructions for posting. Find out what your company's standard procedure is for this.

5.2 Postal services

The Post Office and other courier companies offer reliable transport services for letters and parcels both nationally and internationally. Thanks to these, the UK has one of the best postal communications networks in the world, enabling you, for example, to despatch a package one morning and have it arrive in Hong Kong within 48 hours.

Choosing the right form of postage can save your company money and add to the efficiency of its external communications.

The Post Office annual publication *The Royal Mail Guide* gives details of all postal and other services offered by the Post Office. It is available from Royal Mail Letters (see Useful addresses, p.116), and is updated month-by-month. It includes current tariffs, along with details on packaging and preferred methods of address.

Inland postal services

The Post Office offers a wide variety of services, including discounts for bulk postings, cash-on-delivery, business reply services, etc. Here are a few of the most commonly used.

First-class letters and packets

Items that are sent first class normally arrive at their destination the following day. A fee is charged depending on the weight of the item, and there is no limit on the weight of first-class items.

Second-class letters and packets

Second-class items arrive at their destination on the second or third working day after posting. There is a weight limit on second-class post. Check with the Post Office for details.

It is possible to get a discount if you are despatching large numbers of second class letters. Again, contact the Post Office or consult *The Royal Mail Guide* or the appropriate leaflet for details.

Guaranteed delivery letters and packets

On payment of a surcharge, letters and packets can be sent guaranteed delivery, which means that they have priority and consequently are guaranteed to reach their destination the following day (provided that they are posted before a certain time, usually

5.15 pm on a weekday, and 12.15 pm on a Saturday). You will need to fill in a special delivery form, and hand the item in at the post office and obtain a receipt. If the item fails to reach the destination on the next working day, the Post Office refunds double the Guaranteed surcharge on production of the receipt. You can ring the number on your receipt the following day to confirm delivery.

Recorded delivery
A method by which the Post Office delivers items, and asks for a signature on receipt. They can then provide a record of delivery should there be a dispute. Fill in a recorded delivery form, hand the item in over the counter of the Post Office and pay the surcharge. You will receive a certificate of posting.

Registered post
A method by which you can insure items to be sent by post. The level of compensation depends on the surcharge paid. When the item is delivered, a receipt is signed, and this can be returned to the sender if a second surcharge is paid. Fill in a registered post form and hand it in over the counter of the Post Office along with the item. You will receive a receipt with details of charges paid.

Cash on delivery
The Post Office is able to collect payment for items on delivery if you wish. Items on which payments are to be made must be sent by registered post. Consult the *Royal Mail Guide* or contact the Post Office for details of regulations.

Freepost
A system by which clients can correspond with you without paying the postage. The company operating the system pays a small deposit, a set fee for every item conveyed by Freepost and an additional operating charge. You will need to obtain a licence from the Post Office to run a Freepost system, and to use a special address including the word Freepost. Contact the Post Office for further details.

Business reply service

Similar to Freepost, the Business Reply Service enables you to send out reply-paid envelopes, own-address labels or to print coupons for advertisements. These items will include a special design, and can be used for either first- or second-class post depending on the fee paid by the operating company. Contact the Post Office for further details.

Parcel post

Packets over a certain weight are classed as parcels and must be checked in across the Post Office counter, rather than posted in a letter box. Check with the Post Office for current weight limits and regulations.

There are a large number of other services, including special rates and individual collection from the sender for large numbers of items. Therefore, if in doubt, always check with the Post Office for the best method.

Overseas postal services

Overseas postal services are regulated by the Universal Postal Union, and this means that items posted and paid for in one country will be conveyed in another. Most countries in the world are members.

All packages and parcels sent overseas must be accompanied by a customs declaration.

Letters and packets to Europe

All letters addressed to destinations in Europe are now sent by air. You do not need to mark them for air mail.

Air mail outside Europe

All letters and small packets for destinations outside Europe must be labelled with a blue Air Mail, or *Par Avion* sticker, or marked with these words. The postage rate depends on the weight of the packet and its destination.

Aerogrammes

These are single-letter sheets that may be sent to any country in the Universal Postal Union. Aerogrammes can be bought with postage already paid at the Post Office. Otherwise, aerogrammes can be bought at stationers and the postage paid on posting at the Post office. Aerogrammes should not contain any enclosures.

Surface mail
Surface mail (sent overland or by sea) is obviously slower than air mail, but it is also cheaper.

Swiftair
For items that are going by air overseas, it is possible to pay a Swiftair surcharge. In this way you can hasten delivery by 24 hours, and you can also register and insure them. Hand Swiftair items in at the Post Office and fill in the relevant forms.

International Datapost
For extremely fast delivery of items around the world. The fee charged depends on the destination and the weight of the package. See also Addressing envelopes, p.68.

5.3 Paying postage
There are two major methods of paying for Royal Mail postage: either by buying stamps at the Post Office, or by leasing a franking machine and paying for the postage used at intervals.

Franking machines
Franking machines can be bought or rented. They are operated using a postage card, which works much in the same way as a phonecard. Units are bought from the Post Office, and the card is attached to the machine. When the units run out, the machine stops franking.

Those using franking machines must also fill in franking machine control cards, giving details of units bought and used. These cards must be filled in and returned to the Post Office every week, regardless of whether or not the machine has been used.

The franking machine will stamp ordinary letter envelopes and sticky labels for larger items. All items that have been franked must be handed in over the counter at the Post Office rather than posted in a box.

5.4 Keeping despatch records

It is always desirable to keep a record of the mail that your office sends out every day – if only to keep an eye on the stamps. A postage book is a good way of doing this.

Record the following details for each day:

- date
- balance of stamps brought forward from the previous day
- name of addressee
- location
- posting method
- amount of postage used
- stamps left over in the 'kitty'
- new stamps bought

Special methods of posting can be recorded in a separate book, with receipts or certificates of posting stuck down on the relevant entries. If you use couriers (see below), you can include details of despatches in the same place.

5.5 Courier services

There is now a large number of independent courier services operating in the UK, capable of taking parcels and documents door-to-door at speed either inland or internationally. Items for courier despatch are normally picked up at your office before a certain time, and delivered to the addressee's door. See the *Yellow Pages* for contact details. There may be a certain amount of paperwork to do at your end, so ask the service you are using for instructions. If you use a service regularly, you may like to ask them to give you a stock of forms so that you can fill them in in advance, and avoid waiting charges on behalf of the courier.

Courier charges are usually dependent upon destination and/or weight.

5.6 Red Star

Red Star is a courier service operated by the national railways. Items can normally be picked up at your office for transfer to the relevant railway station, or you can take them there yourself.

They are then taken by the next available train to the Red Star office at the station nearest to the location of the addressee. It is possible to find out what time the item will be waiting at the station, and the addressee can then be alerted.

Red Star also offers a door-to-door service whereby items are picked up at the sender's door (often by motorcycle courier) and at the other end transferred from the station to the addressee's door. This service is not available in all areas of the country, so ring for details before you propose to send a parcel this way.

Red Star is a good way of getting items across the country within a day. It can also offer destinations in the Channel Islands and in Europe.

6
Face to Face
GREETING AND MEETING

6
Face to Face
GREETING AND MEETING

While a great deal of communication now takes place on paper, via computer networks and over the telephone, meetings are still vital to the communication and decision-making process.

The way a company deals with meeting people says a great deal about its internal efficiency and its success as a business, so from the moment a meeting is arranged to the time a visitor leaves the building, the process should involve politeness and efficiency. This section covers ways of keeping a diary so that meetings are not missed, and with receiving and dealing with visitors.

Understanding how a meeting works and how business is transacted through discussion is vital for administrative and executive staff alike. Meetings can take one of several different forms, from the formal Annual General Meeting (which includes shareholders and board members, and must follow the procedures laid down in a company's Articles of Association under the guidance of a qualified company secretary), through presentations to clients, to an impromptu meeting in a colleague's office.

A list of key terms is provided (p.148), along with advice on making arrangements for meetings, drafting agendas, keeping an attendance register, taking minutes and receiving guests. The last part of this section deals with techniques such as how to get your message across and how to make the best use of visual aids in meetings.

6.1 Making appointments and keeping diaries

The efficiency with which your office handles appointments is an outward sign of the state of your company's ability to do business. Arranging and detailing appointments efficiently also enables other people to plan their workload effectively.

One diary or two?

It is often the case that a secretary is in charge of a manager's appointments. Many manager/secretary teams keep two diaries, and systematically keep them both up-to-date. However, the need for discipline in this is paramount, and so it may be easier to keep one large diary for both people, and delegate sole responsibility to the secretary.

Making appointments

- Liaise with the relevant person, and agree several possible times and dates. Write provisional appointments in the diary in pencil.
- Confirm the time and date, both verbally and in writing. Rub out the provisional appointments, and rewrite the confirmed time in the diary.
- List the following details:
  time and date of meeting
  place of meeting
  people involved in the meeting
  subject of the meeting and list of relevant documents that need to be (a) looked over beforehand, (b) taken to the meeting on the day
  note of travel arrangements
  contact number in case something goes wrong on the way
- Remember to leave enough time between appointments for unforeseen problems.
- Update diaries systematically. Intelligence on appointments can be gathered from the following sources:
  correspondence
  telephone calls
  after meetings, when the next meeting may have been arranged
  from the bring-forward file (see Bring forward files, p.106)
- If you are operating a two-diary system, compare them at regular intervals during the day.
- Remember to block-in holidays, note personal appointments (dentist, doctor, etc.), public holidays, important deadlines, birthdays and anniversaries, business trips.
- Leave a separate space for evening meetings and functions.

If your company has a receptionist, it is courteous to let him or her know who is expected to arrive and when. If you do so, visitors are more likely to be greeted with recognition.

6.2 Receiving visitors

The reception of visitors may fall to a receptionist, or to a secretary.

Reception duties

- Keep the reception area tidy. Keep flowers and plants watered and presentable. Empty ashtrays. Replace old and tattered magazines: suitable reading material may include trade magazines, current newspapers or the company's brochure or annual report. Keep yourself smart and presentable at all times.
- If staff are in the habit of sending lists of visitors as an advanced warning system, read them and be prepared for expected arrivals.
- Identify visitors and contact the relevant staff member.
- Ask visitors to sign the visitor's book. In the event of a fire, the visitor's book will act as a register of non-staff members in the building. Make sure, therefore, that you indicate in the book when visitors have left the building.
- Point out the waiting area, or direct the visitor to the relevant floor. It is on the whole better to operate a system whereby all visitors are escorted from reception to their meeting – a secretary or executive may arrive to do so. Never leave reception to do so yourself. Stick to the company's security arrangements.
- Unexpected arrivals (sales people or personal visitors) should be asked who it is they want to see. Be helpful and never dismissive. Contact the relevant person and ask if they have time to receive the visitor. If you have to turn someone away, be polite.
- Never allow unauthorized entry to the building. Make sure that security arrangements protect you from possible attack, and this includes knowing where to get help in an emergency.
- Deal with deliveries promptly and ensure they reach the addressee.

- Stay alert for suspicious packages. If you notice one, do not touch it, but contact the building security or a superior.
- Keep all potentially sensitive papers out of sight.

Useful reference for reception

- List of staff members, giving names, positions and extension numbers.
- Details of local transport services: bus stops, train timetables, etc.
- Telephone directories.
- Details of local parking arrangements. It is also useful to be knowledgeable about local parking restrictions.
- Telephone numbers of local taxi or mini-cab service.

Dealing with delays

It may happen that the person meeting the visitors you have just greeted is not yet available. He or she may have been held up at a previous meeting, for example. In this case, ascertain the length of the wait. Apologize and tell the visitor how long it will be. Make sure the visitor is comfortable, and if possible offer him or her refreshments.

If the delay is likely to be more than a few minutes, the visitor may wish to return another day. In this case it is up to the receiving person to call and reschedule the meeting at a time convenient to the visitor.

Dealing with journalists

Occasionally, a journalist may arrive in reception unannounced. Find out exactly what he or she wants, and contact the person likely to be able to give the information being sought. This may be the company's Press or PR Office, or a particular executive.

Give journalists as much practical help as you can (the same goes for sales representatives and others, who are all simply trying to make a living), but do not pass on information or voice an opinion. Leave this to those authorized to do so. In the face of questioning (even casual comments), simply reply politely that you have no knowledge of the subject. If no-one is available to see the journalist, give him or her the name of the person authorized to speak to the press, and suggest that an appointment is made by telephone.

6.3 Interrupting meetings

It is usually the case that meetings should not be interrupted. Receptionists and secretaries should take telephone messages and pass them on after the meeting is over. If an urgent message comes through, either for the manager or a visitor, it is best to type it out and then pass it to the relevant person as unobtrusively as possible. It is then up to them what response they make. They may simply scribble a reply on your typed message, which you should pass on to the caller, or excuse themselves from the meeting to take or return the call.

6.4 Meetings – key terms

Note: some words are highlighted in boldface. This means you will find them defined in this list.

abstain
To refrain from voting at a meeting.

acclamation
Method of registering a vote whereby those voting call out.

address the chair
Method of addressing a meeting by seeming to speak only to the person in the chair. This method is used to ensure that only one person speaks at a time and that individual conversations do not break out between members.

ad hoc committee
A **committee** that is formed to perform one specific task. After that task is completed, the committee is dissolved.

adjourn
To break off in the middle of a meeting (e.g., for lunch), with the intention of resuming later.

adopt
If the members of a meeting agree the contents of a document (e.g., a report), they are said to adopt it.

agenda
List of subjects to be covered at a meeting, usually following a standard order (see Agenda p.157). Agendas are normally drawn up and circulated in advance of the meeting. Matters that come up too late to be included on the agenda can be raised under **any other business**.

amendment
Alteration to a **motion** suggested by one or more members of a meeting. Amendments must be moved, seconded and voted upon before a motion can

be passed. Amendments that find favour (they are said to be carried) become 'substantive motions'.

annual general meeting (AGM)
A company's annual meeting of shareholders, at which the year's report and accounts are presented and discussed, a dividend is announced, officers are appointed and decisions are made as to the company's future policies.

any other business (AOB)
Heading placed last on an agenda, which indicates that members are permitted to bring up any business that arose too late to be included on the agenda.

apology
Formal (usually written) apology from a person unable to attend a meeting. Apologies are usually read to the members before the business of the meeting gets under way.

attendance register/book
Register that is signed by those attending meetings. Used particularly at annual general meetings and committee meetings. See also Attendance register, p.158.

ballot
Method of voting whereby members write their decision on a voting paper.

board meeting
Meeting of a company's board of directors. See Board of directors, p.8.

carried
A motion or amendment that is agreed is said to be carried.

carry over
If meeting-time is short, a chairperson may be forced to carry over some items to the next meeting.

casting vote
If voting on a **motion** turns out to be equal both for and against, the chairperson may sometimes have the power to cast a vote the way he or she thinks fit and thus effectively make the decision. Such a vote is called a 'casting vote'.

chair
A person who controls and directs a meeting. It is the chair's business to ensure that the meeting is orderly and that as many views as possible are aired. See 6.7 Chairing a meeting.

chairperson's agenda/notes
A special agenda, produced specifically for the person taking the chair at a meeting. It includes extra information to help the chair direct the meeting.

closure
A motion that asks that discussions on a particular subject finish and the meeting proceed to a vote. Sometimes, members who want the discussion closed ask

the chair that 'the question now be put', meaning that the members be asked which way they would like to vote.

committee
A group of people who meet from time to time to make decisions. Most committees perform a specific function. See also **ad hoc committee**; **sub-committee; works committee**.

committee procedure
The procedure by which a committee meeting is called and conducted. The procedure is usually laid down in a company's Articles of Association (see Articles of Association, p.5).

conference
A lengthy meeting attended by delegates either to discuss a list of topics and make policy decisions, or to share knowledge and expertise. Conferences can extend over a period of days and may include a large number of people and events/activities. They are normally arranged by professional conference organizers.

congress
A meeting of representatives of various associated organizations.

consensus
General agreement on a subject.

co-opt
To ask someone to attend a meeting who has not been elected to attend. Such a member is known as a co-opted member and is sometimes co-opted for the purpose of giving specialist advice or to replace an elected member who cannot attend.

delegate
A person who represents a group of people, most often at a conference. The delegate represents the group's views, and in some cases has the power to vote on its behalf.

division
At some meetings, the process of voting is known as 'the division'. The most well-known instance of this is in the House of Commons, where members register their vote by walking through one of two doors.

dropped motion
To be taken up and discussed at a formal meeting, a **motion** must be proposed by one person and seconded by another. If the motion does not have a seconder to speak up for it, it is 'dropped'.

ex officio
A person who is a member of a meeting by virtue of his or her office (e.g. the company secretary or an association's treasurer).

extraordinary general meeting (EGM)
A general meeting of shareholders called to discuss business that cannot wait until the next **annual general meeting**.

for and against
The number of votes cast for and against a motion.

general committee meeting
An ordinary committee meeting, usually held on a regular basis.

general secretary
A person who looks after the administration of meetings. See also **honorary secretary**; **minutes secretary**.

have the floor
When a person stands up to speak at a formal meeting, he or she is said to 'have the floor'.

honorary secretary
A person who performs the function of secretary, usually without being paid. Honorary secretaries normally crop up in associations and clubs.

in attendance
Some meetings meet with certain people 'in attendance'. Such people are not usually full members of the meeting (that is, they are not allowed to vote), but may be present in the capacity of observer.

in camera
A meeting that takes place in private or in secret session.

in the chair
The person who is in control of a meeting (the chair, chairman, chairwoman or chairperson – whichever form you choose to use) is said to be in the chair.

intra vires
Meetings are often limited by the Articles of Association as to what business they can and cannot transact. If the business is within the powers of the meeting, it is said to be *intra vires* ('within the powers'). See also **notice of meeting**; **ultra vires**.

lie on the table
If a committee decides not to act on a certain issue, it is said to allow the issue to 'lie on the table'.

majority
More than half. Certain types of **motion** require majorities of a certain magnitude before they can be carried, and the rules concerning these majorities are usually laid down in the Articles of Association (see p.5). A majority differs from a consensus, which entails general, rather than only majority, agreement.

majority report
A report that is adopted by a majority of the votes.

matters arising
One of the first things that takes place at any formal meeting is that the secretary reads the **minutes** of the previous meeting. He or she will then ask for matters arising, that is, issues that arise from the reading of the minutes.

member
A person who is permitted to attend a meeting and to vote.

memorandum
A document that gives information on a subject that is under discussion. Memoranda should be prepared, and in many cases circulated, in advance.

minority
When voting takes place, the minority is the smaller group, less than half the members.

minority report
A document that is agreed to by only a minority of the members, but which is, all the same, worthy of note.

minutes book
A book in which the **minutes** of each meeting are kept. The minutes book may be bound or loose-leaf.

minutes
A note of the substance of each meeting; see Taking minutes, p.158.

minutes secretary
A person who takes notes at a meeting. The minutes secretary is normally a shorthand secretary. See also **general secretary**.

motion
A proposal put forward to the meeting is known as a 'motion'. If a motion is passed by the meeting, it is known as a 'resolution'. If a motion is altered by agreement of the members, it is called a 'substantive motion'. At most formal meetings, it is necessary to propose and second a motion before it can be discussed.

move
To propose a motion or action.

nem. con.
If a motion is passed unanimously (voted for by all members), it is said to be passed nem. con. (abbreviation for *nemine contradicente*, 'no-one contradicting').

next business
A motion that requests the meeting to delay a decision on the subject in hand and move on to the next business.

no confidence
A chair is normally elected to that position, and is expected to act justly and to follow the rules. If members of a meeting find that they disagree with the actions

of the person in the chair, they may take a vote of no confidence. If the vote is carried, a deputy is elected to take the chair.

nomination form
A form that is sent to those entitled to elect officers. The form usually shows the current holder of the position, and gives an opportunity for voters to nominate or second replacements.

notice of meeting
A document that informs those permitted to attend a statutory meeting when that meeting will take place. The time, date and place of annual general meetings must be notified to the members at least 21 days in advance. The required notice for other ordinary meetings is 14 days. Also known as an 'invitation'.

observer
A person who is called in to observe the running of a meeting. Observers normally have no voting rights.

officer
Those people present at a meeting whose function is its administration.

off the record
The information given or comments made without being noted down in the minutes. Such items are said to be 'off the record'.

on the table
If a **motion** has been proposed and seconded it is said to be 'on the table', and must be discussed.

order
The rules governing the procedures by which a meeting is held. These rules are to ensure that balanced discussions take place and that decisions are made according to the company's regulations.

point of order
A member of a meeting may call the attention of the chair to a point of order. This means that the member is pointing out that something has happened contrary to the procedural regulations for the meeting.

poll
A **ballot** in which members write their names on the voting papers.

president
An alternative title for the person in control of a meeting.

proposition
Similar to a **motion**, but not as formal.

proxy vote
A person who is entitled to vote at a meeting, but cannot attend in person, may ask someone else to vote on his or her behalf. The person asked to do so is

known as a proxy, and they cast a proxy vote as they have been instructed by the person who cannot attend.

quorum
The regulations for most formal meetings indicate that a certain minimum number of people must be present before a meeting can take place. This number is known as a quorum. The first duty of a chairperson is to ascertain whether or not the meeting is quorate.

receive
When members of a meeting agree that they have considered the contents of a document, they are said to have 'received it'.

resolution
A motion that has been passed by the meeting.

rider
Similar to an **amendment**. Riders must be processed in the same way as amendments. That is they must be proposed, seconded and voted upon before the motion can be taken any further.

right to reply
Any person who is adversely criticized or insulted in the course of a meeting has the right to reply.

scrutineer
A person whose duty it is to count votes. Also known as a teller.

second a motion
After a **motion** has been proposed by one member, it must be seconded by another person, who must be prepared to argue for the motion. At formal meetings, motions cannot be discussed or voted upon unless they are both proposed and seconded.

secretary
An officer responsible for the administration of a formal meeting. The secretary is often a qualified company secretary (see Company secretary, p.9), and can advise the chair on points of order as well as ensuring that all regulations are complied with at other stages.

secret ballot
A method of voting whereby members mark a piece of paper, but do not add their name. See also **poll**.

show of hands
A method of voting whereby members indicate their preference by raising a hand.

sine die
A meeting that is adjourned *sine die* is adjourned without the date for the next meeting being agreed.

special committee meeting
Similar to an **extraordinary general meeting**, a special committee meeting is called to discuss business that cannot wait until the next general committee meeting.

standing orders
The rules by which a meeting is conducted.

sub-committee
A committee may order that a second committee be formed (often made up of a few members of the 'parent' committee) to carry out a specific function.

substantive motion
A motion that has been amended by agreement.

table
Any document that has not been sent to the members beforehand but is introduced at the meeting is said to be 'tabled'.

taken as read
In some instances, the **minutes** of the previous meeting are sent to all those involved. In this case, it is sometimes a time-saver to skip the reading of the minutes at the next meeting, on the assumption that members have already read and agreed them. If this happens, the minutes of the previous are said to be 'taken as read'.

teller
See **scrutineer**.

through the chair
At some meetings it may be useful to be able to control speakers, therefore, members are asked not to speak to each other individually, but to hold their conversation in the third person, speaking by way of the chairperson.

treasurer
In a club or association, the treasurer is responsible for administering the finances of the organization and for reporting back. In many cases, the person elected treasurer is an **ex officio** member of the committee.

ultra vires
Outside the powers of the meeting. See also **intra vires**.

unanimous
A decision that is taken with the backing of every member of the meeting is said to be unanimous.

vote of thanks
Some meetings are closed with a vote of thanks, a motion to thank the officials for their administration of the meeting.

voting rights
A person who is entitled to vote at a meeting is said to have voting rights. In

some companies, voting rights are restricted to holders of certain types of shares only.

working party
A group of people asked by a meeting (usually of a committee) to meet at a certain time to perform some specific function, e.g., to produce a report or to look into a certain issue in more detail and come up with proposals.

works committee
A special committee, usually made up of representatives of both workforce and management, to negotiate matters that have relevance to both.

6.5 Checklist for arranging/calling meetings

● Make a list of those who need to be present. Remember that the meeting-time increases with the number of people attending, so keep numbers down to only necessary staff.
● Book a meeting room.
● Circulate those attending with notice of the meeting, agenda and any other information to be read before the meeting.
● Arrange for a person to take notes.
● Make arrangements for any visual aids to be supplied: flip-charts, slide projectors, pointers, overhead projectors, displays, etc.
● Make copies of the necessary handouts.
● Make arrangements for refreshments if necessary.
● Confirm with those attending that they will be able to do so.
● Appoint a chairperson to regulate the meeting, ensuring that all sides are heard and that decisions are made. Prepare a special version of the agenda for the chairperson if necessary.

On the day

● Check that the meeting-room is tidy, well-lit and warm or cool enough.
● Check that there are enough chairs, and that places are set with note pads, pens, drinking water and ashtrays. Make sure that there are enough chairs.
● Make sure that equipment for visual aids are present, and that equipment is working.
● Supply any necessary handouts, and extra copies of the agenda for those who have forgotten to bring theirs.
● If outside visitors are expected, be prepared to greet them at

156

reception. Escort them to the meeting room and offer refreshments.

Afterwards

● Have the minutes of the meeting typed up and circulated among those who attended, including action points and notes of agreements if necessary. A good format for this is a letter, which usually takes the place of minutes after informal meetings.

● Supply any extra information that may have been requested during the meeting.

6.6 Documentation

The regulations concerning formal meetings also cover documentation. Such documentation must be completed accurately according to procedure. However, even for informal meetings, it is useful to provide adequate documentation to facilitate the discussion and co-ordinate subsequent action.

Notice of meeting

The law requires that companies give a certain amount of notice for statutory meetings (e.g. AGMs and OGMs). The length of notice required for an annual general meeting is 21 days. For ordinary meetings, the required notice is 14 days. For other meetings, consult your company secretary or a copy of your company's Articles of Association.

The notice should include details of date, time and venue. A copy of the agenda and any other necessary documents (e.g., a copy of the minutes of the last meeting) should be sent to members along with the notice.

Agenda

Formal agendas (in particular for committee meetings and statutory meetings) normally run in the following standard order:

● Date, time and place of the meeting.
● Apologies (from those unable to attend).
● Reading of the minutes of the last meeting (by the secretary).
● Matters arising from the minutes of the last meeting: people reporting back on action taken since the last meeting.

- Items to be discussed at this meeting. There may be any number of these.
- Any other business. Open call for any business that came too late to be included on the agenda.
- Date, time and place of the next meeting. This is usually proposed on the agenda and then agreed at the meeting.

Most company meetings (especially internal meetings) are much less formal than this, but it is still useful to draw up a defined agenda of items to be discussed, and to circulate it before the meeting, giving participants time to collect their thoughts.

Attendance register

In some instances, it is useful to know who is attending (there may also be a statutory obligation to keep an attendance register). If this is the case, ask participants to sign a list.

Taking minutes

The minutes are a record of the discussion that takes place at the meeting. They should include, in this order:

- Date, place and time of the meeting. Give the subject of the meeting if appropriate.
- A note of the people who attended and their positions, departments or company, usually in alphabetical order.
- Details of apologies.
- Main points of discussion in the order in which they arose, with a note of who raised which point and what the response was. If there is any voting, record the vote on each point.
- Notes of the action(s) agreed upon.

Minutes should be accurate, and they should be checked for veracity with the chair of the meeting. When the draft has been passed, circulate the minutes to all participants.

6.7 Chairing a meeting

A good chairperson is worth his or her weight in gold. The chair must control and direct the meeting, ensuring that business is transacted according to the regulations (if any apply), and that arguments are heard fully and fairly. Meetings that go around in circles and never reach a decision are a waste of time, and they can be tiresome and boring. One of the keys to good meeting practice, therefore, is to find a good chairperson, one who above all is capable of listening rather than speaking. The following are some guidelines for potential chair people.

- Remain impartial. A just chairperson is respected by both sides, and will remain in control by consent.
- Even if you have to be forceful with some members, remain polite. Never lose your temper or appear impatient with anyone.
- Keep your sense of humour, even if the meeting has dragged on several hours over time. But don't be flippant.
- Make sure that both sides in a discussion get a good hearing. To do this, you will need to identify and control the strongest characters, and enable the more timid to have their say without being shouted down.
- Don't allow abrasive personalities to rub you up the wrong way, and learn to defuse situations that look as if they are becoming explosive.
- Stay alert. You must be able to recognize when the debate has diverged from the subject in hand, and to redirect it.
- Transact business as quickly as you can without allowing corners to be cut. It will help if you have ensured that necessary information has been distributed and read beforehand.
- If you are chairing a large meeting, you may find it useful to ask speakers to stand when they speak and to address the chair. In this way you will put a stop to people talking all at once, and enable other members to hear what people are saying.
- If you are chairing a formal meeting, rely on the meeting's secretary to give you guidelines on points of order, and other regulations.
- Be firm and fair, and always play by the rules.

6.8 Effective speaking at meetings

A good performance at informal meetings both inside and out-side the company's walls undoubtedly paves the way for promo-tion. Luckily, effective speakers are not born, they are made, either by training or by experience. Some personnel are trained in the art of speaking, particularly those whose job it is to give presentations. Others may only attend meetings when there are problems to solve, or when a decision has to be taken. Whatever your reason for speaking at a meeting, the following guidelines will help you to say what you have to say effectively and without wasting time.

GREEN NOTE: POLYSTYRENE CUPS

These cups, ubiquitous at most company functions, are made using benzene, a possible carcinogen, and contain CFCs (or HCFCs), both of which damage the ozone layer. It is recommended that that you take your own mug to work, and ask that glasses be used at corporate functions.

Effective speaking – guidelines

- Prepare for the meeting. Ask yourself why you have been asked to attend and what contribution you are expected to make. Read through the documents that have been circulated and make notes on your response to each point on the agenda. Note down also any other concerns you may have on that subject.
- Find out who will be present at the meeting, and what their status is. Consider what their opinions or needs might be in relation to the subject in hand. If you can, discuss the subject with colleagues before you attend. Try to find out who at the meeting will be in agreement with you.
- If you feel the need, write down a full speech (or a list of notes). You may well wish to argue a point or propose a solution. Write down the pros and cons, weigh them up. Remember to take into account the opinions and viewpoints that other people at the meeting might hold.
- At the meeting, don't be overbearing. Wait your turn to speak, and do so with the permission of the chairperson.
- Put across your ideas as suggestions rather than 'the only sane solution', and be prepared to show that you have thought through the alternatives.
- Get into the habit of asking people to agree with you as far as possible. A line of positive responses to the points of your argument make a negative response to your eventual proposal almost impossible.

- Emphasize areas in which there is broad agreement. Include the arguments of others in your own.
- Areas of minor disagreement can be dealt with later – don't blow them out of proportion and spend too much time on them.
- Unless you are an observer, never sit in silence (if you find yourself doing this, perhaps you shouldn't be at the meeting in the first place). If you have nothing to add to the discussion, at least state your agreement with one of your colleagues.
- Try to help the meeting define a solution or come to a decision. Don't be obstructive.
- Remain polite, even-tempered and calm at all times.

Using visual aids

Some meetings are called in order for a member of staff to give a presentation, which may require the use of some kind of visual aid. Flip-charts can be used to record the results of brainstorming; slides, overhead projector transparencies or laminated presentation boards can be prepared with statistical, numerical and other information.

Because the human brain takes in more information through the eyes than through the ears, many managers opt to supplement presentations with visual material. However, undisciplined use of visual aids can confuse the audience and can end up making the presenter look silly.

Only use visual aids in the following circumstances:

- To summarize an argument.
- To illustrate or emphasize a point.
- To demonstrate the workings of a machine or process.
- To clarify complex ideas and information (such as figures and statistics).

Preparing and presenting visual aids is a skill that is honed over time. Here are a few words of advice on preparing and presenting visual aids in meetings:

- Never use too many different types of visual aids. One or two is quite enough.
- Keep your visual aids simple. Use as few written words as possible, limiting the wording to labels and summaries only.

- If producing colour visuals, choose strong colours that contrast with each other. Avoid pastel shades.
- Don't let your creativity get the better of you. Make sure your visuals don't include anything superfluous. Check for relevancy and simplicity.
- Before the meeting, check that all the equipment you need is present and working. Make sure that all members of the meeting will be able to see the visuals.
- If you need to switch off lights to show overhead projector transparencies or slides, make sure that you still have enough light to allow you to read your notes.
- When presenting visuals, avoid turning your back on the audience. Pick a place to stand that does not obscure the visual, and stay there. A speaker who hops about distracts attention from his or her own words and from the visuals on display.
- Never allow a visual aid to speak for itself. Always draw conclusions orally to prevent the audience misinterpreting the message.
- Keep your presentation as short as possible.

*It is now possible for your images (graphs, for example)
to be transformed quickly and quite economically
into slides for projection during a presentation.
A local print bureau specializing in DTP work
should be able to help you.*

For more information on using graphics see Graphics, p.85. Also recommended, for detailed information on all aspects of public speaking from preparation to specific situations, is the *Collins Ready Reference Speaking in Public*.

6.9 Etiquette of informal meetings

So far, this section has dealt with arranged meetings. However, many meetings take place between colleagues on an impromptu basis.

In some companies, the action you take to instigate a meeting with a colleague would depend on whether that colleague is a subordinate, an equal or a superior. In other, more informal circumstances, the etiquette is the same for all. Whatever type of company you work for, if you follow the guidelines below, you should not go too far wrong:

- Unless you are a superior, never 'summon' a person to your office. It is best to telephone through to check availability and then go to your colleague's office.
- If you are superior to the person you would like to meet with, ask them to come to your office, but remember not to be high-handed. Fix a time when a meeting is convenient for both of you.
- If you wish to meet with your superior, it is always best to telephone through beforehand, and to ask to meet in your superior's office. When you arrive, check that your superior is not busy. It is always polite to knock, open the door and then to wait in the doorway until you are invited to go in. It is best also to wait to be invited to sit down before doing so.
- If you have instigated any meeting, make sure that you have all the information you need before you leave your workstation. Make sure also that you have a clear idea what you want to achieve, to save time all round.

Televisual meetings and conference calls

If there is a video-conference linkup at your meeting, make sure that the participants and any visual material are within range of the camera. You may need to hold up flat artwork or charts so they can be seen clearly.

If you take part in a conference call (see p.126), you should identify yourself each time you speak. Other callers cannot be expected to recognise the speaker from their voice alone. Some companies may place a speaker phone on the table at meetings so that a colleague who could not get to the location is able to take part. In this case, make sure you speak clearly and face the general direction of the speaker phone so that your words are picked up.

7
Energetic Electronics
THE ELECTRONIC OFFICE

7

Energetic Electronics

THE ELECTRONIC OFFICE

The advent of electronics and their application to all areas of business and industry have radically changed office life. Out has gone the typewriter, Tipp-Ex and telex, to be replaced for the most part by all manner of sophisticated equipment for text and data capture and manipulation, and communications.

The biggest difference between the office of the past and the office of the present (and the future) is that, because people now have access to equipment that can undertake many different tasks, the distinctions between their roles in the office have become blurred. With the right equipment and training, typists can produce designed reports, secretaries can undertake research and produce financial information, managers can write and mail their own correspondence. Increasingly, machines are used for the more laborious and routine work, which means that almost everyone's job is more varied, demanding and ultimately more satisfying.

However, while electronics gurus claim that the paperless office is just around the corner, old habits die hard, and it seems that in most offices, the hard-copy filing cabinet is here to stay, for a while at least.

There is a bewildering variety of equipment on the market, from the electronic typewriter and calculator to fully-fledged DTP systems, capable of producing high-quality reproductions of colour photographs and combining them with sophisticated typography, and accounting packages that make sure that the operator gets things right. Because each system and package is different, it is nearly impossible to list the facilities available with each one. This chapter, therefore, lists and explains the most common terms related to the electronic office. It also gives general hints on what to look out for when buying equipment, and some advice on maintenance and data security.

The developments in information technology – the ability to store large amounts of information and to retrieve it at the touch of a button, to reproduce electronically photographs, illustrations and text – have necessitated some changes in the law to define and protect the owners of copyright, and those people whose personal information the computers are making available to a wide range of users. A later section in this chapter looks at this legislation and how it affects the ordinary office worker.

7.1 Key terms

Note: some words are highlighted in boldface. This means that you will find them defined in this list.

abort
To stop a computer operation.

acoustic cover
Cover that fits over a piece of equipment to cut down on noise; often used for printers.

anti-static
Anything that cuts out the static produced by electronic equipment; e.g. anti-static mats.

application
A group of tasks that the computer does to fulfil a specific function, e.g., word-processing, accounts, stock control, design, etc. Applications **software** (sold as packages) is required to enable the computer to perform these functions.

artificial intelligence
The name given to the field in electronics research dedicated to making machines act more like people. Artificial intelligence includes making machines understand handwriting and speech, and making them interact with people in the same way as people interact with other people.

ASCII
Acronym for American Standard Code for Information Interchange.

automatic transmission
A system by which quantities of information are stored for transmission to another computer, and then transmitted automatically at a given time, without the need for an operator to be present. Useful for keeping telephone costs as low as possible by transmitting at low-rate times, and for transmitting information across time zones.

background printing
A system by which a computer can be printing one document while the operator is using the terminal for another task. Computers can also undertake other simultaneous tasks in the background.

backing store
A store of data held on magnetic tape or disk for archive use.

back-up
A duplicate copy made of information stored on a disk for security purposes. Some computers back-up automatically on hard disk, but separate back-ups of important information should be made on separate disks and stored in fireproof containers. There are many different types of storage disks available (see pp183–184).

bar code
A series of black and white lines of different thicknesses, which can be 'read' using a light pen or other light-sensitive scanners, and then compared by the computer with a central list to give the appropriate information. For example, supermarkets use bar codes on goods, linked to product and price information and to computerized stock-control systems.

batch processing
A system by which the operator gives the computer a series of tasks to do, and the computer then completes all the tasks in the batch without requiring further operating instructions. See also **interactive processing**.

baud
A unit of data transmission speed; typically, one baud equals one bit per second.

bit
Acronym for 'binary digit'. One single unit of processing power in the binary system used by all computers.

boot
To start a computer running.

buffer
A waiting area for information that is transmitted from a faster to a slower machine. For example, a printer is not normally capable of printing out text at the same speed as it is transmitted from the **CPU**. The extra information yet to be printed waits in a short-term memory (the buffer) until the printer is ready to process it.

bug
An error in a program that causes it to malfunction. See also **virus**.

bulletin board system
An on-line board that allows callers to read or leave messages, converse or play games, and download programs for use on their computers.

byte
Eight **bits**. Computer processing power is now usually reckoned in **kilobytes (k)** or **megabytes (mb)**.

CAD
Acronym for computer-aided design, the umbrella name for computer systems that enable product designers to create design drawings and in some cases simulate test conditions by computer.

carrier
The system that carries information transmitted from one location to another. For example, a telephone company is the carrier of messages sent through an electronic mail system.

CD-ROM (Compact disc – read only memory)
A laser-read disk that stores read-only memory.

chip
A tiny silicon chip that acts as a miniature integrated circuit, enabling computers (and other equipment) to perform a certain function.

clip art
Images stored on disc and ready to be clipped out electronically and pasted onto a document.

clone
A computer compatible with a more expensive computer and able to process programs for the latter.

coaxial cable
A cable that links computers to peripherals, such as printers.

COBOL
Acronym for Common Business-Orientated Computer Language, a computer language often used for programming computers for business use.

communications
An umbrella term for the sending and receiving of information from one computer to another.

compatible
Computers and their systems are compatible when you can read a disk prepared on one machine using a second machine. Compatibility is one of the key concerns when buying computer equipment and software, and there are now a number of 'translation' programs available to ensure that your machine can read copy prepared on another system.

compuphone
A telephone system, controlled by computer, that can store a large number of telephone numbers and dial them automatically.

configuration
The items of hardware that are set up to run together: **CPU**, keyboard, **VDU**, printer, etc.

connect time
The time actually spent connected to an on-line service, such as a bulletin board system.

continuous stationery
Paper specially designed for computer print-out. Continuous stationery is supplied in a single length, and has holes down the outside edges so that it slots into a sheet-feeder for use with a printer. Perforations at the end of each sheet length enable the user to tear the paper into sections suitable for filing.

CPU
Abbreviation for central processing unit, the computer's 'brain-box'.

cursor
A flashing dash or square that appears on the screen to show the user where the computer will place the next character.

cyberspace
The web of computer networks and electronic information services that can be accessed from a computer, using a modem and communications software.

daisy-wheel printer
A printer that has a wheel with the characters placed at the end of each 'petal'. Daisy-wheel printers produce a high-quality print-out.

data
Items of information that can be input to a computer system. Data can appear as words, numbers or symbols.

databank
A system on which information is stored for retrieval by subscribers. Information on databanks is normally updated by the system's operators, but cannot be altered by subscribers.

database
A collection of information that is organized in such a way that it can be analysed by computer.

data input terminal
Any machine that enables the user to input data to the computer. For example, a computer keyboard and **VDU (monitor)**, or an electronic supermarket checkout.

default
In certain software (especially word-processing packages), variables, such as margins, tabs, type-size and font, can all be set as standards. When the operator does not give the computer alternative instructions, it will automatically 'default' to these set values (known as default values).

diagnostic
A system that enables a computer to check for faults in the computer's

programming, and, in some instances, to correct automatically any faults found. Some computers run diagnostics when the machine is booted or switched off.

digital transmission
A method by which information is converted to electronic impulses in order for it to be transmitted (principally along telephone lines). Most computers need a **modem** device to make this conversion.

directory
When filing information on some computer systems, a directory is the intangible equivalent of a filing cabinet. Directories can contain files. Some computer systems use the term 'folder'.

disk (or disc)
A method of storing electronic information using magnetic material.

disk drive
The slot in a computer into which disks are inserted. The disk drive scans the disk using delicate magnetic heads. Disk drives should be treated with care.

diskette
A variable term, often used to mean a computer disk housed in a small hard case (as opposed to a floppy, 5¼-inch disk, for instance).

document assembly
A word-processing system that enables the operator to store standard blocks of text in a memory and call them up when needed to create a new document.

DOS (disk operating system)
A widely used operating system for IBM and IBM-compatible personal computers.

dot-matrix printer
A printer that forms the characters using tiny pins. When impressed on the paper, the pins form the characters from tiny dots.

download
Receive a program, file, or other data from another computer via a modem.

drag
To position the pointer on an object, press and hold the mouse button, move the mouse and release the mouse button.

DTP
Abbreviation for desktop publishing. An umbrella term for the software and hardware technology that makes it possible to put together books, brochures, reports and other publications, and which involves processing photographs, text, graphics and illustrations (theoretically) without leaving your desk.

electronic accounting machine
A computer system that is designed to perform many accounting functions and, sometimes, to control the accounting procedure.

electronic cottage
A high-speed intercommunication between computers at different locations has made it possible for some people to dispense with travelling to work, choosing instead to work in the comfort of their own homes, while staying in constant contact with their office. In these cases, the home is sometimes known as an 'electronic cottage'.

electronic data transmission
Essentially the same as **digital transmission**.

electronic diary
Software that enables the user to create a computerized diary for one or more people. The diary or diaries can be accessed from a number of networked terminals.

electronic filing
An umbrella term for the things users do to file the information on their computers in a logical place. See 3.4 for hints on good electronic filing. The term is also used for a specific system by which users can transmit information to electronic storage areas at another location on the network.

electronic mail (e-mail)
An umbrella term for systems that allow users to send each other messages, either from one machine to another within a network, or via telephone lines to an outside user. See pp.128–129.

electronic writing pad
A machine that has a flat, sensitive surface, capable of recognizing handwriting and converting it for display on the screen.

e-mail
See electronic mail.

enhance
To pick out certain words and phrases in text using enhancements such as **bold**, *italic*, underline, etc.

escape
A command sometimes used to get out of a document or file.

exit
A command sometimes used to get out of a computer application, or to get out of a file.

extended keyboard
A keyboard that is larger than the standard QWERTY typewriter keyboard. It contains extra **function keys**, a number pad for calculations, cursor control keys, etc.

field
In a database, a field is the area in which a certain item of information is placed.

For example, if the database included company name, address and telephone number, there may be fields for each of these items. When a database is asked to sort information to produce reports, it sorts according to field.

file
A single computer document. The size of the file (the maximum limit of which varies according to the software used) depends on the operator; it may, for example, contain a single letter, or many letters. Files can be kept together in electronic directories or folders.

floppy disk
A term used to describe any computer disk that is inserted into a computer's disk drive (as opposed to a **hard disk**).

folder
A container for documents, programs and other folders on the desktop or in directory windows.

footer
A section at the bottom of a word-processing page into which standard information can be keyed. In most word-processing packages, the information in the footer is automatically printed at the foot of each page of the document, and can include an automatic page-numbering facility. See also **header**.

font
A collection of letters, numbers and symbols in a distinctive typographic design. Most programs come with a variety of different fonts, which you can use to alter the look of your document or artwork.

format
A method of preparing a floppy disk for use with a certain software system. Most disks need to be formatted (also called 'initialized' before information can be stored on them.

function key
The keys (usually marked F1, F2, F3, etc.) which enable the user to specify functions within the software used (e.g. search and replace).

graphic user interface (GUI)
A program that allows users to interact with a computer by pointing to graphics on the screen, generally using a mouse rather than typing in instructions.

graphics
Any illustrations drawn using a computer. They may include graphs, icons, pie charts and line drawings or plans. **DTP** software enables the user to produce very sophisticated graphics.

graphics tablet
An input device that transforms images drawn on its flat surface into images displayed on the computer screen.

hard copy
A copy of part or all of the information on the disk printed out onto paper.

hard disk
A magnetic disk that has a very large memory. A hard disk is usually supplied as part of a PC's **CPU**.

hardware
The physical machinery component of a computer system, e.g., **CPU**, **VDU**, keyboard, etc. See also **software**.

header
A section at the top of a word-processing page into which standard information can be keyed. Headers operate in the same way as **footers**.

help
Some software systems have built-in information files, which may be accessed in various ways, e.g. by entering the word 'help' or by pressing the F1 function key.

highlight
In word-processing packages, highlighting is the method of selecting parts of text for a particular operation, e.g., for enhancement or deletion.

hot zone
In word-processing, the area at the end of a line of text. The hot zone is defined by the operator as a certain number of characters from the right-hand margin. Any words that fall within this zone are automatically hyphenated or taken to the following line.

hypertext
Documents presented in an interactive computer environment; allows users to branch from one screen display to other text, graphics, or video.

icon
A tiny picture on the screen, which, when selected, enables the operator to carry out some operation. Icons are most often found in **DTP** software and can be compared to the written menus of word-processing and other packages.

information superhighway
A proposed national infrastructure of cable and telephone lines that would make voice, data, and video communications available to everyone.

information technology (IT)
An umbrella term covering all the technology used to input, store, retrieve, manipulate and transmit information.

initialize
Initializing is the same as **formatting**.

ink-jet printer
A printer that magnetizes the ink to a letter shape to form letters on the paper. The system is very fast.

input
To introduce information onto a disk (by keying, by scanning, etc.). See also
output.

installer
A program that you use to install or update your system software or to add
resources such as networking software.

interactive processing
A method of processing information where the user and computer interact with
each other throughout the process. See also **batch processing**.

interactive terminal
A terminal at which interactive processing takes place.

interactive video
A computer-controlled, video-training system that enables the student to
interact with the video, commonly by making decisions between given
alternatives.

interface
The area or device at which two pieces of computer equipment connect with
each other.

keyboarding
A term increasingly used instead of 'typing'.

keying in
To input information to the computer using a keyboard.

key to disk
To input information to the computer using a keyboard.

kilobyte
1024 **bytes** = 1 kilobyte (K). One kilobyte is equal to about 205 five-character
words on the screen.

laptop computer
A portable computer.

laser disk
Also called an optical disc, a small disk on which digital data are stored as minute
pits and bumps, and which is read by a laser beam: an audio compact disc and a
CD-ROM are examples.

laser printer
A sophisticated, electronically controlled printer that makes an image using
lasers. Laser printers are fast, quiet and can produce top-quality copies. Colour
laser printers are also available.

light pen
A light-sensitive device used for 'reading' bar codes and for use with certain
VDUs and **electronic writing pads**.

line printer
A printer that produces each line of text at once, rather than character by character. Line printers are extremely fast.

list processing
A system that enables the user to merge information from two or more different files. Often used to print out standard letters with variable addressee information (in this context more often called 'mail merging').

lock
To prevent files or disks from being changed or deleted (but they can still be opened or copied).

log on
A term used to describe the process of entering a system, normally requiring the use of a security code, and normally when dealing with a central computer.

magnetic disk
Another name for a **hard disk**.

magnetic tape
A medium used to store computerized information, access to which is not required in a hurry.

mail merge
See **list processing**.

mainframe
A very large computer that has a large memory. Mainframes can process information from a large number of terminals at one time.

main logic board
A circuit board that holds RAM, ROM, the microprocessor, custom integrated circuits, and other components that make the computer work.

megabyte
One million **bytes**. Megabytes are units of storage capacity available on a **hard disk**.

memory
A measure of a computer's capacity for processing, which includes the operating system of the machine and the information you have chosen to manipulate or store. Memory is measured in **bytes**.

menu
A list giving a number of tasks that the user can ask the computer to perform using the software package that is running.

merging files
Same as **list processing**.

microcomputer
A small computer, also called a personal computer (PC), in which the **CPU** is

contained in one ore more silicon chips. Your word-processor or desktop computer is probably a micro.

microfiling
A system (sometimes computerized and centralized) by which documents are photographed onto microfilm and stored in archives. Microfilm is accessed manually through a reading device, often connected to a copier for production of selected hard copies.

microprocessor
Same as a **chip**.

mini computer
A computer that is only 'mini' in relation to a mainframe.

modem
Acronym for modulator/demodulator. It is a device that enables computer signals to be turned into audio signals to be transmitted via telephone lines.

mouse
A device that can be attached to a computer keyboard, which enables the user to move the cursor around the screen and to make selections by clicking a small button. A mouse is most useful when using **DTP** and graphics packages that require free movement of the cursor across the screen.

MS-DOS
Microsoft Disk Operating System, a common operating system for PCs.

multimedia
Manner of computer display of information, using text, graphics, sound, and video.

multitasking
In a computer, the process of performing, concurrently, two or more tasks.

network
A collection of devices such as computers and printers that are connected together. A network is a tool for communication that allows users to store and retrieve information, share printers and exchange information.

numeric pad
On an **extended keyboard**, the set of keys to the right, laid out like a calculator.

off-line
When a computer or a peripheral is disconnected from the network it is said to be 'off-line'.

on-line
When a computer or peripheral is connected via a network to other devices, it is said to be 'on-line'. This terms has now expanded to include being on the Internet, or with the facilities to do so.

operating system
The software that forms the basis of a computer's 'intelligence'. It links the electronic parts of the machine to the software you have chosen to run.

optical character reader (OCR)
A device that scans typed text and transfers it to the computer disk. OCRs reduce the need for keying words to disk. However, the OCR has not yet been perfected, and many will only read certain typefaces. They may also mistake some characters for others ('i' for 'I', for example). When using an OCR, therefore, it is vital to proofread the text.

output
Information, etc. that is produced by a computer. See also **input**.

PABX
Abbreviation for Private Automatic Branch Exchange. A switchboard system that enables outgoing calls to be dialled direct, leaving only incoming calls to travel via the central switchboard, thus speeding up telecommunications.

paperless office
An office system in which electronics have completely replaced the need for paper. Mail is transmitted electronically across telephone lines and flashed onto the screen before being stored. Documents are transmitted to a central point, filed and backed up automatically. Electronic diaries are kept and updated on-screen. While many companies are finding ways of reducing their need for paper copies, there is a long way to go before the filing cabinet and the post box disappears for good.

peripherals
Any computer device that is connected to a main computer. For example, your printer (the peripheral) may be connected to your word-processor, or your terminal (the peripheral) may be connected to a central mainframe.

personal computer (PC)
Same as a microcomputer, consisting of a **CPU**, a **VDU** and a keyboard.

Prestel
An information system supplied to subscribers by British Telecom and transmitted to terminals via the telephone lines. Prestel is an interactive system.

program
A complex set of instructions that tells the computer what to do.

prompt
An on-screen message from the operating system or a software application, usually asking for the next entry.

punched cards
Cards used to input data to a computer. Each card is punched with holes in various places that act as codes that can be interpreted by the computer.

RAM
Acronym for Random Access Memory. Computer disks with random access memory can be accessed by the user and the information that they have stored can be manipulated. The user is able to access the information at random, almost instantaneously. RAM can be considered as work space. The greater the number of **bytes** on your RAM disk, the larger your work space. See also **ROM**.

ribbons
There are various types of ribbon available for computer printers. They include high-quality carbon ribbons and fabric ribbons. Consult your printer's handbook for details of the type of ribbon appropriate for your model.

ROM
Acronym for Read Only Memory. This type of memory can be read, but it cannot be manipulated by the user. It contains the machine's **operating system**.

save
When information is written to a computer's screen it is most likely that it is being held in a temporary memory space. When the user gives a 'save' command, the computer transfers the information to a permanent memory space. Information that is not made permanent in this way will be lost if the machine is turned off or crashes for any reason. It is, therefore, essential to 'save' regularly as you work.

scanner
A device used with **DTP** software that is capable of transferring drawn materials and photographs to disk for subsequent manipulation.

screen-typer
A word-processing set-up that consists of an electronic typewriter, a screen and a disk drive.

search and replace
A facility that scans through text on command, looking for given strings of characters, and automatically changing them for given alternatives. A 'global search and replace' is the same process applied to very long documents or groups of documents.

security code
A typed code required by the computer before the user can access the information stored. Security codes can prevent unauthorized access to sensitive information, and most systems offer this facility.

security disk
A back-up disk. The security disk is often a second back-up, located for safety at another site.

179

shared logic
A computer configuration in which the **CPU** and **software** are shared by
several individual terminals.

simulation
A computer-created model of a real or imagined situation or phenomenon,
such as an airplane flight.

software
A program that enables the computer to carry out specific tasks. Some
computers can store the software on a built-in hard disk, whereas others
require that the software is loaded from a disk each time the computer is
switched on.

split screen
A facility in some software that enables the user to call up two files or
documents and view them at the same time.

spreadsheet
Software that enables the user to prepare documents such as financial forecasts.
Spreadsheets can be set up so that users enter only the information, and the
software does all the required calculations instantaneously.

stand-alone
Any computer system that does not rely on a mini-computer or a mainframe.

status line
At the bottom or top of a word-processing screen, the graphics that show the
'status' of the cursor: which horizontal column it is in, which vertical line it is on,
which page of the document it is working on, and where the tabs, etc. have
been set.

system disk
A disk that contains the information that tells the computer how to perform the
particular functions that have been loaded (word-processing, accounts,
illustration, etc.).

terminal
The point at which you the user come into contact with the computer.
Terminals generally consist of a **VDU** and a keyboard connected to a **CPU**.

tractor feeder
A device on a printer that facilitates the use of continuous stationery. The paper
is clipped to the tractor feeder, which then draws it through the printer at the
appropriate speed.

user-friendly
Software that is 'user-friendly' is used easily. It helps the user by providing
information at the help command, and gives messages that are easy to
understand.

VDU
Abbreviation for Visual Display Unit – the screen, or monitor.

virtual reality
The use of computers to create the illusion that the user is actually inside a three-dimensional simulation of an environment.

virus
An 'infectious' computer disease that is capable of destroying the machine's basic programming, spread through disks, the Internet and occasionally by e-mail. Virus warnings are circulated from time to time and it may be helpful to have a virus protection program on your computer, or a program which will correct problems should they arise.

voice recognition
The ability of a computer (actually its input device) to translate spoken words into digital signals.

window
An area of a display screen set off for separate handling of materials, overlapping other areas as needed.

word-processor
A computer system that is designed solely for use as a word-processor. Most PCs can operate several kinds of software that enable them to perform such functions as word-processing, accounts, and to manipulate databases.

workstation
An area in the office that is built around a computer. It may include a **VDU**, a **CPU**, a printer and a keyboard. Good workstation design is the key to maintaining the health of the operator. See 9.3 Using workstations for further details.

wraparound
A word-processing facility that writes automatically from one line to the next without the operator touching the carriage-return key.

7.2 Buying computer systems

Keeping pace with technology is often difficult, and some managers find it hard to decide which system they should buy, and when. Here are some hints:

● Work out what your needs are and what they are likely to be over the next five years. Prioritize them. Get the input of those who will be using the system.

● Keep up to date with computer information given out in your trade press or in national computer magazines.

- Discuss specific systems with potential operators and their trainers, as well as with salespeople. You may also try to find companies that already use the system you are contemplating buying, and you could get a user's view from them. Remember that your decision will affect the operator from day to day – consult him or her.
- Ask about compatibility. If you already have a computer system, or if you have a client or colleague firm with whom you need to be compatible, get a disk and try it out with the system you are considering buying.
- Don't expect computerization to pay for itself too quickly. Familiarization and integration with other office systems takes time.
- Look into the possibility of networking the individual machines in your configuration.
- Discuss maintenance contracts, guarantees for supply of materials and other after-sale support.
- Look carefully at job specifications – the introduction of electronic equipment will inevitably change working practices.

7.3 Care of electronic equipment

Some parts of electronic equipment are extremely delicate. Proper care will ensure that you do not lose and misplace vital information, that your equipment lasts as long as possible without disintegrating, and that staff are protected from repetitive strain injury and other health risks (see 9.3 Using workstations).

Care of equipment

- Keep the atmosphere free of smoke and dust, which can accumulate on the delicate heads inside disk drives.
- Keep screens clean using the special kits available from manufacturers.
- Never drink liquids near a keyboard.
- Ensure that cables are secured in such a way that staff cannot trip over them.
- Ensure that your power supply is protected from surges (adaptors can be obtained for this purpose). Do not use sockets that take computer cables for other appliances.

- Check manufacturer's instructions on paper for use in printers, especially in laser printers.
- Never cover the air vents of electronic equipment, and make sure that they are not placed in direct sunlight, which may cause overheating.
- Do not move computer equipment more than necessary and take great care when doing so.
- Make sure that disk-heads are cleaned regularly using a cleaning diskette, and following the manufacturer's instructions.

Care of floppy disks

- Store floppy disks inside their protective envelopes, away from magnetic fields (especially coiled telephone wires). Do not place next to the telephone, on top of disk drives, or near radios or other audio equipment.
- Keep floppy disks out of range of liquids such as tea and coffee.
- Never touch the magnetic material exposed through the keyhole of a magnetic disk.
- Never write on a floppy disk label with a ballpoint pen – the pressure will corrupt the disk. Use a felt-tip pen or write the label before sticking it to the disk.
- If information stored on a floppy disk is not to be erased, use the read/write protect mechanism to 'lock' the disk and to alert other users.
- Keep archive disks in fireproof containers.
- Never force a floppy disk into a disk drive.
- Never bend floppy disks. When sending them by post, make sure that they are packed so that they cannot be bent, and mark them 'Electronic Media – Do Not Bend'.

7.4 Hints for easy-access electronic filing

- Name electronic folders and documents using full words that can easily be interpreted by other users, or develop a 'company' system using a series of codes, perhaps the first and last two letters of each word.
- Make back-up copies of *all* work on floppy disks, an external disk drive, such as a second hard disk, a Syquest or zip drive, at

regular intervals. It may be necessary to detail one person to do this for all operators.

● Always set the calendar mechanism on your computer (you may have to do this when you first switch on every day) so that old copies of files can be identified by their date.

● Make a typed index of the files on your hard disk so that others can access it easily. Keep the index up to date.

● Always label floppy disks and store in an indexed filing system.

● Apply the same disciplines to electronic filing as you would to paper filing (see 3.1 Filing).

● Periodically, weed out old files to make space for new ones, otherwise, the computer's memory will become clogged and its operating will become slower. Eventually, you may inadvertently lose information when the computer decides that it has no more memory left.

7.5 What is a Database?

A database is a large, complex list of facts and information – usually containing text and numbers and possibly also images, sounds, and video or film clips. Typical databases include telephone directories, airline flight guides, and bibliographic references, but databases have been used to store all kinds of knowledge. Databases are distinguished from mere lists by one essential feature: upon request, a specific group of disparate facts can be extracted from the collection.

Some electronic databases, including computer versions of many reference books, are linked to telephone lines so that people can reach them by dialling through a modem. This type of arrangement is referred to as an on-line database

A typical database is designed around a central core list of facts. These facts are grouped in discrete 'records', each containing data associated thematically. In a telephone book, each person's entry is one record. Records, in turn, contain 'fields', each with a different type of information: in a telephone book, one field is slotted for a last name, another field for a first name, a third for an address, and a fourth for the phone number itself. Fields make an electronic database searchable. Thus, anyone can request all records in which the field for last name contains the name Jones. Electronic databases can also be rearranged ('sorted') in the order of fields: for example, the same database of phone numbers can produce a printed copy of a telephone book or a guide in which information is listed according to addresses.

All databases permit users to add new information or to update old facts. On computers, new information is entered into an on-screen 'form'. Usually, forms are designed to streamline the task of entering facts.

To help people retrieve and print facts, databases use reports – commands for sorting lists and formatting their appearance on the printed page.

7.6 Photocopiers

Photocopiers now come in many shapes and sizes, and, driven by electronic technology, they are capable of carrying out some complex tasks. Proper care of a photocopier ensures that it is always working when you want to use it, and that it does not cost a fortune in maintenance and repair fees. Making sure that you get your photocopying right first time saves paper and money in copy charges.

Photocopier care

- Clean the glass surface regularly using the kit supplied by the manufacturer or other specialist suppliers. Such kits can also be used for cleaning computer screens.
- Give the photocopier enough space to breathe. That is, leave space between the machine and the wall for adequate ventilation.
- Like computers, photocopiers respond badly to hot, humid or smoky conditions.
- Listen to your photocopier. If it begins to 'grumble', call a maintenance engineer to check it.
- Before photocopying onto transparency or onto unbonded recycled paper, check for guidelines in the operating manual, or ask a maintenance engineer.
- Follow carefully instructions for loading paper cassettes and clearing paper jams.

Photocopying tips

- Check that you have the correct paper in the cassette before you start.
- Check that the photocopier is programmed correctly. Many photocopiers return to a default setting after a certain time (normally one copy at A4 size), but if your copier does not have this facility, you will save paper if you check first.
- Make sure that any liquid paper or glue is dry before putting the document into the copier.
- If you have a number of sheets to copy, put them through the machine starting with the last. This way your copy of the document will come out in the correct order.
- Transparencies can be used to superimpose one piece of text or an illustration onto another.
- Be careful when dealing with the inside workings of photocopiers – they can become very hot indeed.
- When putting special copying paper into the photocopier (e.g., coloured paper or letterhead) remove all standard paper from the cassette to avoid copying on to the wrong type by mistake.
- Keep photocopying paper in a dry place. Paper that is damp jams the machine.
- Dry powder toner can get everywhere if you are not careful, and it is difficult to remove from clothes and skin. Cover the toner bottle with a plastic bag before removing it from the machine, and seal the bag to avoid spillage.
- Some photocopies have difficulty 'seeing' light blue and pencil marks. Avoid using them if you want your marks to show up.
- If your document is typed close to the edge of the paper, reducing the photocopy size to 99% will give you a margin without visibly reducing the typesize.
- Always close the lid of the photocopier before starting to copy. Never look directly at the light emitted by the machine – it could damage your eyes.
- Don't photocopy documents that are still stapled. Remove the staples before you start and replace them after you have finished.
- If you have a number of copies to make, check the first copy individually before setting the machine for the rest.

> ## GREEN NOTE: PHOTOCOPIERS
> ● *Copying on both sides of the paper saves trees, and a bin beside the photocopier encourages staff to collect waste paper for recycling.*
> ● *Many photocopiers have an energy-saving facility which switches the machine off while not in use, but keeps it warm so that you don't have to wait too long before you can start to copy. Use the facility as a matter of course to save on electricity consumption.*

7.7 The Data Protection Act 1984

This legislation covers personal information (e.g., exam results, income details, etc.) stored on any computer system other than those for private or recreational use, or those kept by the police and the Inland Revenue.

Under the Act, organizations that store such information on a computer system (not by more traditional filing methods) must register with a central registrar and must give details of the type of information they are holding and what they use it for. Companies also have a duty to ensure that information is accurate, up to date and protected from unauthorized access. Those people whose details are stored in this way have the right to find out what the information consists of.

A copy of the Data Protection Act 1984, and a guide to the Act are available from Her Majesty's Stationery Office (address in Useful addresses, pp.115–116).

7.8 The Copyright Designs and Patents Act 1988

A copy of this act is available from Her Majesty's Stationery Office. In general, the Act deals with the ownership of written works (including statistical information), works of art, photographs, artworks, designs and patent inventions. In principle, an original work belongs to the originator, and no-one is allowed to reproduce that work without the originator's permission.

7.9 A Beginner's Guide to the Internet

The Internet is a worldwide network of computers, which hold data that you can access directly from your computer. Access is channelled through high-speed links provided by commercial organizations called 'service providers'. If you have a modem on your computer, you can sign up with a service provider, choose the software you wish to use, and begin exploring.

There are over 15,000 discussion groups on the Internet, and you can participate in discussions on different topics, and receive information about specialized subjects, as well as subscribing to mailing lists. If you are required to do research for your company, you will find the Internet invaluable, as it gives you access to libraries and research centres around the world. You will also be able to order flowers, book travel arrangements, hire cars, sample products and purchase many other services. It is possible to make purchases using a credit card, although there have been reported   instances of criminals gaining access to credit card numbers used in this way so you may decide on a more secure payment method.

When you are connected to the Internet, you can communicate with any of the 50 million or so users, either live or by sending e-mail messages. You can subscribe to newsgroups or mailing lists, and receive information about products and services. You can also access electronic data stored in the computers that form the Internet.

To visit Internet sites, you will need a Web browser (see p.190), such as Netscape Navigator or Internet Explorer. To visit a specific site, type in the address exactly as it appears, and press the return key. If you use a site frequently, some systems will let you select it as a 'favourite spot'. You can then just click for access without retyping the address every time.

Choosing a service provider

Before signing up with a service provider you will need to ask questions about the cost – and make sure you read the small print. There can be many hidden costs, on top of the standard monthly fees. Try to ensure that you get unlimited access to the Internet for your fee. Some providers charge extra if you spend more than a certain number of hours per month on-line. Ask about helplines and the number of PoPs they have (the number that subscribers use to dial into their service provider; if there are too few lines, or their coverage is not international or extensive in this country, you may wish to choose another).

You'll need to know what software is provided – ideally, you will need a Web browser (see p.190); an FTP program (File Transfer Protocol), which allows you to gain access to any of the files and programs available on the Internet and transfer them to your hard disk; an e-mail program (see pp.128–129); and a news-reader.

You may need help installing the software if the process is not automatic, but most display clear step-by-step instructions on screen when you load the installer disks and helpline numbers that you can call for assistance if you get stuck.

What is the World Wide Web?

The World Wide Web (WWW), often referred to simply as the Web, is a service that allows computer users to navigate the Internet quickly and easily. Using hypertext (hypertext mark-up language or HTML) links for organizing and displaying informa-tion on the Internet, the Web enables users to jump from one document to another, simply by pointing to a highlighted phrase ('link'), then clicking a mouse button. The pages of the Web cover a vast range of topics, presented in an attractive, interesting and accessible form.

The Web was developed in 1990 at the European Organization for Nuclear Research (CERN), as a way for scien-tists to share documents. By 1995 it was the fastest-growing service on the Internet. At present, the Web is being used mainly as an information resource, but numerous additional applica-tions are possible. For example, a growing number of companies are establishing Web sites to promote products and sell merchandise.

You may decide to look into the benefits of organizing a web site for your company. They can be designed and established quite easily and could be a good marketplace for your company's products. Ask your service provider for information or look under Internet providers in the *Yellow Pages* for a range of com-panies that specialize in Web site design.

A Web site is distinguished by the prefix http:// in its address. Http, which is short for Hypertext Transport Protocol, refers to the method of transporting documents between Web servers and browsers. Using the Internet is similar to working with a multimedia CD ROM – clicking on a 'live' area takes you to a different, related screen. You can also e-mail through the Web, using the e-mail facility in your Web browser.

A Web browser is a program that enables your computer to download and view pages of the Web. A plug-in is a program that adds features to a Web browser so that it can handle files containing different elements, such as 3-D and multimedia. You can download new plug-ins and upgrades for existing ones, usually from the software developer's 'home page'.

Useful terms

Anonymous FTP
A means by which you can log on to a remote computer using an FTP program.

Archie
A database of files stored on FTP sites.

BBS
A single computer or network that you dial direct to access services.

channels
Channels are used by people to talk to one another on IRC (Internet Relay Chat) networks. Every channel is run by an operator who sets the channel mode (restricting access, perhaps).

FTP
A protocol for transferring files on the Internet.

home page
A set up by a Web user – companies may offer free samples, or do research, and individuals may simply provide details of their personal history or interests.

hypertext
Text containing links to other pieces of text, either within the same document or in another one. Most Web pages are based on HTML (see p.189).

Java
A programming language that enables Web pages to contain miniature programs that appear as animation, sound, scrolling text or interactive features.

IRC
Networks on the Internet, where you can hold conversations, or chat with other users.

newsreader
A newsreader program is required to access newsgroups on your provider's service.

PoP
The telephone number that customers use to dial in to their service providers.

posting
You 'post' a message on when you write to a newsgroup, and it is read by a group of people.

search page
Provides a direct link to many of the major search 'engines' and directories. Netscape offers one on http://www.netscape.com/home/internet-search.html.

Telnet
Telnet is a program that allows you to log on to a remote computer and access services from your PC.

URL (Uniform Resource Locator)
An Internet address, providing a standard way of referring to Internet resources.

Usenet
The main network of newsgroups (really discussion and debate groups) available on the Internet.

CAUTION

● *To protect your computer from viruses, be sure to scan every file that you download with one of the anti-virus programs that are available either on the Internet, or through your main software supplier.*

8
Buying and Selling
TRADING AND ACCOUNTING DOCUMENTS

8
Buying and Selling

TRADING AND ACCOUNTING DOCUMENTS

All businesses have a duty to keep accounts and it is in their own interest to document trading carefully.

8.1 Key terms

Note: some words are highlighted in boldface. This means that you will find them defined in this list.

a/c
Abbreviation for account.

account
A facility that enables financial transactions to take place. A bank account, for example, or a credit account with a supplier.

accounts
Records of all financial transactions.

a/c payee only
Words written between the parallel lines of a **crossing** on a cheque. They indicate that in theory the cheque may only be paid into the account of the named person, but in practice it is still possible to transfer the cheque to a third party by **endorsement**.

air waybill
A document drawn up by an airline detailing the goods that a consignor has transferred for transportation by air. It is a form of receipt similar to a **bill of lading**.

APR
Abbreviation for annual percentage rate.

BACS
Abbreviation for bank account clearing system, in which a company can pay invoices or salaries directly into the payee's bank account, usually on the same or an allocated day.

bank charges
Banks charge fees to customers depending on the services rendered (e.g.,

cashing cheques, stopping cheques, for funds transfer, etc). Charges vary from bank to bank and from year to year. They are usually deducted from the balance of the account at the end of each month. Many banks waive their charges in certain circumstances, for example, if an account is a certain amount in credit.

bank reconciliation
An accounting procedure that enables a bank account holder to determine the exact state of the account. The bank statement lists transactions up to a certain date. By reference to the paying-in book and the cheque book, it is possible to add to the total on the statement debits and credits up to date. A written reconciliation should include: the total on the statement; the dates, details and amounts of further credits; the dates, details and amounts of further debits; a grand total representing the current state of the account.

bank references
A statement made by the bank for the use of a company's suppliers, indicating that the company (the buyer) is creditworthy. See also **trade references**.

banker's card
An alternative name for a **cheque guarantee card**.

banker's draft
A **bill of exchange** that is bought from a bank and sent to the payee. Banker's drafts can be bought in major world currencies and crossed to prevent fraud.

bank giro credit
A method of paying in money to a bank branch for credit to an account not held at that branch. Paying-in slips are often titled 'bank giro credit'.

bearer cheque
A cheque that is made out to 'the bearer' (the person who presents it at the bank). Bearer cheques are payable in cash over the counter. They are, however, not very secure in that anyone can cash a bearer cheque.

bill of exchange
A document that allows the transfer of a specified amount of money from one person to another on a given date. A cheque is a bill of exchange, and so is a bank note.

bill of lading
A document that gives details of the transfer of goods from the consignor to the master of a ship. It is a form of receipt.

blank cheque
A cheque that has not been filled in with details of payee or amount, but which has been signed. Obviously, blank cheques are vulnerable to fraud and theft. An upper limit to the cheque may be written at the top or bottom or top of the cheque. See Cheque, p.207.

budget account
A type of bank account on which the bank offers a certain amount of credit in return for regular payments of a certain amount.

cash card
A plastic card that enables the user to withdraw cash from a bank account by way of a service till. Security is provided in the form of a secret Personal Identification Number (PIN).

charge card
A plastic card and associated account, which enables the user to buy goods and services (though usually not to draw cash). The account must be paid in full at the end of each month, and so charge cards are not the same as credit cards. The American Express card, for example, is a charge card.

cheque
A bill of exchange, which, after cash, is most widely used for transferring funds from one person or company to another. A cheque is essentially a request that the bank pay the named payee the sum written on the cheque. Cheques that are not presented within six months of their date become invalid and are known as 'stale cheques'. The terms on which a cheque is drawn is determined by the **crossings**. It is against the law to issue a cheque knowing that it will be **dishonoured**. See Cheque, p.207.

cheque guarantee card
A plastic card that guarantees to the seller that a cheque will be honoured up to a certain limit (given on the card, but usually £100). It is now almost impossible to use a cheque without presenting a guarantee card. Some cheque guarantee cards now also double as **payment cards** and **cash cards**.

clearing house system
This system is the basis of commercial branch banking in the UK. It enables payments to branches of each of the main banks to be sorted and made to the relevant bank quickly. Because of this system, it takes only about three to four working days for a payment to clear and be credited to the correct account at the correct branch.

commercial bank
Most of the banks in the UK are termed commercial banks. The major commercial banks are Lloyds, National Westminster, Barclays and the Midland. Each bank offers a variety of banking services for individuals and companies, as well as loans, small business advice, international banking services, insurance services and foreign exchange. Services and charges vary between the banks.

commission
A percentage of the value of a transaction, paid to an agent (such as a sales representative) as a fee for services rendered.

consignment note
A document that gives the carrier of goods the right to collect the goods and to transport them to their destination. It usually gives details of the goods, their weight and value.

counterfoil
Part of a document, that is retained by the person making the transaction, to act as a receipt and a record. Counterfoils are most familiar on cheques and paying-in slips (see illustration 8.2-2, p.209), and should be filled in fully and accurately.

credit card
A plastic card that enables the user to buy goods and services on credit (e.g. Visa and Mastercard). The account is held by the issuer of the card and a credit limit is established. The user receives a statement each month and must pay off a minimum amount (if not all) of the debt at that time. Credit card operators usually charge a very high rate of interest. See also **charge card**.

credit note
A note to the buyer that the account with the supplier is in credit. Credit notes are usually printed in red. They are issued when goods are returned to the supplier, and can be set against the next invoice.

credit transfer
Money may be moved from one bank account to another by way of a credit transfer. This is often the method of paying employees a monthly salary, and can also be used to pay suppliers.

crossing
Indication on a cheque that certain conditions apply to the drawing of a cheque (e.g. that it may only be paid into a bank account). The crossing usually appears as two lines, with details written between the lines. See also **a/c payee only**; **endorsement**; **general crossing**; **not negotiable**; **not transferable**; **open cheque**.

current account
A type of bank account for everyday use. Facilities on current accounts include cheque books and cards, standing orders and direct debits. Some banks now also offer interest-bearing current accounts.

customs declaration
A document that states the nature and value of goods that are being imported or exported through customs.

cycle billing
A method of sending out bills in batches at various times during the month. It enables suppliers to deal with their billing in batches and ensures that customers are billed once in the period (but not necessarily at the end of the month).

debit card
A plastic card that can be used to purchase goods and services. It operates much in the same way as a cheque, debiting the sums direct from the user's current account.

deductions
Sums of money taken off payment due. Employees are subject to various deductions from their gross salary, including **National Insurance** contributions and **PAYE**.

deposit account
A bank account specifically for moneys that will not be required for everyday use. Most deposit accounts attract interest. See also **current account**.

direct debit
A method of making payments that are due regularly (e.g., rental fees and regular bills). A direct debit mandate is made out by the buyer in favour of the supplier, who then enforces it. Amounts (which can be varied from payment to payment) are then taken directly from the bank account on a certain specified day each month.

dishonoured cheque
A cheque that is not paid by the payer's bank, perhaps because there is not enough money in the account to cover it. See Cheque, p.207.

drawer
The party that presents a cheque or other **bill of exchange** for payment.

EFTPOS
Abbreviation for electronic funds transfer at point of sale, a computer system that enables retailers to connect directly with the purchaser's bank account in order to extract funds immediately, facilitated by use of a plastic **debit card**.

emergency code
A code that enables accountants to deduct tax from an employee's earnings on an emergency basis (and at a higher rate) until the true tax status of the employee is established. Presenting the employer with a **P45** should reduce the amount of time spent under the emergency code.

endorsement
If the payee named on a cheque does not have a bank account, it may be possible to have the cheque paid into another person's account. This is done by the payee writing their name on the back of the cheque. The cheque then becomes a third party cheque and can be paid into any bank account. Because of rising cheque fraud, some banks now refuse to take third party cheques that have been endorsed in this way, and many cheques are 'crossed' with the words: 'account payee only' to prevent endorsement and, through that, fraud.

estimate
A rough indication of the price of a job, often supplied by traders whose costs are subject to fluctuation. See also **quotation**.

Eurocheque
A cheque that can be exchanged for any foreign currency. See Eurocheques p.296.

general crossing
Crossing that indicates that a cheque must not be cashed on production, but that it must be paid into a bank account. A general crossing may consist of two parallel lines only, or of two parallel lines with the words '& co.' written between them. See also Cheque, p.207.

gross
A sum of money due before any deductions have been made. Therefore, an employee's gross earnings are earnings before tax, **National Insurance** contributions and other agreed payments have been made. See also **profit**.

imprest system
The most common method of organizing **petty cash**. See 8.3 Petty cash p.211.

income tax
Tax on money earned, payable to the state via the Inland Revenue. See Income tax, p.213; 8.6 Money matters for sole traders.

in hand
Some companies ask their staff to work a period of time (say, a week) 'in hand'. This means that the employee works week one without being paid. Work done in week one is paid at the end of week two. When the employee leaves the company, he or she is paid two weeks wages in one lump sum.

Inland Revenue
A body that is responsible for the administration of the UK's taxation laws, including income tax. The employees of the Inland Revenue have wide powers to investigate the financial affairs of individuals and companies (including access to otherwise confidential bank accounts) to ensure that the correct amount of tax is paid. See Income tax, p.213; 8.6 Money matters for sole traders.

insurance
A scheme that provides compensation in the event of loss or damage of property or other mishap in return for regular payments to the scheme. Insurance schemes are set up by insurance companies, and terms vary from scheme to scheme. The UK runs a **National Insurance** scheme which offers a wide range of benefits (including access to the National Health Service, social security benefits, sick pay and a state pension) in return for payments (contributions) linked to earnings. See also National Insurance contributions, p.212.

interest
The amount paid on a sum of money borrowed or deposited in an interest-bearing bank or building society account. Interest is normally given as an annual percentage rate (**APR**), and the rate of interest payable can fluctuate.

international payment service
A service that enables payments to be received from and paid to companies or individuals anywhere in the world.

inventory
A list of the equipment owned by a company.

invoice
A document that requests payment for goods or services rendered. Details include: the selling company's name, address, VAT registration number (if appropriate); the buying company's name and address, with order details (such as an order number or the name of the person requesting the goods or services); details of the goods or services rendered; amount due and when; discounts for fast payment. See also Invoice, p.216.

joint-stock bank
An alternative name for a **commercial bank**.

legal tender
The bank notes and coins that make up a country's currency. From time to time, the government decides to issue new notes or coins, and the old forms cease to be legal tender.

loan
A sum of money borrowed from a company, individual or lending institution. Loan schemes vary from lender to lender, but all commercial lenders charge interest on the loan, and request that it be repaid by a certain date. There may also be an arrangement fee to be paid.

market intelligence
Information about a certain business or industry. Some banks offer a market intelligence service.

National Girobank
A banking system that is run through the Post Office by the Alliance and Leicester Building Society.

National Insurance
A national scheme that requires contributions to be made by all individuals; offering in return access to the National Health Service, a state pension at retirement age, unemployment and other benefits. See National Insurance contributions p.212.

net
A sum of money after all deductions have been made. For example, net profit is

the amount of profit made after taxes have been deducted. An employee's net income is the money received after **National Insurance**, **income tax** and **pension** deductions have been made. See also **gross**.

N/F
No funds. Used on a cheque that has been returned unpaid to the **drawer** because the account on which the cheque is to be drawn has insufficient funds to cover the amount payable.

night safe
A safe that is normally found in the outside walls of commercial banks, in which customers may deposit money and other valuable items after the bank has closed. Customers who wish to make use of a night safe service are normally issued with a lockable bag and a key to the safe.

not negotiable
A cheque that is **crossed** and marked with the words 'not negotiable' may be passed to a third party for paying in (see **endorsement**). However, the person who has agreed to pay the cheque in is warned that if the cheque is unpaid, he or she (as opposed to the bank) will be the party that loses out. See Cheque, p.207.

not transferable
A cheque that is not to be transferred to a third party by **endorsement** is **crossed** and marked with the name of the person to be paid – 'pay J. Smith only'. Alternatively the words 'not transferable' may be used and the words 'or order' printed on the cheque crossed out. See Cheque, p.207.

open credit
A method of cashing cheques at a branch other than that at which the account is actually held. At branches of the bank in the UK, open credit can be obtained by special arrangement with the branch. Open credit can also be arranged with overseas banks. See Open credit, p.296.

open cheque
A cheque that is not **crossed** and so does not need to be paid into an account. It may therefore be exchanged for cash over the counter of a bank.

order
A document that indicates to a seller what it is the purchaser wants to buy. An order is drawn up by the purchaser and normally includes the following: name and address of the purchaser and of the seller; date of the order and any reference number; details of the goods or services required; latest delivery date; instructions for delivery.

overdraft
When the holder of a bank account draws more money than is actually in the account, the account is said to be overdrawn and the excess amount is known

as an overdraft. Authorized overdraft facilities can be arranged with the bank and interest and an arrangement fee is usually payable. Unauthorized overdrafts can be costly in terms of bank charges and should be avoided if possible.

P1
An **Inland Revenue** document known as a tax return. Self-employed people are required to fill our tax returns at the end of every financial year to indicate profits and expenses and to give details of personal life that may affect taxation. Tax liability is calculated on the basis of the information given on the P1. Employees are likely to receive only one P1, at the end of their first year at work. The P1 is accompanied by a P3, giving instructions as to how to fill in the P1.

P2
An **Inland Revenue** document sent to employees by the Inland Revenue detailing the allowances (i.e. sums of money that people are entitled to earn before they must start paying tax) for which they are eligible and giving the individual's tax code.

P3
See **P1**.

P6
An **Inland Revenue** document, similar to a **P2** that details an employee's **tax code**, but which is sent to the employer.

P7
The **Inland Revenue**'s guide to the **PAYE** system, for employers.

P11
A record held for each employee, showing the tax deductions that have been made. At the end of each year, the employer sends a P14 to the **Inland Revenue**, as an account of deductions for all employees.

P14
See **P11**.

P15
An **Inland Revenue** 'coding claim form'. This form is filled in by employees who cannot produce a **P45**, and gives the Inland Revenue similar information as the **P1**.

P45
A form handed to an employee on leaving a job. It should be taken to the next employer or to the unemployment benefit office. It gives details of earnings and of tax paid in the current year, along with the correct **tax code** and **National Insurance** record, so that the employer knows how much tax and National Insurance to deduct from earnings. Those who cannot present a P45 are issued with a **P15** so that a tax code can be requested from the **Inland Revenue**,

and will be charged at a higher rate of tax until the correct code is issued.

P46
An **Inland Revenue** form filled in by the employer when a new employee cannot produce a **P45**, requesting a **tax code**. It is sent to the Inland Revenue along with form **P15**, which is filled in by the employee.

P60
An **Inland Revenue** document detailing the employee's tax and **National Insurance** contribution record for the previous tax year. P60s should be kept safely as they are proof of payment.

PAYE
Abbreviation for pay-as-you-earn, the system whereby the earnings of employees are charged **income tax** at source (i.e. earnings are paid minus the deduction for income tax). See Income tax p.213.

payee
A person to whom a cheque is made out. See Cheque, p.207.

paying-in slip
A form on which is written the details of money to be paid into a bank (see Paying-in slip p.208).

payment card
Alternative term for a **debit card**.

pay slip
A document that is given or sent to an employee detailing gross earnings along with any deductions. Every employee is entitled to receive a pay slip of some sort under the Employment Rights Act, 1996 (see The Employment Rights Act, 1996, p.248).

pension
Money paid to a person who is no longer working, either due to age or illness. Widows and ex-servicemen may also receive a pension. See Pensions, p.213.

petty cash
All companies need to make small payments for day-to-day expenses. They therefore hold a small amount of money at the office, and operate a system to monitor outgoings. See Petty cash p.211.

PIN
Acronym for Personal Identification Number, the secret security code issued to users of **cash and credit cards**.

postal order
A **bill of exchange** that can be bought from Post Offices. Postal orders can be bought for very small sums and are useful for sending small payments by post.

Postcheques
A service offered by the **National Girobank**, similar to the **Eurocheque**.

Postcheques (backed up by a guarantee card) can be cashed for local currency in Europe, Iceland, parts of the Mediterranean and the USA.

poundage
A fee paid to the Post Office when buying **postal orders**.

PR
Abbreviation for 'please re-present'. A cheque returned to the payee may be marked with these letters, indicating that the cheque should be presented again to the bank, at which time there should be funds available to enable the cheque to clear.

profit
A company's earnings after all costs have been taken into account. Gross profit is profit before tax has been paid, and net profit indicates profits after tax liabilities have been dealt with.

pro forma invoice
An invoice issued before an order is placed or before goods are delivered, which provides details of the goods and the cost.

quotation
A firm indication of the amount of money payable for goods or services. See also Quotation, p.203.

R
The person who writes out a cheque may indicate on the line giving the amount in words that a receipt is required. This is done using the abbreviation 'R'.

R/D
Abbreviation for refer to **drawer**. When written on a cheque, it indicates that the payee must return the cheque to the drawer, either because some of the required information is missing (e.g. a signature) or because there are no funds in the account to cover the cheque. See also Cheque, p.193.

receipt
A document that shows that money has been received. Companies that wish to claim **VAT** on a payment should ensure that the receipt gives the selling company's VAT number.

remittance book
A log of money being paid to the company either by post or by courier. Some companies require that those responsible for handling incoming correspondence indicate payments in the remittance book.

remittance advice
A document sent out with payments giving details of the payment as advice to the payee. Details may include: the payer's name and address; the invoice or statement number and date; details of goods or services; the amount of the remittance. The person responsible for incoming correspondence should always

check that the remittance enclosed tallies with the amount stated on the remittance advice and follow up any discrepancies.

requisition
An internal document within a company requesting supplies.

salary
An employee's earnings, usually paid monthly by cheque or directly to the employee's bank account.

SERPS
Acronym for state earnings-related pension scheme. See also Pensions, pp.201–202.

schedule D
A system of income tax involving the self-employed. See also Registration as a sole trader, p.217.

SO
Abbreviation for **standing order**.

special crossing
One of a number of **crossings** that indicate how a cheque can be drawn.

stale cheque
A cheque that has not been presented for payment within six months of its date is no longer valid, and is known as a stale cheque.

standing order
A request to the bank that a regular payment is made to a certain payee on a certain day of the month. Standing orders differ from **direct debits** in that the request comes from the payer and not the payee.

statement
An indication of the state of an account. A bank statement, for example, shows the state of a bank account. See illustration 8.2-3, p.210. A supplier may send customers statements covering invoices that have not yet been paid. Action taken on receipt of a supplier's statement depends on the terms of the original invoice.

stopped cheque
A payment of cheques that have already been issued may be stopped by the account holder by arrangement with the bank. To stop a cheque you will have to give the account number, the cheque number and the payee. A charge may be payable. A guaranteed cheque can not usually be stopped.

SWIFT
Acronym for The Society for Worldwide Interbank Financial Telecommunications. SWIFT is an electronic network enabling payments to be made and other financial information to be exchanged between subscribers worldwide.

tax code
An **Inland Revenue** code which, when used with the correct calculation tables, indicates the amount of tax that should be deducted from an employee's gross earnings.

tax return
Inland Revenue documents, which are filled in by employees after the first year at work (and sometimes yearly thereafter), and by self-employed people at the end of every tax year. The information given enables the Inland Revenue to work out how much **income tax** each person should pay. With self-assessment, many more people have to complete a tax return, and you are given the option of assessing your own income and tax payments, based on a series of calculations that are supplied for you.

telegraph payment
A method of paying people in other countries, also known as telegraphic transfer (TT).

trade references
A statement by a current supplier that a buying company is trustworthy. Trade references or **bank references** are often required by suppliers when setting up an account.

Transcash
A **National Girobank** system of paying people via the Post Office. Payments are made to the Post Office in cash using a Transcash form, and then credited to the payee's National Girobank account.

TT
Abbreviation for telegraphic transfer. See **telegraph payment**.

turnover
The total value of goods or services sold in one period (usually a year).

VAT
Acronym for value-added tax, a kind of purchase tax levied on goods and services depending on their value. Those liable for VAT are traders turning over a certain amount per quarter. As soon as a company's turnover reaches this level, it must register for VAT and display the registration number on all relevant documents (especially invoices and receipts).

  The company probably pays VAT on expenses such as materials and then charges VAT on goods sold. At the end of every quarter, the amount of VAT paid on expenses is subtracted from the amount received from customers, and the remainder is payable almost immediately to the Customs and Excise (the government department that administers and enforces the VAT system). Some goods are zero-rated or exempted from VAT (for example, books and children's clothes) but the level of VAT (a percentage) and what goods attract

VAT can change from year to year. At the time of publication the rate was 17.5%.

wages
An employee's earnings, usually paid on a weekly basis in cash.

zero-rated
Certain goods (e.g., books, food and children's clothes) do not attract **VAT**. These items are said to be zero-rated.

8.2 Basic banking documents

All office staff should have a knowledge of the basic banking documents, and understand how to decipher them.

Cheque

A cheque is basically a document that bears an order to the account-holder's bank to pay the named person a certain sum of money. The process in general works as follows. Cheques are issued by the account-holder and presented to the payee's bank.

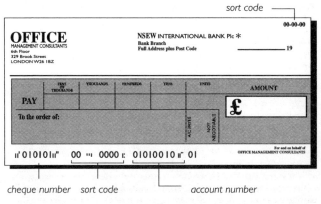

Illustration 8.2-1 A company cheque, which differs from personal cheques only in format. This style is often supplied for use with computerized accounting systems and is usually accompanied by a tear-off remittance advice.

The payee's bank puts the cheque into the clearing system, and the paying bank eventually authorizes payment and transfers the given sum from one account to the other. The whole process should take about three working days, but with some cheques (e.g., building society cheques) it may take up to 10 working days.

Cheques are normally issued in books or in another format (which usually also includes an attached remittance advice for use with a computerized payments system – this type of cheque is illustrated below). Each cheque has its own number through which it can be traced and stopped if necessary. In circumstances where an account-holder does not have a cheque available, a counter-cheque can be issued by the bank, but a small fee is usually charged for this service.

Cheque counterfoils should be filled in at the time of writing the cheque for future reference. Illustration 8.2-1 shows one type of company cheque.

If you are accepting a cheque for payment, check:

● That the amounts in words and figures tally with each other.
● That the date is no more than six months ago (if it is more than six months old the cheque is invalid).
● That the cheque has been signed.
● That the name of the payee is correct.

If you are accepting a cheque with a cheque guarantee card, check the following details before writing the number of the cheque card on the back of the card (if the account holder is allowed to do this him/herself, the guarantee is invalid):

● That the signature on the cheque is the same as on the back of the card (watch the person write the signature if you can).
● That the cheque card is not out of date.
● That the card and the cheque relate to the same account (compare the sort code, branch name and account number).
● That the cheque card has not been tampered with in any way.
● That the cheque card is not listed on any 'wanted' lists sent to you by the issuing company.

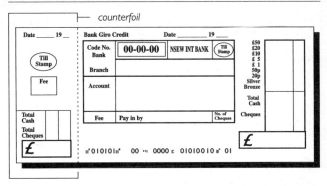

8.2-2 A standard form of paying-in slip with its counterfoil. Space is given on the back of the form to list details of cheques and postal orders, and should be filled in, along with the counterfoil at the time of deposit.

Paying-in slip

This form is sometimes known as a bank giro credit. It should be filled in with all the relevant details when paying in cash, cheques or postal orders to the bank. Personalized paying-in slips are available in books (sometimes now included in cheque books) with details of the account already filled in. Alternatively, paying-in slips are available at banks. They can be used to pay sums into an account held at that branch or at another branch, or at another bank (although a fee may be charged for this service). Illustration 8.2-2 shows a standard paying-in slip.

WARNING
The paying-in slips issued for use on certain accounts should not be used for paying in to other accounts. The specific information on such slips is printed in magnetic ink, capable of being processed by computer, and so, even if you cross the information out, the credit may still be credited to the account for which the slip was issued.

NSEW INTERNATIONAL BANK Plc ✱

STATEMENT OF ACCOUNT
OFFICE MANAGEMENT CONSULTANTS
ACCOUNT NUMBER 01010010

Date	Particulars	Payments	Receipts	Balance
1997	Opening balance			1425 33
3 OCT	070402	251 91		1173 42
4 OCT	070403	26 00		
	SUNDRY CREDIT		364 92	
	XYZ ACCOUNT D/D	100 00		1412 34
6 OCT	070405	43 00		
	070406	92 00		1277 34
10 OCT	070404	142 00		1419 34
15 OCT	ABC ACCOUNT S/O	150 00		1269 34
18 OCT	SUNDRY CREDIT		1054 00	2323 34
20 OCT	BGC		200 42	2523 76

8.2-3 A standard bank statement.

Bank statement

Details of all transactions carried out on a certain account, sent to the account holder (usually monthly) by the bank. Those receiving bank statements should check the details against the counterfoils in cheque books and paying-in slips. Bank statements only show transactions at the bank up to the date given. There may be cheques still in the clearing system for credit or debit. It is therefore wise to undertake a reconciliation to ascertain the state of the account up to date.

Bank statements often use abbreviations, and they should also include a key explaining what the abbreviations mean.

```
┌─────────────────────────────────────────────────┐
│  Folio _____           Date _____ 19__        │
│                                                   │
│           PETTY CASH VOUCHER                      │
│                                                   │
│  For what required:                  £    p       │
│                                                   │
│                                                   │
│                                                   │
│                                                   │
│  Signature _____          │
│                                                   │
│  Passed by _____          │
│                                                   │
└─────────────────────────────────────────────────┘
```

8.3-1 A standard form of petty cash voucher.

In illustration 8.2-3, S/O means standing order, D/D means direct debit and BGC stands for bank giro credit. The letters O/D next to a balance figure in the last column is often used to indicate an overdraft.

8.3 Petty cash

Petty cash is a sum of money kept in a safe place in the office to pay for small day-to-day expenses. Petty cash should be kept in a lockable box, drawer or cupboard. Most companies use the imprest system (see below) when organizing their petty cash.

The imprest system

This system enables administrators of petty cash to keep track of outgoings and to record them in a simple manner.

The system is started by placing a specific sum of money in the petty cash box, usually £100, known as the float.

When employees wish to take cash to cover small expenses, a petty cash voucher is made out (books of vouchers can be bought from office suppliers, detailing the name of the person taking the money, the expense, the date and the amount taken. It is authorized by the system's administrator. The employee also hands over receipts where possible.

So at all times, the amount of cash in the box plus the amounts indicated on the petty cash vouchers add up to the amount of the float. When the float is reduced below a given level, a petty cash account is made out detailing the expenses. A further sum is requested to take the float back up to its original level, and the cycle begins again.

8.4 Employee money matters

Accounting procedures related to the payroll are normally dealt with by the company's accounting personnel. However, all employees should understand their basic rights and the normal procedures so that they can double-check pay-slips and keep an eye on other matters, such as pensions. The legislation concerning the payment of employees is discussed in section 10.2, Employment legislation.

Wages and salaries

The term 'wages' usually refers to money paid to an employee at the end of each week, and most often in cash. Salaries are paid monthly, usually by cheque, or by direct payment to the employee's bank account (using BACS).

In either case, employees all have a legal right to receive a pay-slip detailing the following:

● basic pay for the period
● pay for overtime or bonuses
● any allowances (e.g., for work clothing or petrol for a company car)
● statutory deductions (income tax and National Insurance)
● voluntary deductions (e.g. contributions to an occupational pension scheme, etc.)
● total net pay for the period

National Insurance contributions

National Insurance contributions are normally deducted from employees' earnings at source. The amount due under the scheme depends on the amount the employee is earning.

See also 8.6 for advice on National Insurance contributions for self-employed people.

Income tax

Like National Insurance, income tax is usually deducted from an employee's earnings before they are paid (under the PAYE, or pay-as-you-earn, system). The percentage rate of income tax payable by each person depends on how much is earned, and the rate increases in 'tax bands'. At the start of each financial year, the government sets the rates payable by people in each band, and also sets allowances, money on which income tax is not payable.

For example, a single person's tax allowance (there are other allowances depending on the employee's personal circumstances) may be set by the government at around £3,800. This is the amount he or she can earn in a year before tax becomes payable. Any amounts earned over that threshold become liable for tax at the given rate, say 20 or 25%.

Personal information and tax records are transferred between the employee, the employer and the Inland Revenue on any one of a number of Inland Revenue forms, all with the suffix 'P': see 8.1, Key terms for details.

Pensions

All employees are entitled to a state pension on retirement provided that they have paid the requisite number of contributions over the better part of their working life. The basic state retirement pension is paid to all who have made the minimum number of contributions.

A more valuable state pension is payable to those who have contributed at a higher rate to SERPS (state earnings-related pension scheme). It is now possible to decide whether you wish to be part of this pension scheme or whether you wish to 'contract out' of the scheme and arrange your own personal pension plan. If you plan to 'opt out' of SERPS, make sure you get good independent financial advice (see below).

Personal pension plans

If you decide to arrange your own personal pension plan, it is wise to do so through an independent financial adviser who is a member of a professional body such as FIMBRA (Financial Intermediaries and Brokers Regulatory Authority). A scheme is normally devised whereby you decide how much you want to contribute each month, and the money is then invested on various financial markets. If all goes well, the profit on these investments increase and eventually you have enough money to provide a retirement pension. You may find that if you contract out of SERPS, your employer will match your own contributions to a personal pension plan.

Occupational pension schemes

Some companies operate their own occupational pension schemes, into which both the company and the beneficiary pay contributions. These schemes can supplement state pensions.

If you leave your present employer, it is possible to cease the payments and still receive the (reduced) benefit of the scheme when you retire, or in some instances (especially if the employer is a local authority) to transfer the plan to your next employer. It is wise to find out the situation when you start or leave employment.

Expenses

Each company has different methods of dealing with its employees' expenses, and different regulations as to what can be claimed back from the company and by whom. Those in possession of company cars may be able to claim for petrol, for instance, and those making business trips will normally be able to claim for all accommodation, meals, etc.

If you are entitled to claim for expenses, you should obviously keep all receipts, and ensure that they all give VAT registration numbers for the seller's company.

The main problem with expenses is how to claim for small out-of-pocket expenses for which no receipt is obtainable – newspapers, cups of coffee, fares for public transport. Such expenses can add up, but they are a nightmare that most accounts departments could do without. One solution is to allow the person a *per diem* (per day), a small amount of money for every day of the trip to cover such expenses.

Your company will no doubt issue you with instructions on how to account for and claim expenses, and it saves the accounts department time if you follow them.

8.5 Trading documents

Most office staff will come across the following documents.

Price list

A price list is exactly what it says, a list of prices issued by a supplier. Most price lists give a date of issue, and users should check that the price list being referred to is current. Prices are often subject to change without warning and so should be checked with suppliers before issuing an order.

Prices may include a sum for VAT, but most often do not, they should also give an indication of whether prices include transportation to the buyer. Check for details of quantity discounts or for cash or immediate payment.

Estimate

An estimate is a statement by a supplier (usually of services rather than goods) that gives the probable price of a finished job. An estimate does not constitute a binding agreement to stick to the price stated.

An estimate usually breaks the services down into stages, listing estimated sums for such items as materials, time, etc. It may also include an indication of the delivery date.

Quotation

A quotation is a statement by a supplier (usually of services rather than goods) giving an accurate account of the price of the job for the benefit of the customer. Wherever possible, orders should be issued on the basis of a quotation rather than an estimate. Check details such as delivery date, inclusion or not of VAT and discounts for fast payment.

The quotation should also tell you for how long the goods or services are on offer at the quoted price.

Order

An order is a document that requests goods or services from a supplier. It will normally be a firm order, for which all negotiations (e.g., on price and payment schedules) have been completed. An order may include the following information:

● The buyer's name, address and VAT number.
● The seller's name and address.

- The date of the order, the name of the person authorizing the order (and probably his or her signature) and any reference number (this will be used to connect the order with the later invoice for payment).
- Details of the goods or services required and their price (before VAT is added).
- Delivery information and a date by which delivery must be made.

A firm order is generally looked upon as a promise to pay for the goods detailed (provided of course that there is nothing wrong with them).

Invoice

An invoice is a document sent to a buyer, detailing the goods or services bought and the amount of money payable and by what date. Most invoices give the following information:

- The name and address of issuing company (the seller).
- The seller's VAT registration number.
- The name and address of the receiving company (the buyer), and the name of the person responsible for the purchase and the reference of any buying order (see Order)
- The date of the invoice.
- The details of the goods or services bought.
- A note of the price agreed and VAT payable.
- The details of discounts for quantity or for speedy settlement of the invoice.

If invoices remain unpaid, the buyer may receive reminders. In some cases, companies have great difficulty collecting money from their customers. They therefore 'sell' the debts owing to them to a company known as a factor. The factor collects the debts on behalf of the seller and deducts a commission for the service. Monies paid to suppliers through factors, should be sent to the factor (not the supplier). Cheques should be made payable to the factor.

8.6 Money matters for sole traders

The financial affairs of sole traders are considered by the law to be inseparable from their personal financial affairs. Therefore, it is most important to keep rigorous accounts and all the other documents required. Sole traders are subject to personal taxation on their profits at the usual rates. Registration for VAT is only necessary if you are turning over a certain amount per year. Contact your local VAT office for details.

All sole traders are advised to engage the services of a qualified accountant who is experienced in dealing with the Inland Revenue.

Registration as a sole trader

When you decide to become a sole trader, you will need to register with the Contributions Agency (which deals with National Insurance payments) and with the Inland Revenue. The local office of the Inland Revenue will register you for Schedule D taxation and send you a registration number. You will then receive a tax return every year.

It is advisable to pay basic National Insurance contributions by direct debit (usually drawn every quarter). You will then be sent a record of your contributions and asked, on the basis of the profit declared to the Inland Revenue, to make up the contributions to a level that will permit payment of a state pension and access to other services and benefits.

Your bank account

If the Inland Revenue decides to investigate your financial affairs, inspectors will have access to any bank and building society accounts. It is therefore a good idea to open a new account for your business, and to transfer a certain amount of money each month to a separate account for personal use. Legitimate payments into your bank that are not earnings can then be paid into your personal account. Both accounts will be liable to scrutiny, but at least your affairs will be clear.

Records you need to keep

You will need to keep strict records of income and outgoings related to your business. This not only shows the Inland Revenue that you are organized and honest, but will reduce the amount of work your accountant will have to do in preparing an end-of-year statement (and so reduce the fee).

● *Cash book* Keep a month-by-month list of invoices you have sent out, and of your expenses.

● *Receipts* You will need to keep receipts relating to your expenses, which can include materials, rent of premises, telephone, electricity and gas bills, etc. Your accountant will be able to advise you what legitimate expenses you may be able to deduct from your earnings to arrive at a taxable profit figure. Capital expenditure (e.g. for durable equipment) can be written off against expenses over a period of time. Your accountant should be able to advise you.

● *Banking documents* You must keep all bank statements, along with paying-in books and cheque books. It is advisable, when paying in sums to keep a precise record of all details.

● *Invoices* Keep copies of all invoices that you send to clients, preferably using a sequential numbering system so that the Inland Revenue can see that no invoices are missing.

The general state of your accounting documents and procedures will tell the Inland Revenue a lot about the accuracy (or otherwise) of your declared profit. It is therefore in your interests to keep your documentation clear and up to date.

8.7 Foreign exchange

Banks and other agencies that buy and sell foreign exchange often quote prices in the following way:

	WE BUY	WE SELL
US$	1.8	1.6

This indicates that if you want to buy US dollars with pounds sterling, you will get 1.6 dollars for every pound you spend. If you want to sell US dollars and buy sterling, you will be paid £1 for every 1.8 dollars you have.

However, percentage commissions are payable on each transaction, and you will probably find that commission in the UK is a higher rate when you sell your sterling to buy dollars than when you return and you want to sell your dollars for sterling.

8.8 Metric/imperial conversion tables

It has now been many years since the UK officially replaced the old imperial system with the more modern metric system for measurements and quantities. However, the old system still holds sway in some instances and in the USA metric is not usually used.

Metric units

Metric units work in a simple manner: the root of the word (metre, litre, gram, etc.) tells you the basic unit, and the prefix gives you the size of the measure in relation to the basic unit. For example, centimetre denotes one metre divided by ten, a kilogram is 1,000 grams. Here are the metric prefixes:

Prefix	Factor	Prefix	Factor
deca	10 (= x 10)	deci	10^{-1} (= one tenth)
hecto	10^2 (= x 100)	centi	10^{-2} (= one hundredth)
kilo	10^3 (= x 1000	milli	10^{-3} (= one thousandth)
mega	10^6 (= x one million)	micro	10^{-6} (= one millionth)
giga	10^9 (= x one thousand million)	nano	10^{-9} (= one thousand millionth)
tera	10^{12} (= x one million million)	pico	10^{-12} (= one million millionth)

Imperial units

Imperial units are based on various historical measurements.

LENGTH	12 inches (in) = 1 foot (ft)
	3 feet (ft) = 1 yard (yd)
	220 yards (10 chains) = 1 furlong
	1,760 yards (8 furlongs, 5,280 feet) = 1 mile
AREA	144 square inches (sq in) = 1 square foot (sq ft)
	9 square feet = 1 square yard (sq yd)
	4,840 sq yd = 1 acre
	640 acres = 1 square mile (sq mile)
VOLUME	1,728 cubic inches (cu in) = 1 cubic foot (cu ft)
	27 cubic feet = 1 cubic yard (cu yd)

CAPACITY	4 gills (20 fluid ounces) = 1 pint
	2 pints (40 fl oz) = 1 quart
	4 quarts (160 fl oz) = 1 gallon
	2 gallons = 1 peck
	8 gallons (4 pecks) = 1 bushel
	8 bushels (64 gallons) = 1 quarter
	1 barrel (oil) = 50.4 gallons (US 42 gallons)

WEIGHT	16 drams = 1 ounce (oz)
	16 ounces = 1 pound (lb)
	14 pounds = 1 stone
	2 stones (28 lb) = 1 quarter
	4 quarters (112 lb) = 1 hundredweight (cwt)
	20 hundredweight (2,240 lb) = 1 ton

Converting Imperial to Metric

LENGTH

inches to millimetres	x 25.4
inches to centimetres	x 2.54
inches to metres	x 0.254
feet to centimetres	x 30.48
feet to metres	x 0.3048
yards to metres	x 0.9144
miles to kilometres	x 1.6093

AREA

square inches to square centimetres	x 6.4516
square feet to square metres	x 0.0929
square yards to square metres	x 0.8316
square miles to square kilometres	x 2.5898
acres to hectares	x 0.4047
acres to square kilometres	x0.00405

VOLUME

cubic inches to cubic centimetres	x 16.3871
cubic feet to cubic metres	x 0.0283
cubic yards to cubic metres	x 0.7646
cubic milescubic kilometres	x 4.1678

CAPACITY

fluid ounces to millilitres	× 28.5
pints to millilitres	× 568.0
US pints to millilitres	× 473.32
pints to litres	× 0.568
US pints to litres	× 0.4733
gallons to litres	× 4.55
US gallons to litres	× 3.785

WEIGHT

ounces to grams	× 28.3495
pounds to grams	× 453.592
pounds to kilograms	× 4.536
pounds to tons	× 0.0004536
tons to tons	× 1.0161

Converting Metric to Imperial

LENGTH

millimetres to inches	× 0.03937
centimetres to inches	× 0.3937
centimetres to feet	× 0.032808
metres to inches	× 39.37
metres to feet	× 3.2808
metres to yards	× 1.0936
kilometres to miles	× 0.6214

AREA

square centimetres to square inches	× 0.1552
square metres to square feet	× 10.7636
square metres to square yards	× 1.196
square kilometres to square miles	× 0.3861
square kilometres to acres	× 247.1
hectares to acres	× 2.471

VOLUME

cubic centimetres to cubic inches	× 0.061
cubic metres to cubic feet	× 35.315
cubic metres to cubic yards	× 1.308
cubic kilometres to cubic miles	× 0.2399

CAPACITY

millilitres to fluid ounces	x 0.0351
millilitres to pints	x 0.00176
millilitres to US pints	x 0.002114
litres to pints	x 1.760
litres to US pints	x 2.114
litres to gallons	x 0.2193
litre to US gallons	x 0.2634

WEIGHT

grams to ounces	x 0.0352
grams to pounds	x 0.0022
kilograms to pounds	x 2.2046
tons to pounds	x 2204.59
tons to tons	x 0.9842

US Imperial units

Also called Customary Units, US Imperial Units differ slightly to UK Imperial Units. Here are the differences:

1 US pint = 16 fluid ounces
2 US pints (32 fl oz) = 1 quart
4 US quarts (128 fl oz) = 1 gallon
1 US ton (also known as the short ton) = 2,000 pounds

Temperature

To convert Celsius (centigrade) to Fahrenheit:
   multiply by ⅘ and add 32.

To convert Fahrenheit to Celsius:
   subtract 32 and multiply by ⅚.

9
Healthy, Safe and Secure
HEALTH AND SAFETY AT WORK

9
Healthy, Safe and Secure
HEALTH AND SAFETY AT WORK

It is in every company's best interest to ensure that its staff is protected from danger of injury, and that working conditions are within the law. This section deals with issues related to health and safety at work, giving information on employers' and employees' duties under the legislation as well as advice on how to avoid injury.

9.1 Legislation on health and safety at work

The major legislation covering health and safety at work is embodied in the Health and Safety at Work Act 1974 (HASAW) and the Office, Shops and Railway Premises Act 1963. They set out the responsibilities of employers to protect their employees. Employees also have a responsibility under HASAW to protect themselves and fellow workers. A third Act, the Employer's Liability (Compulsory Insurance) Act 1969, states that employers must insure against accidents at work and that up-to-date certificates of this insurance must be displayed where all employees can see them. Employers' duties under these Acts include:

● To provide a safe place in which to work, with safe access to it.
● To ensure that machinery and equipment, storage and
  transportation facilities are all safe to operate.
● To ensure that relevant employees are trained and supervised
  in the use of equipment, especially dangerous equipment,
  which must be provided with adequate safety guards.
● To ensure that visitors to the company's premises are also safe
  from injury.
● To issue a written policy on health and safety.
● To keep a record of accidents (see Keeping an accident record
  book, p.231.)
● To provide clean premises without slippery floors and
  obstructions, and to ensure that the premises are not
  overcrowded.

- To provide adequate lighting, heating (the usual minimum is 16°C/61°F), ventilation and washroom facilities, along with eating and seating facilities.
- To ensure that people are not asked to lift a load that is likely to injure them.
- To ensure that fire precautions are taken and first aid facilities provided.

In large companies, personnel departments are responsible for monitoring conditions and working practices to ensure that they are safe, and unions have safety representatives with whom employers should consult.

A copy of each of these Acts appears in a booklet entitled The Guide to Health and Safety at Work Act 1974 is available from many large bookshops or from HSE Books, on 17987 881165.

9.2 Preventing accidents in the office

Most accidents in the office are falls or 'collisions' with obstructions, electrical accidents, and accidents with machinery. Back injuries, often sustained when lifting heavy objects, are becoming very common, and can sometimes cause lifelong back problems.

Preventing falls and 'collisions'

- On the stairs, look out for worn stair treads and broken bannisters.
- Look out for worn or torn carpets.
- Avoid slippery surfaces; mop up immediately any spilled liquids, etc.
- Broken glass should be swept up immediately. The slivers should be wrapped in a thick wad of newspaper and marked so that others treat it with care.
- Secure trailing leads and wires of any kind.
- Never leave desk and filing cabinet drawers open.
- Don't stack furniture, boxes, etc. in corridors where people can fall over them, and especially not on fire exit routes.
- Don't place furniture so that sharp corners protrude.
- Don't put too much weight on the open top drawer of a filing cabinet – it may topple over on top of you.
- Don't overstack shelves or allow stacks to protrude over the edge.

Checklist for electrical dangers

Check for:

- Loose connections
- Worn insulation cables
- Broken switches and sockets
- Worn appliances
- Liquids near power sources
- Trailing electrical leads

When operating dangerous machinery

- Always read the instructions.
- Make sure you know how to cut off the power supply in an emergency.
- Don't clean the machinery, or put fingers inside, when the equipment is running.
- Don't meddle with safety guards.
- Always guard your fingers when using guillotines, staplers, knives and scalpels, etc.
- Tie back long hair when operating machinery with moving parts, remove dangling jewellery, ties and other accessories that might also get caught.
- The insides of photocopiers and other equipment can get very hot. Read warning instructions and take safety precautions to avoid being burned.

Avoiding back injuries when lifting

- Always bend your body at the knees rather than at the waist. In this way, the weight is transmitted to your legs rather than your back.
- Don't be tempted to take too much in one journey.
- Always make sure that you can see over a load.
- If you can, share heavy loads with another person.

9.3 Using workstations

Many people believe that working at workstations that include VDUs present health risks to the worker. These are said to include: radiation risks to unborn babies; eyesight problems; epilepsy; headaches; stress; skin problems; and musculo-skeletal problems, together known as repetitive strain injury (RSI).

The government maintains that none of these problems (including radiation-linked risks) are the product of the VDU itself, but are more the effect of long hours working without sufficient breaks at poorly designed workstations. Despite these assertions, however, RSI accounted for more than half of all occupational injuries reported in the UK in 1997.

To minimize the risk of health problems when working with VDUs:

- Do not work for long periods without a break. Frequent breaks away from the workstation (which do not include activity involving the lower arms and wrists) are recommended. Breaks should include some form of movement or exercise. Ask that your work is reorganized to allow you to take breaks.

- Ensure that the VDU screen is clean of dirt, smears and fingerprints. Arrange the workstation so that there are no reflections on the screen, and set the brightness control to suit the lighting in the office. The words on the screen should be clearly visible.

- Find a chair that can be adjusted to suit your height, and make sure that it supports your back.

- Pay attention to your posture. Adjust your chair so that your arms below the elbow are horizontal when you are keying. Don't slouch, and make sure that you have a curve in your lower back, supported by the back of your chair. When keying, keep your wrists straight. Make sure that they are supported if possible, and that they are not resting on a sharp desk-edge.

- Adjust the angle of the screen to suit the height and position of the chair. Place documents in a stand.

- VDUs cannot cause epilepsy, but if you already have photosensitive epilepsy, you may be at risk.

- Make sure you have some greenery in the office – plants help to absorb the positive ions produced by computer equipment, and will keep the environment more people-friendly.

- Ensure that you have a supply of fresh air; constantly recycled air can lead to chronic illness, asthma and a host of other health conditions. If your windows are sealed, invest in an ionizer, which emits negative ions into the air. Make sure you take a walk outside each day, even if it is only for ten minutes.

● Try to ensure that you get a little natural sunlight each day, and position your desk near a window, if possible; a large number of office workers report suffering from depression, particularly in the winter months, which is attributed to the absence of natural light.

If you are concerned about poor working conditions, the EC (European Commission) has issued a directive on workstations, listing employers' responsibilities regarding workstation design and operation. New workstations must already comply with this directive, and existing workstations must be in compliance by the end of 1996. It includes provision for appropriate eye-testing and prescription of spectacles if necessary (paid for by the employer); monitoring of workstations; planning of breaks (with job restructuring if necessary); and adequate training. A copy of the directive can be obtained from HMSO (see Useful addresses, pp.115–116)

9.4 First aid

Each employer has a duty under The Health and Safety at Work Act to provide first aid for employees. First aid covers medical treatment for minor injuries (for example, cuts and sprains) that would not otherwise be treated, and emergency treatment to keep a person alive until fully qualified medical personnel arrive (for example, while waiting for an ambulance in the event of a heart attack).

The first aid kit

Every office should have a first aid kit. The Health and Safety Executive recommends the following contents:

20 sterile plasters, assorted sizes
2 sterile eye-pads with attachments
6 triangular bandages
6 safety pins
6 medium-sized unmedicated dressings
2 large unmedicated dressings
3 extra-large unmedicated dressings
1 card giving first aid instructions

All dressings should be sterile and individually wrapped. If there is no mains tap water available, the kit should also include sterile water or saline solution in sealed containers for eye irrigation.

Remember to replace any item that is used as soon as possible.

First aid instructions

In offices, which are considered to be low-risk environments (compared, that is, to construction and industrial sites, for example), there should be at least one qualified first aider for every 50 members of staff. As a general rule, it is best to leave first aid to qualified people, but a basic knowledge of first aid techniques is always desirable. The card that should be kept in your office's first aid kit gives detailed instructions. Here are some general guidelines:

In all situations, the casualty should be sitting or lying down. If you think you will need medical help, send for an ambulance by dialling 999. Be prepared to give an accurate description of the injury.

Breathing
- If the casualty is not breathing, but has a pulse, place him or her in a horizontal position, face up.
- Open the mouth and clear it of any foreign material.
- Lift the chin forward with one hand and press the forehead back with the other. Maintain this position throughout.
- Kneel down beside the casualty, and while keeping the head tilted backwards, open the mouth and pinch the nose.
- Take a deep breath. Seal your mouth over the casualty's and breathe out deeply into it. The casualty's chest should rise.
- Remove your mouth and let the casualty's chest fall. If the chest does not rise again, check that the head is tilted back fully. Continue to inflate the casualty's lungs with your expired air at a rate of 12–15 breaths per minute until the casualty is breathing. If this does not restart the breathing check the pulse in the casualty's neck. If not pulse is felt, the heart has stopped – start chest compressions immediately.
- When breathing restarts, place the casualty in the recovery position as shown on the first aid instruction card in your first aid kit.

Unconsciousness
- Open the casualty's mouth and make sure that the tongue is not blocking the throat.
- Place the casualty in the recovery position.

Bleeding
- Sit or lay the patient down to slow the heart rate and lessen the blood flow.
- Elevate the injured area to allow the effects of gravity to slow the blood flow.
- Inspect the injury for foreign bodies or debris; remove anything that is not embedded.
- Apply direct pressure if no foreign bodies are present; apply indirect pressure if foreign bodies are present
- Apply a wound dressing to give direct or indirect pressure as appropriate.
- Do not use tourniquets or constrictive bandages.
- Immobilize the injured area by permanent elevation, e.g., place an arm in a triangular sling or raise the legs by placing the feet on a soft pad.
- Recheck wound dressings for secureness and effectiveness.
- Treat for shock – keep the patient calm, resting and warm and give plenty of reassurance.

Suspected broken bones
- Do not move the casualty unless he or she is in immediate danger.
- Support and secure the injured parts so that they cannot move.

Burns and scalds
- Reduce the spread of heat by placing the affected area under gently running cold water, or by immersion, for at least 10 minutes.
- Remove anything constrictive near the affected area, e.g., rings, jewellery, boots or shoes, in case swelling occurs.
- Do not remove any clothing that may be sticking to burns but remove any clothing that may continue to scald.
- Do not apply lotions, oils or cream.
- Apply a sterilized dressing but do not apply pressure.

● If the burn is large, apply a sterile dressing and send the casualty to hospital.

Eyes
● Wash your hands.
● To remove a foreign body, irrigate the eye with clean, cool water.
● To remove chemicals in the eye, flush continuously with clean, cool water for at least 10 minutes.
● If the eye is injured, cover it with an eye pad and send the casualty to hospital.

Electrical injuries
● Do not touch the casualty until the current is switched off. If this is not possible, stand on some dry, insulated material and use a wooden or plastic implement to separate the casualty from the electricity source.
● If breathing has stopped, start mouth-to-mouth resuscitation while an ambulance is being called.

Keeping an accident record book

In cases where injuries sustained at work are serious, it is possible for the casualty to claim compensation. It is important, therefore, to keep an accurate record of all injuries, however minor, and of the first aid action taken. This record book should include all of the following information:
● Name and address of the casualty.
● The casualty's occupation.
● Date of the entry into the book.
● Date and time of the injury.
● Place and circumstances of the accident, clearly described.
● Description of the injury and the treatment given.
● Signature of the person who made the entry into the book. If this is not the casualty, give the signatory's address.

Contact the Health and Safety Executive for information on first-aid training courses. HMSO publishes the approved Code of Practice (COP 42), *First Aid at Work*, which gives detailed guidance on first aid. For the address, see p.114.

9.5 In the event of fire

Once they break out, fires can spread rapidly from their point of origin. On discovering a fire, or on hearing the fire alarm, it is essential to act quickly and to follow the correct procedure. You will find instructions on how to do this posted at intervals in your office building.

IMPORTANT

However small the fire may seem to be, you should always raise the alarm and call the fire brigade.

Protecting against fire

- Paper-based refuse should be kept in a separate place until it can be removed. Do not allow such waste to accumulate.
- Paints and other flammable liquids should be stored in metal containers, preferably outside the building.
- Do not cover heaters, and maintain a clear space behind refrigerator motors and near the air intakes of other machinery.
- Do not smoke in store-cupboards and dispose of cigarette refuse carefully.
- Switch off all equipment at night (especially gas-fired equipment), and pull out the plugs.
- Do not wedge open self-closing fire-doors.
- Do not obstruct fire exits or corridors.
- Have fire-fighting equipment checked regularly.
- Ensure that sprinkler systems, fire doors, etc. are working at all times.
- If you are new to a building, find out where the fire escape routes are, and where the designated meeting area is. Make sure that you understand the fire procedures for your building.

Fire-fighting equipment

All offices should be fitted with fire extinguishers and other relevant equipment. There are several different types of fire extinguishers available, each designed to fight different types of fires.

TYPE OF FIRE	EXTINGUISHER
Wood, paper, fabrics	water or similar extinguisher
Flammable liquids, or solids that turn to liquid (e.g., greases, fat, oil, etc.)	foam extinguisher, CO_2 dry powder extinguisher or halon extinguisher
Electrical appliances	turn off power supply. CO_2 dry powder or halon extinguisher
Small fires in containers of cooking fat, or in clothes	light-duty fire blanket

It is advised that some members of staff are trained in the use of fire-fighting equipment, in order to take the fastest possible action before the fire brigade arrives. Further information can be obtained from your local fire brigade.

GREEN NOTE
Halon fire extinguishers, which are used for electrical fires, contain the chemical Halon 1211. It is believed that this chemical accounts for up to 30% of ozone depletion in the Antarctic. Testing extinguishers containing halons can lead to leaks of this damaging chemical. Exchange halon fire extinguishers for CO_2 dry powder extinguishers. Take advice on how to dispose of halon extinguishers safely.

Providing for the disabled
If members of staff include the deaf, blind or partially sighted, people with impaired mobility, or the mentally handicapped, managers should take advice on fire alarms or signals and procedures for evacuation. In any event, one person should be detailed to guide each disabled member of staff to the point of safety, and to remain with him or her until the all-clear is given. Contact the Disablement Resettlement Officer (DRO) at the

local Jobcentre, who can put you in touch with specialist advisors for expert advice on the best alarm systems and the most effective procedures for evacuating disabled staff. Alternatively, contact the relevant disabled association (e.g., Royal National Institute for the Blind).

9.6 Smoking in the office

It is now generally agreed that smoking is harmful both to smokers and to those around them. While the numbers of people smoking have in recent years been reduced enormously, 32% of women and 35% of men still smoke.

Because of the health risks of smoking, and most particularly of 'passive smoking' (that is, breathing in the smoke of another person's cigarette), many restaurants, places of entertainment and public transport amenities have taken action either to segregate smokers from non-smokers or to ban smoking altogether.

Smokers who smoke in an enclosed space such as an office are forcing their non-smoking colleagues to inhale their cigarette smoke. This can give rise to minor ailments such as irritated eyes and nose, and sore throats. It can also exacerbate asthma and other allergic disorders such as hay fever. In the long term, passive smoking could lead to lung cancer in a person who has never smoked.

Smoking also has other effects. The smoke is harmful to electronic machinery, especially to computer disk drives. It also leaves a bad smell on clothes, furnishings and in the air. Tar is deposited on walls, ceilings and many other surfaces, so that the company needs to redecorate more frequently and has to spend more money on cleaning.

Reducing or banning smoking in the office leads to a healthier and happier workforce, and creates a better environment in which to work.

Under the Health and Safety at Work Act, it is any employer's duty to ensure that employees are safe from health risks while at work, and this includes the risks from passive smoking. It is now widely agreed that employers should take the health of their non-smoking employees as a priority over those who smoke, and establish the non-smoking office as the norm.

How to establish a non-smoking policy:

● Consult with the workforce to find out about passive smoking.
● In consultation with all parts of the workforce (including the union if there is one), formulate a policy on smoking. This could be one of three main alternatives:
that smoking is banned altogether from the interior of your building;
that smokers are segregated from non-smokers in separate offices, and smoking is banned in common areas;
that smoking is banned in all parts of the building except in designated areas (such as a smokers' rest area).
● Give your employees notice that you intend to implement the agreed policy (say, three months).
● Make sure that employees understand the rules and that they know what disciplinary action will be taken against them, should they breach the rules.

Further information on establishing a policy on smoking in your office can be obtained from ASH (Action on Smoking and Health) Workplace Services:

ASH
Workplace Services
16, Fitzhardinge Street
LONDON
Tel: (0171) 224-0743
Fax: (0171) 224-0471

Alternatively, contact the Health and Safety Executive (see Useful addresses, pp.115–116).

9.7 Office security

Many offices are vulnerable to some sort of theft or break in. The vast number of thefts take place during normal office hours, and are carried out by people who simply walk in off the street.

Here are some things you can do to prevent loss of posses-sions:

● Make sure that all entrance ways are secure. The most secure method is to install a locked door, operated by intercom and automatic lock. If this is not possible, receptionists or security

235

guards should challenge all those whom they do not recognize as members of staff and ensure that they are escorted to the relevant office or turned away. Companies with large numbers of staff should ask both staff and visitors to sign in and out every time they enter or leave the building. Many companies issue identification labels to ensure that unauthorized people can easily be identified.

- All members of staff should keep an eye open for 'strangers', and make a habit of challenging them. A polite 'Can I help you?' should do the trick.
- Do not leave valuables lying about on desks or in coat pockets. Keep valuables (handbags, wallets, etc.) with you at all times, or lock them in secure drawers. Never leave personal valuables at the office overnight.
- Keep petty cash and other company valuables in a safe.
- Make sure that all windows are closed and locked (even on upper storeys) outside working hours. If you do not have a security guard, detail one person (and a deputy) in each department to check that this is done every day.
- Install a reliable alarm system.
- Only issue building keys to certain members of staff. Keep a record of who holds keys. Investigate the circumstances of lost keys. Never issue keys to temporary staff.

If your office contains valuable equipment, it is a good idea to record the serial numbers and to keep the record in a central place. Alternatively, have each item stamped with your company's postcode (the local Crime Prevention Unit can advise). This will help with insurance, as well as in the identification and recovery of stolen goods.

If you think that your office building has been broken into overnight, make a list of the items that are missing and check for possible entry-points. Do not touch anything until the police arrive.

9.8 Alerting emergency services

Emergency services include the following:

Ambulance
Police   DIAL 999 for any of these
Fire brigade

- Ask for the service you require.
- Give the telephone number and location shown on the phone from which you are calling.
- Wait to speak to the emergency service.
- Give the address where help is required (usually written above the telephone in telephone boxes and at emergency lines).
- Stay on the line and be prepared to give any other information required.

10
Personnel Matters

10
Personnel Matters

All companies are organizations made up of people who each take a particular role. Choosing the right people and looking after their needs can only be beneficial to the company, but recruitment and dismissal (and the treatment of staff in between) are all governed by law.

This section looks at matters that may affect people during their employment. It starts with a list of employment terms and goes on to give brief outlines of the major legislation governing employment. There is some advice on finding the right staff and, from the other point of view, finding the right job. There are also notes on sexual harassment and on how to manage your time effectively and reduce stress.

At the end of the section is a discussion of how best to arrange an office at home and how to avoid some of the pitfalls of doing so.

Matters relating to protecting employees from injury while they are at work (covered by the Health and Safety at Work Act) are discussed in section 9.

10.1 Key terms

Note: some words are highlighted in boldface. This means that you will find them defined in this list.

ACAS
Acronym for Advisory Conciliation and Arbitration Service. ACAS works to improve relations between employers and employees. ACAS does this principally by drawing up and issuing codes of conduct and acting as an independent arbitrator.

ante-natal leave
Women who have worked for two full years or more for the same employer are entitled to time off work to attend ante-natal care when they become pregnant. See also **maternity leave**.

appraisal
A periodical review of an employee's work, involving in most cases a discussion

between employer and employee. A satisfactory appraisal can be linked to pay increases, but appraisals can also be used to identify problems in working practices and to set targets for the following period.

bank holiday
All employees are entitled to take bank holidays off work. If they are required to work on a bank holiday, they should be granted another day off **in lieu**, or paid at an overtime rate. See also **public holidays**.

breach of contract
If an employer or employee does something that is contrary to the terms laid out in the **contract of employment**, that person is said to be in breach of the contract.

Commission for Racial Equality
A body set up to provide information and to advise on matters relating to the Race Relations Act. See p.250.

compassionate leave
Absence from work due to personal matters such as death or illness in the family. Many companies allow employees a reasonable amount of paid leave in such circumstances.

constructive dismissal
If your employer changes the terms of your contract in any fundamental way, and those changes are not acceptable to you, you may resign and then claim constructive dismissal. If your employer changes the terms of the contract, decide immediately whether or not those changes are acceptable. Do not work under the new rules, otherwise you may be said to have accepted the changes and will not therefore be able to claim constructive dismissal. See also **unfair dismissal; wrongful dismissal**.

contract of employment
A document that sets out the terms and conditions of your employment. See 10.5, Your contract of employment.

contractual maternity pay
An agreement between employer and employee (laid out in the contract of employment) with regard to payments for leave while pregnant. See also **statutory maternity pay**.

contractual notice
An agreement between employer and employee (laid out in the contract of employment) with regard to notice of termination of a contract of employment. See also **statutory notice**.

contractual sick pay
A procedure and amounts payable by the employer for time spent off work due to illness, as set out in the contract of employment.

core time
In the flexitime system, the core time is the period of time for which the employee is expected to be at work.

custom and practice
A legal term referring to a **contract of employment**. Just as contracts can be made verbally, without pen touching paper, so they can be changed by custom and practice. For example, an employee's contract may state that the job involves certain duties. With time, the employee starts to take on other duties without complaint (or without choosing to claim **constructive dismissal**), and when the extra duties can be said to be established as custom and practice, they are seen in the eyes of the law to have become an implied part of the contract of employment.

direct discrimination
In the law relating to sex and race discrimination, direct discrimination takes place when an employer (deliberately or not) treats an employee of one sex or racial group differently to an employee of another. See also **indirect discrimination**.

disciplinary procedure
Many large companies have a set procedure for dealing with matters of discipline. It can consist of a set number of stages, involving verbal and written warnings and eventual dismissal. The disciplinary procedure should be set out in a contract of employment. **ACAS** has produced a code for disciplinary procedures, it is available from ACAS or from Jobcentres.

dismissal
The termination of a **contract of employment** by an employer. Dismissal is one of the matters covered in employment law, and it is possible to claim to the courts that you have been unfairly or unlawfully dismissed (see below). See also **constructive dismissal**.

Employment Appeal Tribunal
The body that sits above an Industrial Tribunal in the legal system, set up to hear appeals against decisions considered to be unfair or wrong.

equal opportunities
A blanket term for encouraging businesses to view all their employees (and potential employees) equally, regardless of age, gender, race or disability.

Equal Opportunities Commission
A body set up to monitor the working of the law relating to equal opportunities, and to provide information and advice.

expressed terms
In a contract of employment, the expressed terms are the items actually written into the contract. These can be contrasted to **implied** and **imposed terms**.

fixed term contract
A contract of employment that is not for permanent employment. In a fixed term contract, the employer and employee agree at the outset that the employee will cease work on a certain date, or when a certain project or task is completed.

flexitime
Some companies operate a time-keeping system whereby their employees are asked to work a certain number of hours regularly, but the starting and finishing times are not set. Instead, employees agree to be at work during the **core time**, and to work a minimum number of hours during a period. In this way, staff can (within the limits of the core time) please themselves what time they start and finish, and if they work more than the minimum number of hours in the period, they are often entitled to 'flexidays' – time off to compensate them for the overtime.

grievance procedure
Many larger companies have a set procedure for dealing with employee complaints. The grievance procedure (if there is one) should be set out in the contract of employment, and gives an opportunity for all concerned to hear grievances and solve problems in an acceptable way.

gross misconduct
Extremely bad behaviour – such as fighting or stealing from the company – is desscribed as gross misconduct and can lead to **summary** (or instant) **dismissal**.

implied terms
A contract of employment sets out the terms of the agreement between employer and employee. Those written down in the contract are known as **expressed terms**. However, some terms of employment are so obvious that it is not usually considered necessary to include them in writing, and they are known as implied terms. They may include honesty and obedience. See also **imposed terms**.

imposed terms
In a contract of employment, terms that are not written into the contract, but nevertheless must be complied with. Such terms are imposed by law, and they include compliance with the Health and Safety Regulations and other laws. See also **expressed terms**; **implied terms**.

indirect discrimination
In the law relating to sex and race discrimination, indirect discrimination occurs if an employer does something (deliberately or not) that makes it less likely for a person to apply for, or be accepted for a job on grounds of race or gender. See also **direct discrimination**.

Industrial Tribunal
A legal body that hears claims under employment law.

in lieu
Instead of. An employee may be offered time off in lieu of a bank holiday worked, or pay in lieu.

job evaluation study
Under the Equal Pay Act (1970), it is an offence to pay one person less than another when the two are doing **like work** or work of equal value. In cases brought before a tribunal, a job evaluation study may take place in order to determine whether one person's job is similar or of equal value to that of another.

lay off
In hard times, an employer may not have enough work for employees to do. In these instances the employer may choose to lay workers off, that is to ask them not to come to work. While laid off, employees do not receive any pay. After four weeks of being laid off, employees are entitled to claim redundancy pay from their employer.

like work
Employees are entitled to the same pay as others doing substantially the same work. At a tribunal, the employer will need to show that there is a distinct and meaningful difference between the work carried out by the two workers (known as a material difference). If no material difference can be found, the tribunal will rule that the two jobs are 'like work' and enforce the rule that like work must attract like pay.

material difference
See **like work**.

maternity rights
After two years' working for the same employer, women who become pregnant are entitled to maternity rights, which include the right to take time off work for ante-natal classes, and to take paid leave for a period before and after the infant is born.

National Insurance (NI) contributions
These are payments made to the state by all working people to cover state pensions, health services, etc. Employees have part of their NI contribution paid by the company and the rest is taken from their wages at source.

National Insurance number
A reference number issued to everybody when they become eligible for work, relating to each individual's National Insurance records. You will need the number on many occasions, so keep it safe and memorize it if you can.

notice
A period of time between being notified of the termination of a contract and stopping work. Both employees and employers must give the required notice before terminating a contract of employment. The law lays down statutory notice periods (the length of notice increases with the length of service, up to a maximum of 12 weeks), and the contract of employment may improve upon these (called contractual notice).

occupational pension
A pension fund set up by the employer for those in his or her employment. See also **SERPS**.

pay-slip
A document that must be issued to all those on the pay roll, detailing wages and deductions.

P45
A document that is drawn up by your employer when you leave the company, giving details of the tax and National Insurance you have paid. Take your P45 with you to your next employer or when you want to claim unemployment benefit; it will speed up the process of calculating tax and benefits.

public holiday
All employees are entitled to take Christmas Day (throughout the UK) and Good Friday (in England, N. Ireland and Wales) as public holidays. Those who are asked not to do so are entitled to time off or pay at an overtime rate **in lieu**.

racial discrimination
Under the Race Relations Act, it is unlawful to discriminate (treat differently) any person on the grounds of their race, colour or ethnic origin. See The Race Relations Act, p.250, for further details.

redundancy
Being made redundant, when an employee is no longer required in the company. In some cases employees who are made redundant are eligible for redundancy payments. As for other types of employment-linked benefit, redundancy pay can be statutory or contractual.

self-employed
People who work for themselves are said to be self-employed. Self-employed people pay their own tax and **National Insurance (NI) contributions**, they can choose what work they do and when they do it. In general they also use their own materials and equipment.

SERPS
Acronym for State Earnings-Related Pension Scheme. This scheme operates by taking part of the **National Insurance (NI) contributions** paid by

employer and employee and investing it in an additional state pension scheme, over and above the basic scheme offered by the state. If you are 'contracted in' to SERPS (i.e. you have agreed to being part of the state pension scheme) and you have paid the requisite number of NI payments at a higher rate, you will be eligible for a pension from the state when you reach retirement age. You may also receive benefits from an occupational pension scheme and from a personal pension plan. You may choose to 'contract out' of SERPS, and instead set up a personal pension plan. People who are self-employed are not eligible for SERPS.

sex discrimination
Treating an employee differently because of their gender or (mostly in the case of women) because they are married. See The Sex Discrimination Act, p.236.

sexual harassment
An umbrella term covering a wide range of unwanted attention of a sexual nature. See 10.4, Sexual Harassment at work..

short-time working
If an employer finds that the company has less work than anticipated, he or she may opt to reduce employees' hours, and this is known as 'short-time working'.

state retirement pension
A basic pension scheme operated by the state. Employees pay a minimum number of **National Insurance (NI) contributions** and then receive a basic pension on retirement. See also **SERPS**.

statutory maternity pay
If you have been working for the same employer for more than two years and you become pregnant, you are entitled to be paid at a certain rate for the time you spend away from work shortly before and then after the birth. While there are statutory provisions for maternity pay, some employers may agree to pay you more than the statutory minimum. Such an agreement should be written into your contract of employment, and is known as contractual maternity pay.

statutory notice
Under the law, employees and employers are entitled to a certain amount of **notice** of termination of a contract of employment. The law sets out statutory minimum periods of notice, known as statutory notice. The period of the statutory notice depends upon the length of service of the employee, rising gradually to a maximum of 12 weeks.

statutory sick pay (SSP)
Arrangements for payment to an employee who cannot work due to illness. The system for statutory sick pay entitles the employee to be paid (by the employer, who then claims the money back from the state), but not for the first three days of illness. The amount of money an employee will be paid when sick depends on his or her earnings. SSP is normally paid for up to 28 weeks.

summary dismissal
Instant dismissal. If employees are guilty of **gross misconduct** they are liable to summary dismissal.

Trades Unions
Organizations that were set up to represent the rights of employees. Every person has a basic right to become a member of a trades union and not to be victimized for doing so. Each member of a union must pay union dues (a kind of subscription), and this is often stopped from their earnings at source. Any person not wishing to be a member of a trades union may ask that the contributions are not deducted. The representatives of trades unions can help by advising you of your rights, and they can sometimes be involved in grievance procedures. The central trades union body is the Trades Union Congress (TUC) (address on p.116).

unfair dismissal
Dismissing an employee on unfair grounds. These may be grounds related to gender and race, or other unreasonable grounds. If a claim for unfair dismissal is brought, the employer must prove to a tribunal that the dismissal was carried out in a reasonable way (following the disciplinary procedure if there is one or reasonable in comparison with the disciplinary code drawn up by **ACAS**) and that the reasons were not discriminatory.

victimization
Treating an employee differently for some reason, such as because he or she has been active in bringing a legal claim against the employer, or because the employee is a member of a **trades union**.

wages council
Any of a number of bodies set up in certain industries to give regulations and guidelines on such matters as minimum pay, working conditions, etc.

wrongful dismissal
Dismissing an employee in such a way that the dismissal breaks the terms of the employment agreement, e.g. by not giving enough **notice**.

10.2 Employment legislation

The law with regard to employment is embodied in six principal
Acts of Parliament: the Employment Rights Act, 1996; the Equal
Pay Act 1970; the Sex Discrimination Act 1975; the Race
Relations Act 1976; the Disability Discrimination Act; and the
Health and Safety at Work Act 1974.

Employment legislation changes from year to year, with the
introduction of amendments by the British parliament and by
the legislative body of the European Community.

If you think that you have a claim (i.e. if you think that your
employment rights have been infringed) under any of these Acts,
it is vital to get immediate advice, either from a lawyer specializing in employment law, or from another organization such as a
Citizens' Advice Bureau or Jobcentre. Each Act sets out time limits for bringing your claim to court. If you fail to do so within that
time, you lose your chance to redress the balance.

Obviously, many grievances are redressed by a caring employer as soon as an employee complains, so it is not always necessary
to apply to be heard in court or at an Industrial Tribunal.
However, it is still always best to get specialist advice as soon as
you can. Some of the rights under these Acts only apply to you if
you have worked for your employer (or an associated company)
for a certain amount of time. On the whole, self-employed workers are not protected in the same way as the employed.

The following notes give some idea of your rights under the
first five of the above Acts and how to go about making a claim
against your employer. The Health and Safety at Work Act is covered in 9.1.

The Employment Rights Act 1996

This Act covers most aspects of employment: contracts, dismissal,
maternity rights, trade unions, etc. You are given the basic protection afforded by the Act if you work as an employee (not as a
freelancer or self-employed person).

Rights include
- The right to a pay-slip itemizing pay and deductions.
- The right to written terms of employment (after working for
  13 weeks).
- The right to time off to attend an ante-natal clinic, to

maternity leave, and to have the job held open for a certain length of time after your baby is born. These rights do not yet apply to fathers.

- The right to join a union.
- The right to take time off (within reason) for public duties.
- The right not to be dismissed unfairly, and to receive redundancy pay.
- The right not to have unlawful deductions made from your wages by your employer, or deductions that have not been agreed by you.
- The right to have your contract of employment transferred to a new employer in the event of the business being sold.

How to make a claim

If you think your rights have been violated, take immediate advice at a local Law Centre or Citizens' Advice Bureau. If your claim is likely to succeed under the Act, a claim will be made to an Industrial Tribunal.

The Equal Pay Act 1970

This Act covers equality in pay between people doing jobs that are either equal in value or substantially the same in the work they involve. It was enacted principally to try to bring the pay for women more into line with that of men, but men as well as women may claim under the Act.

You may have a claim if there is someone who is doing the same job as you, but who gets paid more. Alternatively, you may be able to point to a person doing a completely different job, but whose work could be said to be of equal value to the company.

How to make a claim

The Equal Opportunities Commission can provide information, or you can get leaflets from the Jobcentre or Citizens' Advice Bureau. Your claim may then be taken to an Industrial Tribunal.

Most claims under current employment legislation must be brought before a Tribunal no later than three months after the act or incident in question. Therefore it is vital to take immediate advice if you think you have a claim.

The Sex Discrimination Act 1975

The Sex Discrimination Act makes it illegal for employers to discriminate against people (usually women) on the grounds of their gender or of their being married.

Discrimination includes
- Refusing people employment on grounds of their gender.
- Treating people differently on grounds of their gender.
- Advertising for staff of one gender rather than another, when gender is immaterial to the job advertised.
- Refusing to give you the promotion prospects offered to other people on grounds relating to your gender.
- Victimizing you because you have made a claim (or supported someone else's claim) under the Act.

Matters of pay differences on the grounds of gender are covered under the Equal Pay Act p.249.

How to make a claim
Get information from the Equal Opportunities Commission, a Jobcentre, Citizens' Advice Bureau or Social Security Office. Claims are brought to an Industrial Tribunal.

The Race Relations Act 1976

This Act makes it illegal for an employer to treat you differently on grounds of your race, colour or ethnic origin.

Different treatment includes
- Refusing to give you a job on these grounds.
- Advertising for people of a certain race, colour or ethnic origin, unless this is material to the job.
- Segregating you from other members of staff.
- Paying you less or refusing to give you the promotion prospects offered to others.
- Victimizing you because you have made a claim (or supported someone else's claim) under the Act.

How to make a claim
The first thing to do is to seek guidance from the Equal Opportunities Commission, the Commission for Racial Equality, a Jobcentre or Citizens' Advice Bureau. You will normally be

given a questionnaire, which you should take to your employer and ask that it be filled in. Your claim may then be taken to an Industrial Tribunal.

The Disability Discrimination Act 1995

This act makes it illegal for employers to discriminate against anyone with a disability (physical or mental impairment) which has a substantial and long-term adverse effect on their ability to carry out normal day-to-day activities.

Discrimination includes:

* Advertising jobs in a way that indicates that a disabled person is less likely to be appointed.
* Refusing you employment on the grounds of your disability.
* Employing a disabled person on less favourable terms and conditions than those granted to other employees.
* Refusing a disabled person the promotion prospects, transfer or training opportunities offered to others on the grounds of disability.
* Harassing or dismissing a disabled employee.
* Failing to comply with an employer's duty to make 'reasonable adjustments' (such as acquiring and modifying special equipment, or allowing the person time off for assessment or treatment).
* Victimizing a disabled person for making a complaint or bringing proceedings alleging discrimination.

How to make a claim

Get information from the Equal Opportunities Commission, a Jobcentre, Citizens' Advice Bureau or Social Security Office. Claims are brought to an industrial tribunal.

Further reading

An excellent book which covers employment law in accessible terms is *Your Rights at Work* by Jacqueline Middleton (published by Optima). Alternatively, the Information Section of the Employment Department (address overleaf) can provide authoritative booklets on request.

Information Section, Department of Education and
    Employment
Caxton House
Tothill Street
LONDON
SW1H 9NF
Tel: (0171) 273-3000

10.3 Formulating an equal opportunities policy

The law on equal opportunities makes it an offence for any
employee to discriminate between staff on grounds of race, gender or disability. Companies large and small are advised to operate an active equal opportunities policy, not only because they
may find themselves on the wrong side of the law, but also
because it benefits the company, its industry and the national
economy to make employment choices in terms of ability and
thus to make good use of the skills available in the workforce.

An equal opportunities policy should penetrate all aspects of
personnel management, including recruitment, training and
promotion. It should cover race, gender and disability, but some
organizations also include older people, ex-offenders and homo-
sexuals in their policies.

To implement an effective equal opportunities policy, The
Equal Opportunities Commission (their address is given in
Useful addresses, p.116) recommends the following steps:

- Formulate an equal opportunities policy in consultation with
  all managers and staff.
- Set out the steps that the organization needs to take to operate
  the policy successfully.
- Inform all staff (especially those involved in recruitment) of
  the policy and ensure that they understand the things they
  need to do to bring their working practices into line with it.
- Survey the company to find out what is happening, and as the
  policy starts to be implemented, monitor its progress at
  regular intervals. Look into promotion policies and ensure
  that staff are promoted on objective criteria only.
- When formulating job specifications, ensure that they are
  objective and related to the job.

- When asking prospective employees for interview, offer preselection training to enable them to perform at their best in tests and interviews.
- Look into the possibility of instituting some kind of flexible working: flexitime, job-sharing, part-time working, etc., to enable mothers with young children to do their jobs properly.

If you think that you have been dismissed, denied a position or passed over for promotion on grounds of your race, gender or disability, contact The Equal Opportunities Commission or The Commission for Racial Equality (both addresses are given in Useful addresses, p.116) for information on what to do.

10.4 Sexual harassment at work

Sexual harassment is the term given to a number of forms of behaviour, and the definition is not clear cut. The European Commission defines sexual harassment very broadly as 'unwanted conduct of a sexual nature, or other conduct based on sex affecting the dignity of women and men at work'. Harassment can include:

- Unwelcome attention of a sexual nature.
- Making lewd suggestions, or comments or insults of a sexual nature.
- Passing around sexually explicit material that embarrasses or offends other members of staff.
- Indicating that promotion may be offered or pay increased in return for sexual favours, or alternatively that a person may lose their job if favours are not granted.
- In the worst cases, sexual assault and rape.

Most cases of sexual harassment involve a number of incidents over a period of time. However, one single act, if it is serious enough, can be regarded as harassment.

If you think you are the victim of sexual harassment

Sexual harassment can be extremely damaging and disturbing to the victim, and it must not be tolerated for any reason. Everybody at work has a right to their dignity and respect from every other colleague (including the boss). Both women and men (and it is important to remember that men can fall victim as well as women) can seek redress under the Sex Discrimination

Act 1975 (see p.250), and in the event of being forced to leave your job, you may be able to claim constructive unfair dismissal. However, you may not need to go to an Industrial Tribunal, and, indeed, this is often the last course of action a victim wants to take.

- In the first instance, make it clear to the person concerned that their conduct is unacceptable. A firm negative response may well put an end to this kind of behaviour (some people do not know what is offensive or when they have gone too far). You may like to take a colleague with you when you do this. In any case keep a log of the actions that are unacceptable to you and a note of what you did about it.
- If any of your other colleagues have been harassed by the same person, ask them to keep a record, a number of complaints from different people in concert will help your case. Talking to colleagues at work will also provide you with (often badly needed) emotional support.
- If the person persists in their conduct, bring it to the attention of a superior, your personnel officer or employee representative in the union. Ask them to take action to warn the person off, and perhaps to take disciplinary proceedings. In many cases, the person whose conduct you find unacceptable is your immediate boss. If this is the case, and you have no-one else to discuss the matter with, go to his or her boss, or get in touch with a local Citizens' Advice Bureau.
- Don't be afraid to take the case to a Tribunal if all else fails – you will have the support of many of your colleagues.

What the employer can do

Sexual harassment can disrupt working practices, drastically reduce morale and in some cases lose the employer good members of staff. It is in every employer's interest to show employees that such behaviour will not be tolerated, and that it will be met with disciplinary proceedings and even dismissal. If employers fail to do this, they may find themselves liable for prosecution under the Sex Discrimination Act (see p.250).

Draw up and circulate a policy against sexual harassment. Let staff members know who they can turn to if they are being harassed, and assure them of confidentiality and a sympathetic, objective hearing. Take appropriate action against offenders.

Further information

Two booklets are available, both entitled *Sexual Harassment in the Workplace*. One tells employees their rights and remedies, and gives advice on what to do if they are being harassed, and the other tells employers how to organize and operate an anti-harassment policy. They are available from the following address:

> ISCO 5
> The Paddock
> Frizinghall
> BRADFORD
> BD9 4HD

Alternatively, telephone the Department of Education and Employment's Sex and Race Equality Division on (0171) 273 4849 for copies. Quote reference PL924 for the employee's leaflet and reference PL923 for employer's information. You can also get general advice from ACAS, The Equal Opportunities Commission, the Trades Union Congress (addresses in Useful addresses, pp.115–16), Citizens' Advice Bureaux and Jobcentres.

10.5 Your contract of employment

A contract of employment sets out the terms and conditions of your employment. In many cases, employers issue a full written contract, but you may alternatively receive a letter giving some basic details. Every full-time employee is entitled to receive a document stating the terms and conditions of their employment after working for 13 weeks.

In cases where no written contract is received, there is still a verbal contract between employer and employee, an agreement to provide services in exchange for money.

All employees are protected by the law. Some rights under the law only apply after you have worked for a certain period of time (e.g., you are only eligible for statutory maternity pay and time off if you have worked for more than two years for the same employer). These laws apply whether you have a contract or not.

Your contract should cover the following issues:
- Job title and a description of the duties expected of you.
- Pay and method of payment: weekly, monthly, in cash, by cheque, or by direct payment to your bank account.

- Details of any other 'perks' associated with the job: for example, a company car or membership of a healthcare scheme. Alternatively, details may be given of payments for buying and cleaning of uniforms or work clothes, or for supplying tools and equipment.
- Basic hours (including details of the flexitime system if there is one), arrangements and payments for overtime, holiday entitlement.
- Length of notice required for termination of the contract on either side.
- Arrangements for sick pay.
- Details of pension arrangements, if there are any over and above the normal state schemes.
- Details of the grievance and disciplinary procedures if these have been arranged.
- Any other conditions of your employment. For example, the office in which you are going to be working may have been declared non-smoking. Alternatively, the employer may give details of appraisals and periodical pay rises, or in a few cases, ask you to sign the Official Secrets Act as a condition of your employment.

You should ask questions on all of these points at the final interview, before accepting the position, and come to a verbal agreement. If you receive a written contract, you should check that it tallies with the verbal agreement already made.

Most of these issues are covered by legislation or by codes of practice laid down by advisory bodies such as ACAS and the Equal Opportunities Commission. If they are not covered in your contract, your rights are the statutory rights embodied in employment legislation or codes of practice. For example, if you and your employer do not agree notice periods, you will still be entitled to statutory notice. Equally, any notice period agreed that is less than the statutory period, is not upholdable in law. The same applies to sick pay, pensions, statutory maternity pay, etc. Equally, if there is no disciplinary procedure, and an employee brings a claim, the Tribunal will compare the actual events with the code of practice for disciplinary procedures drawn up by ACAS.

10.6 Finding staff

It is axiomatic that a company is only as good as its staff. Recruiting people is not simply a matter of getting the best, but also of finding someone who is suitable for the particular role you have in mind and someone who will fit in to your company.

The recruitment procedure is costly and can lead to a certain amount of disruption. If you offer the job to the wrong person, who may leave the company after a comparatively short time, there will be more disruption and you may have to go through the entire process again. It is therefore important to get it right first time.

The key to finding the right person for the job is preparation and objectivity.

Writing a job specification and profile

When a vacancy arises, the first thing to do is to put together a job specification, detailing all the duties necessary. If you are not the person for whom the new employee will be working, get that person's input. If the job is already carried out by someone, ask them to list the duties that make up their job and the kinds of skills necessary.

Look at all these suggestions objectively. It may be that you really do not require a secretary, but a PA or office manager, or that the job could be divided up between existing members of staff. Find out if there are any problems associated with the position as it exists now. Ask colleagues of the outgoing person, and try to remedy problems before you go about finding a new employee.

Once you have a satisfactory job specification and you are sure that it accurately describes the duties required to be carried out, consider the qualifications and skills that will be required, and try to picture the kind of person you want to be doing the job. Take heed of the legislation that relates to equal opportunities (see 10.3), and make sure that you are not excluding certain types of person unnecessarily (or illegally). Make a list of the skills that you consider absolutely necessary, and then make a separate list of the skills and personality traits that you consider desirable in the ideal candidate.

Advertising the job

By now you should have a fair idea of the type of person you need. On the basis of the job specification and profile, you should be able to draw up a job advertisement. Make sure that the advertisement is fair and honest. List any conditions that may either prohibit some people from applying (e.g., special working hours, certain skills requirements, etc.) or that may attract candidates (e.g., perks, promotion prospects, comfortable offices, etc.).

Candidates can come from a number of sources:

- Recruitment consultancies or agencies, who often screen candidates for requirements and suitability before recommending them for interview. There are agencies specializing in most business sectors. Look out for one with a reputation for good judgement, and one that specializes in finding people at the level you require. Agencies will normally charge a finder's fee if their recommendation leads to employment, usually based on the successful candidates earnings in the first year. While agencies save you time by screening out unsuitable candidates at an early stage, they normally only represent people actively looking for jobs. Other methods (possibly combined with the services of an agency) can produce candidates that may not have previously considered a change of job, but who were tempted by your advertisement.

- Trade publications and national or local newspapers. National newspapers will ensure that you have the widest possible choice of candidate. Trade publications usually bring candidates already working in your field.

- The grapevine can produce a number of suitable candidates, and has the benefit of personal recommendation.

- In-house advertising of positions can be mandatory in certain companies. If it is not, consider the kind of response you may get from advertising the job in-house. It may be better not to do so if there is a risk of disappointing existing employees by turning them down.

- A file of speculative applications may yield someone who seems to be suitable.

If you have decided to go through an agency, and are unsure which agency to use, get in touch with The Federation of

Recruitment and Employment Services Ltd, which has a large number of member agencies, all with a high standard and agreed code of conduct. They produce an annual listing of members in the UK:

> The Federation of Recruitment and Employment
>   Services Ltd
> 36–38 Mortimer Street
> LONDON
> W1N 7RB
> Tel: (071) 323-4300

Application forms

Many employers send application forms to those responding to their advertisements. These have the advantage of ensuring that you get all the information you need before selecting candidates for interview. CVs are the alternative, but many prefer application forms because they enable the selector to compare like with like.

Your company may already have a standard application form. If not, you may wish to design your own. You may like to cover the following areas:

- Personal details: name, age, date of birth, nationality, marital status, address and contact phone number.
- The job: job for which application is being made, reference number (if any), date available to start, previous applications to the company, where the candidate found out about the job.
- Education: names of schools and colleges, qualifications gained, positions of authority, prizes or awards; professional qualifications and membership of professional bodies.
- Skills: any other skills such as languages, driver's licence, keyboard skills with particular software packages, etc.
- Work history: ask for a chronological record giving details of position held, dates, reason for leaving. You may also like to ask for current earnings if that is relevant.
- Physical fitness: this section could give a list of ailments (such as diabetes, heart condition, high blood pressure, etc.), and ask whether a person is a smoker or non-smoker.
- Leisure interests: ask for a list.
- Ask the candidate also to answer questions giving more general information such as why they want this particular job,

why they wish to leave their present employment or what
qualities they think they may bring to the job.

You may also wish to ask for a passport photograph to be sent
with the application form, which is always useful in putting faces
to profiles.

Once you have received application forms or CVs you can
start to make a selection, using your profile for the job. Weed
out those candidates who do not have the qualifications and
skills you listed as being necessary. Then prepare to interview the
rest.

The interview

Conducting interviews is a skill acquired with experience, supple-
mented with a natural talent for understanding people. There
are many different methods of organizing an interview, and
many books on the market covering the theory of interviewing.
There are also different levels of interview and different types.
You may decide that more than one person needs to be present,
or that you require a whole panel of people. The following is a
list of guidelines for one-to-one interviewing:

- Prepare for the interviews. Read through each CV or
  application form carefully and make notes of any particular
  questions you want to ask. Make sure you take your notes to
  the interview. Prepare also a list of standard questions that you
  want to ask all candidates in the areas covered by the
  application form: background, education, training, work
  experience.
- When arranging interviews, leave enough time to cover the
  questions you want to ask (and for the candidate to ask
  questions), and for you to make notes after one interview and
  to read through the application form for the next candidate.
- Do all you can to put candidates at their ease – anxious
  candidates will not perform at their best, and you will not get
  a clear picture of them. Arrange to use a waiting area that
  gives easy access to the lavatory, with refreshments and
  reading matter provided (it might save time if the reading
  matter took the form of a job profile and a survey of the
  company). Interview people in a quiet place away from other
  employees. Make sure that somebody is prepared to greet
  candidates as they arrive.

- Let the candidate do most of the talking. If you do not get a full enough answer, draw the candidate out: 'What makes you say that?', 'Do you think that is important?', 'Do you think that is always the case?', 'Could you explain that for me?'. If you still cannot get a satisfactory answer go back to the question later.
- Take notes, but make them discreet and few, there should be time between interviews to put down fuller notes.
- Give the candidate time to ask you questions, and be honest in your replies. Make sure the candidate understands the conditions of employment, and can agree to them.
- Take as much time as you can within your schedule – never interview people in a hurry.
- Never offer a candidate a job on the spot.
- At the end of the interview, tell the candidate what to expect as the next stage in the process.
- When deciding on candidates try to be objective, comparing like with like. If you find that none of the candidates are suitable, start the process again rather than feeling pressurized into employing second best.
- Always let candidates know your decision as soon as you can, as a common courtesy, but also to keep the good name of your company untarnished.

10.7 Finding a job

How you conduct your search depends on what stage you have reached in your career.

For those who are unemployed, the government now runs a variety of courses and schemes, designed to get you back to work by teaching you how to apply for jobs, how to draw up a CV, and in some cases, how to decide where to go from here. Details are available at your local Jobcentre.

Sources of employment

Jobs can materialize from a number of sources:
- Advertising in the trade press, national and local newspapers.
- Through a Jobcentre.
- Through a 'recruitment consultant', an agency specializing in screening people for potential employment and then

recommending them to companies looking for staff. See also information on The Federation of Recruitment and Employment Services Ltd, p.259.

- Through chance contacts, colleagues in other companies and friends.
- Temping is an opportunity to get your foot in the door to a job (see The temporary option, p.268 for details).
- Speculative applications.
- On the Internet; a wide variety of jobs are now advertised on web-sites of companies looking for employees, and those of newspapers.

Before you start your search, list your skills and experience, along with the characteristics of the kind of job you want. With this information clarified in your mind, you will be more able to spot a suitable job when it is advertised, and to send clear messages to potential employers about what you want.

Don't be afraid to let friends and contacts know that you are looking for a new job. You never know – a friend of a friend may well be looking for someone with just your skills. However, if you are already in employment, telling outside colleagues of your desire to move could be detrimental to your present firm's image, so be discreet in your enquiries.

Drawing up a curriculum vitae (CV)

Your CV is the most important career document you will ever draw up. It should tell the reader – a person whom you hope to persuade to give you a job – what your skills, qualifications and experience are. On another level, its layout and overall presentation should prove beyond any doubt that you think clearly, are neat and literate. A CV is a preliminary to an interview. The prospective employer will decide on the basis of your CV and covering letter (see below) whether or not to interview you.

Various companies and employment agencies offer a CV writing service, but the price is usually high, and such services are normally geared towards highly paid executives looking for top positions.

You should always include the following information:

- *Full name, address and telephone number* (beware of using your office number unless your boss knows you are looking for a new job).

- *Date of birth, age, nationality, marital status.* Some people (especially married women) prefer not to give their marital status at this stage, afraid that they may be discriminated against before being given a chance to prove their worth. The choice is yours.
- *Education and training.* List schools and colleges in chronological order. Give the institution's name and location (the town name is usually enough), and the dates you attended. Give the academic qualifications you achieved. If you have a string of GCSEs, you may not have enough space to list them all. Instead, simply give the number of subjects. However, if the advertisement specified certain qualifications, you must mention them.

  Under the heading of education, you should also give any other training: secretarial or administration qualifications, for example. Some employers expect you to prove that you have the qualifications you list, so be prepared to take certificates to interview.
- *Any other skills,* e.g., driving licence. It is only necessary to give positions held at school or college if you have only recently left. Language skills are increasingly important to employers, so list them if you have them.
- *Employment record.* List the jobs you have held in *reverse* chronological order with dates, starting with your most recent job. Give the name of the company and its location (the full address is not necessary), and its business if that is not clear.

  State your job title and list responsibilities. If you think of your responsibilities in terms of the skills required to carry them out, your worth as an employee will be that much clearer. Give also an outline of any outstanding success you have had. Don't leave any gaps in your employment record. If you were unemployed, say so (in these days of high unemployment time spent without working is no longer unusual), but tell the prospective employer what you did with your time: practised your computer skills, learned shorthand or brushed up on a language, for example.
- *Interests.* Give a short list of things you are involved in in your spare time. This is important in that an unusual hobby will give you a talking point, and any outside interests will show you to be a well-balanced individual.

- *Referees.* It is not always useful to give the names and addresses of referees at this stage. If the advertisement specifically requests this information, however, add it to your covering letter (see below). If you decide not to give referees, write on your CV 'Details of referees available on request', for example.
- You may like to submit a passport photograph along with you CV (even if this is not specifically requested). It helps selectors remember you, and a cheery smile among a pile of applications may put you at a psychological advantage.

You should be able to squeeze all this information on to one sheet of A4 paper, typed! The task is made easier if you have access to a computer which allows you to change the sizes of the type (beware of making the type too small), but the real key is concise writing.

In describing your experience, keep your sentences short and accurate (you may not even need to use full sentences, with the advantage of reducing your use of the word 'I'). Use as many positive and active words as you can: undertook, specialized, devised, organized, took responsibility for, successfully, created, oversaw, growth, liaised, etc.

Make use of headings, and enhance them using boldface or underlining, to make your CV more easy to read.

Resist the temptation to include absolutely everything you have done. If you do this, you will have nothing to discuss at the interview. The aim is to make the employer interested enough to interview you and find out more (without being mysterious).

Never lie on your CV. If you do get the job, and you are caught out, you may have broken the terms of your employment contract, and you could face instant dismissal.

When you have finished, ask someone else to proofread your CV. Spelling mistakes are inexcusable and may lose you the chance of an interview.

Keep master copies of your CV in a safe place. Update it regularly.

The covering letter

Covering letters are sent to advertisers along with CVs and are just as important in assessing your suitability for the job. Set out your covering letter as you would any other business letter (see

Layout, p.56.). Check the advertisement for instructions. You may be asked to hand-write your covering letter. If not, and your handwriting really is illegible, you may decide to type it.

Before starting on your covering letter, read the advertisement carefully. Try to picture the type of person the advertiser is looking for. You will find that various key phrases come to the fore. Your covering letter must let the employer know that you have read the advertisement and that your CV shows you have the required skills and qualifications.

The subject line should include the job title and any reference number given in the advertisement. It is a formal letter, and so should begin 'Dear Sir', or, if a contact name is given, 'Dear Mrs Such-and-Such'. You should close in the usual formal fashion.

The first paragraph should give the date of the advertisement, the publication and the job: 'I am writing in response to your advertisement for an office manager which appeared in *The Evening News* on 28th January 1998.'

The next paragraph should go on to say what you are currently doing and the kind of job you are looking for (closely following the clues in the advertisement, of course). 'Potential', 'challenge', 'exercising skills', 'making use of experience gained'; these are all key phrases that you could use to put a positive light on your wish to change jobs.

The third paragraph should outline the skills you have acquired that make you an ideal candidate for interview. You may be asked to provide referees, and should give them at the end of the letter. If the advertisement does not specify this, you should say that you can supply references on request (see below). When you sign off, say that you are enclosing your CV as requested, and, should your application be of interest, you would be pleased to attend for interview at the employer's convenience.

Again, it is important to keep your letter concise and, above all, positive, without bragging. When it is written, proofread it, or have a friend do so. Make sure that you get it in the post before the closing date, and that you have followed all the instructions in the advertisement.

Section 2.3, Letters and letterwriting, gives more general hints on writing an effective letter.

Application forms

Some employers prefer to ask you to fill out an application form rather than send a CV. If you are confronted with a form, photo-copy it and fill in the photocopy first, so that when it comes to the original, you don't make any mistakes.

- Read the instructions carefully, and follow them to the letter.
- Consider the questions (especially the essay-type questions usually found at the end of application forms) carefully. Look for clues in the advertisement as to what the selector wants to read.
- Never lie on an application form.
- Answer all the questions, in neat handwriting. If you are a typist and you are sure you can fill in a form using a typewriter, then do so unless the form specifically requests handwriting. Make sure there are no spelling mistakes. Erase rather than crossing out mistakes (but try not to make mistakes in the first place).
- You may find it useful to send along your CV as well as the application form, perhaps if you feel the CV gives more information that might be necessary.
- Make sure your application form is in the post in good time to make the deadline.

References

The people you chose to be referees depend on how long you have been working. If you are moving into your first job, it is usual to use a person of standing who knows you well (a business person, your clergyman, etc.) as a personal referee, and to use a member of school or college staff as an academic referee.

After this stage, however, it is important to use people who have employed you. It is normal to cite two referees, but always check the instructions of the potential employer for variations.

Choose people who are likely to give you a good reference, and ask their permission before you hand over their name and address. To speed the recruitment process, some employers like to be able to telephone referees. Do not give telephone numbers unless you are sure that the referee will not mind being dis-turbed.

In some cases, a previous employer will give you a written testi-monial, which you can give to a potential employer. If this is the case, photocopy the original, and send out the photocopy. You might find it advantageous to do this when sending out a CV, even if not requested in the advertisement. Keep the original in a place where it cannot become crumpled and dirty.

Interviews

Interviews are held to find out if you are the right person for the job. If you are asked to attend an interview, it is likely that you already have the majority (if not all) of the skills considered necessary. It only remains for you to find out if you want to work for this employer, and for the employer to find out if you would fit into the role. Interviews are therefore not a form of examination, they are an opportunity to tell the interviewer why you are the person for the job and to find out more about the company.

There are many books on the market giving interview techniques, and if you feel you consistently let yourself down in interviews, then you should certainly do some reading. The following are a few guidelines to remember:

- Prepare for the interview. Consider what kind of person the employer is most likely to be looking for. Find out all you can about the employer in advance, and be ready to show that you have done your homework.
- Make a list of reasons why you consider yourself to be suitable. You may already have done this thinking for your covering letter or an application form.
- Be prompt, polite and smartly turned out. Follow instructions you have been given such as bringing with you a photograph, a copy of your CV, school certificates, your P45 or National Insurance number, etc.
- Don't smoke in an interview unless invited to do so.
- Be honest. Give as much information as you can to enable the interviewer to make a clear assessment of you. Listen to the questions and give full answers
- Make a list of questions you want to ask at the interview, and make sure that these questions demonstrate your interest in the company, your eagerness to be promoted and to work hard. Try to avoid making your first questions 'When can I go on holiday' or 'When do I get my first pay rise'. Some candidates are reticent about asking about earnings, but it is important to do so if this information has not already been

given. Try to cover all the areas that would be covered in a standard contract of employment, but avoid going over any ground that you should already know about (from reading information already supplied to you).

● Above all, try to relax. Get a good night's sleep before the interview and avoid alcohol.

The temporary option

People with office skills have the option of doing temporary work, through a temp agency. Temporary jobs can be anything from a morning to a couple of days or weeks. In some instances, long-term temporary positions are available – positions that are open for two months or more.

Temping is a good way to see yourself through periods of unemployment. But some people make a conscious decision to forego full-time employment because they have other commitments, and temping is one way of earning a living while at the same time giving you time to do other things.

If you are looking for a permanent job, it is often the case that temping can introduce you to a company that later decides to make you an offer of a permanent job. The advantages of this are clear: both employer and employee have already experienced and clearly approve of each other's working practice, and the employee has already been trained while acting as a temp.

Whatever your reasons for wanting to work in this way, temping can keep you busy, give you experience of a wide range of industries and a number of jobs depending on your skills.

Some temp agencies offer their clients a broad list of people with general office skills and experience: word processing, secretarial and PA work, book-keeping, data input, etc. Others specialize in certain activities or cater for specific industries: e.g. some supply qualified drivers, warehouse staff or computer operators, while others have built a client base in advertising, accounting, law and medicine, etc.

Agency commission

Temp agencies work on a commission basis. That is, they charge their clients so much per hour for your services and they pay you at a lower rate, taking the difference as profit.

Temping is a partnership between you and the agency. If you

are good at what you do, they make a profit. If they find you
enough assignments, you make a living.

How to find a suitable agency
● First of all, list your skills and experience.
● Look through your copy of the *Yellow Pages* and pick out a
  number of agencies that cover your field.
● Call the agencies that seem to cover your field. They will be
  able to tell you immediately whether or not they are taking on
  new recruits. Be prepared to tell them what your skills are and
  how much time you have available. (Note: at least one of
  Britain's major agencies will not take you on unless you are
  free to work over a period of at least six months.)
● Arrange to meet the person in charge of recruiting temporary
  staff (usually called the temp controller). You will be asked to
  bring a copy of your CV. The interview may take up to three
  hours, so make sure you leave enough time.

Temp agency interview
● Treat this interview as you would any other. Dress smartly and
  arrive on time. Don't forget your CV (see pp.262–264), and if
  you have a P45, it is a good idea to take it, along with a note of
  your National Insurance number.
● If you say you have typing skills, you will be asked to do a speed
  test.
● Some agencies will then ask you to take a written test, which
  includes tests of spelling, mental arithmetic, filing, knowledge
  of word processing.
● You will then have time to discuss the way the agency works,
  and the kind of work you would be prepared to do. At this
  stage, it is just as important to find out what the agency can do
  for you as to let them know all the things you can do for them.

At work
Here are some guidelines for good temping practice:
● Stay in touch with your temp controller. Let him or her know
  where they can contact you, and if you decide to take a
  permanent job, let the agency know.
● Make sure you understand the agency's rules for filling in
  paperwork, especially with regard to pay. If you fill out the

paperwork incorrectly, you could lose money that you are
entitled to.

- Always arrive at the client's office on time. You should have
  been given a contact name, and you should ask for that
  person at reception. Make sure you find out what the
  company's working hours are, and work the same hours.
  Do not work overtime unless you are specifically requested
  to do so.
- Dress in a way that is suitable for the client company. On the
  first day, it is advisable to dress up rather than down.
- Make yourself familiar with the office layout (find out
  especially where the fire exits are).
- Be personable, listen carefully to instructions and ask if you do
  not understand something.
- Don't touch equipment you do not know how to operate. If
  you have been requested to use unfamiliar machinery, ask for
  a quick lesson.
- When you have been working for an hour or so, ask that your
  contact check that you are doing the job correctly, and iron
  out any problems. Continue to do this regularly throughout
  the assignment.
- If you have finished a task, ask whether there is something else
  you can do. Try not to be idle.
- Do not make personal telephone calls. Ask for permission if
  you need to use the phone.
- Follow the guidelines on safe working practices as you would
  in a permanent job.
- If you have any problems with your assignment, discuss them
  in the first instance with your temp controller at the agency.

Training

Most temp agencies realize that their greatest asset is the skill of
the people on their books. They also understand that it is important that these skills are updated to keep them marketable, and
so offer training sessions free of charge or for a small fee. If there
are obvious gaps in your skills (perhaps you are familiar with
computers, but not with a system that is in demand, for example), ask if the agency can offer training.

Some people sign on with more than one agency. There is
nothing dishonest in this, but do let each agency know that
you may be working through another from time to time.

10.8 Managing your time

Every person in a company is a manager – a time-manager.
Regardless of your position or the limits on the freedom to
choose how you spend your time, time-management is the key to
efficiency. Planning your time so that you avoid both crises and
monotonous routine will enable you to produce high-quality
work, and more of it.

Identifying priorities

The basic skill in time-management is identifying priorities. To
do this you must have a clear idea what your function in the company is, and how your position relates to that of your superiors
and subordinates.

Make a list of all the things you are expected to do in your job,
and the targets you have been set. What are the most important
parts of the job? What could be delegated (if you have these
powers)? What parts of your job could be called routine?

The next thing to do is to analyse how you spend your time.
Include time spent away from your tasks socializing. How does
this relate to the priorities of your job? How much of your work is
the result of crises? How much is routine? How could you reduce
the time spent on routine work, leaving more time for priority
work?

This analysis will tell you how your current working practice
relates to the aims of your job. The next things to do is to shuffle
tasks until you are spending the majority of your time on the
most important aspects of your job.

Continue to monitor how you spend your time. If you find
that you are overloaded with unimportant work, consider how
you could reduce it. If you are in a position to delegate, then do
so. It may be that new technology could take the drudgery out of
unimportant routine work. Look into acquiring the relevant
equipment and suggest the changes to your manager.

Before you start on a task, always spend a moment considering how best it can be done, rather than jumping straight in.

Setting deadlines

Work expands to fill the time allotted. This means that if you set a deadline that is too far ahead, the work will still take that amount of time. However, if you set deadlines that are too tight, you will overstretch yourself (and the staff you may manage), and reduction in quality may lead to crises (time-wasters in themselves). With experience, you will learn to tell how long a task should take.

Get into the habit of demanding deadlines, constantly asking, 'When would you like this to be finished?'. Set time limits for meetings and learn to reduce the amount of time in meetings spent fruitlessly 'chin-wagging'.

Your body clock

Each individual's body clock operates differently. Some people are at their sparkling best in the morning, while others are not fully awake until lunchtime. Some come alive after two o'clock, while others are beginning to flag by four. Plan routine tasks for the times when you are not at your best. Make use of your 'quality time' to do the things that are most important to your function as you have defined it.

Effective reading

For many people in business, the need to know what is going on in the industry, in the company or in a specialist field is vital to their job. But many simply cannot find the time to stay up to date with all the reading they have to do. Here are some hints for effective reading, to help you get through that pile of reports, trade magazines, publicity material, internal memos, etc.

- Sort the reading material into piles according to priority: urgent; important; unimportant. Decide whether some material could be delegated to others. Always be selective about your reading matter. Intelligent selection will ensure that you miss nothing of importance.
- Read headings, conclusions, and introductions (in that order) first. This may be all you need to read.
- Look over the entire document first. Get an idea of its

structure before starting to read in earnest. You may get some clues as to what parts of the material you can afford not to read.

- Write notes on the document as you read.
- Don't read word-for-word, don't say the words to yourself as you read (this slows down your reading speed). Instead look for shapes of sentences, and you should be able to grasp what is being said quicker than you can read.
- Stay alert while reading – going back over a sentence time and time again may mean that your attention has wandered.
- Ensure, however, that you have taken in what you have read. Write yourself a quick synopsis of the document, and use this to confirm your interpretation to the author/sender. This is particularly important if the document you are reading is a brief. Not everyone find written communication easy, and their 'vision' may not have been accurately reflected in the brief.

Time-management guidelines

- Reduce time-wasting to the minimum, and encourage others to do so. Chit-chat in the office involves not only you, but also disturbs others. This requires discipline, but it does not mean that you should be unfriendly.
- Protect your time if you can. Make it clear in the friendliest possible way that interruptions are not welcome at certain times.
- Analyse your body clock and set routine tasks for the times when you are not so alert. Mid-afternoon is usually a low period for many people, whereas early mornings are usually ideal for 'close work', creative endeavours and figures.
- Constantly analyse your time use and actively organize your time so that you are spending as much as possible on priority tasks.
- Always set judicious deadlines for yourself and others. If you are working on instructions for a superior, ask for a deadline and get some idea of the importance of the task. If you find that you cannot meet a deadline, tell the person to whom you are reporting as soon as possible, and set another realistic deadline. Never avoid calls, or present a series of deadlines that you know you don't have a hope of meeting.

- Keep meetings as brief as possible. You may even opt to be present only at the parts of meetings that relate to you, excusing yourself when a discussion turns to matters that do not involve you.
- If you are a manager, learn to delegate work. Most managers find effective delegation difficult at first, but experience makes it easier.
- Tread a middle path between monotonous routine and crises.
- Always consider how you can best achieve a task before you start.

10.9 Dealing with stress

All workers, in whatever position, are susceptible to stress, which can take its toll on a person's physical health and private life, as well as on the quality of their work. Stress can be caused by over-work, undefined goals and priorities, unrealistic deadlines and expectations. It can appear as one or a combination of a number of symptoms:

Symptoms of stress
- Physical symptoms such as ulcers, headaches, skin conditions, nausea and fatigue.
- Mood swings – exhilaration as well as depression.
- Inability to define priorities or organize workload.
- Severe frustration over failures.
- Bad temperedness with superiors and subordinates.
- Poor physical fitness.
- Constant work overload: full in-tray; unpreparedness for meetings; failure to meet deadlines; the need to take work home or constant late working.
- Inability to take even the shortest of holidays.

Ways to reduce stress
- Plan and prioritize. Delegate work. Set realistic deadlines.
- Get a clear view of your role within the company and the expectations people have of you.
- Identify tasks that you hate doing, or that you find stressful. If your job is full of these, you may need to consider changing jobs.

- Discuss problems and grievances with a sympathetic person. Make changes in your working practice to overcome them.
- Plan holidays and days off.
- Take frequent short breaks while at work. Do not work through your lunch break. Get into the habit of leaving the building for a short while at lunchtime, if permitted, but at least leave your workstation.
- If you find you are doing tasks for which you have no training, ask to be trained properly.
- Get enough sleep. Avoid working late if you can, and reduce the amount of work you take home by making better use of time in the office.
- Check that your workstation is arranged to reduce physical stress. See 9.3 Using workstations for details.
- Try to avoid drinking too much coffee and tea, which can actually make your tired and irritable when the effects wear off.
- Eat little and often throughout the day, which will prevent blood sugar drops that may be exacerbating the problem.
- Ensure that you get enough exercise – a long walk at lunchtime can clear your head, and works to relax you so that you feel more alert and able to cope with the stresses of your job.
- Personalize your office space as much as possible, ensuring that you have a comfortable, practical chair, and plants, which can help to reduce the positive ions in the air that can lead to the symptoms of stress.

10.10 Working from home

More and more people are taking the decision to work from home, either retained as permanent members of staff, but working on a part-time basis, or as fully fledged self-employed freelancers. Here are some tips to help you work efficiently at home.

- Set aside a place dedicated to work, preferably a whole room (with a door that closes) – avoid working on the kitchen or dining-room table.
- 'Go to work' just as you would if you were leaving for the office. Set aside particular times for breaks and finish work at a given time.

- Build up a routine – self-discipline is a necessity when working at home. It will also help your employer assess how you are getting on.
- Avoid the temptation to work long hours, just because you are at home. Set yourself realistic targets, but leave time for relaxation.
- Dress properly as if you were going to an office. Don't work in your dressing gown.
- Make sure that other members of your household understand that when you are in your workspace, you are working and should not be disturbed. It is almost impossible to work effectively when you are constantly being interrupted, especially by the demands of babies and small children. If this is the case, engage a child-minder and make sure that he or she knows that, even though you are in the house, you are only to be disturbed in an emergency.
- Have a separate telephone installed so that you do not have to leave your workspace to take calls, or be interrupted if a call is for someone else in your household. This will also help when it comes to accounting for telephone costs. If you cannot do this, consider installing an answerphone, and leave a message telling callers that you will return their call at a given time.
- If you have a computer or other special equipment, make sure that your home power supply is adequate to the task.
- Organize your workspace exactly as you would organize an office, with a logical filing system. Keep it tidy.
- If you live alone, working from home can become very lonely. Make plans to get out and see friends or to telephone friends and colleagues. Try to make contact with the outside world at least once a day.

11
Party Time
BUSINESS ENTERTAINING

11
Party Time
BUSINESS ENTERTAINING

The term 'corporate entertainment' covers a wide variety of activities, and many of these are aimed at securing the goodwill of clients. Entertaining clients can range from Ascot or the opera, to lunch or dinner at a local restaurant, to a cocktail party or evening reception. Other forms of entertaining can involve members of staff, such as retirement parties, annual dinner-dances or celebrations of a particular success.

It rarely falls to one person to arrange large events – some businesses specialize in arranging corporate entertainment on behalf of companies, and many companies that entertain on a large scale usually employ specialists to take care of this aspect of their business. However, you may be asked to co-ordinate a dinner or reception, or to arrange for a table at a restaurant. This section gives guidelines and checklists for those who are asked to arrange functions.

11.1 Restaurants

It is useful to keep a good restaurant guide handy in the office, so that you can make a suitable recommendation if the need arises. Also, keep a note of restaurants you or your colleagues have been to and enjoyed (you could keep addresses and comments in your address file) so that you have a good knowledge of what is available in the local area.

When asked to make a reservation, you will need to know:
● the time and date
● the number of people
● any special food requirements (e.g. vegetarian, non-smoking)
● any other requirements (disabled access, for example)

Make the reservation in the host's name a few days in advance, and remember to confirm on the day (you should also have a confirmed number of guests by then). Take a note of any particular dress codes and check for special requirements.

Make sure that guests know where the restaurant is and the name in which the table has been reserved. The host should try to get to the restaurant a few minutes before the guests so that they can be greeted on arrival.

In general, it is the host who should pay the bill, and it is usually better to leave the table to do this.

11.2 Catered functions

How you deal with the organization of a catered function (a reception, party, dinner-dance, etc.) depends largely on whether you are dealing with in-house catering staff and using your own company's premises or outside contractors. The following checklist covers most of the items you will need to consider. For the more ambitious function, you will need to start work well in advance.

Checklist

- Find out about the scale of the function (i.e. the number of guests involved), the venue and the purpose, along with a budget for the function. Consider whether you will also need the services of a guest speaker (see 11.4 Speech-making).
- Draw up a preliminary guest list.
- Research possible venues (you may need to visit a venue to check toilet, cloakroom facilities and the size and layout of the function room). After consultation, make a firm booking.
- Arrange for invitations to be printed (see 11.3 Invitations) and sent out. Book the guest speaker or ask members of your company if they would be prepared to make a speech. You may also require the services of a master of ceremonies – choose someone who is authoritative as well as good-humoured and witty.
- Take advice on catering. Most caterers can offer a number of menus designed for specific occasions – you may require basic finger-food, a buffet or a full-scale sit-down dinner. Compare prices and services and make a booking, letting the caterer know how many you are expecting. Make sure that you know what the caterer is supplying in the way of food, drink (including non-alcoholic beverages), crockery and cutlery, glasses, napkins, decorations, etc. Make sure you make a note

of any special food requirements – such as vegetarian or Kosher.

- Research and book a band for live music if necessary. Don't take any risks with music – try to see the band you are considering 'in concert' before making a decision.
- Start a register of invitation replies.
- Make arrangements for decoration of the venue (e.g. flower arrangements). The caterer may well arrange to do this for you.
- Devise a seating plan if necessary.
- In the week of the function, check and confirm all arrangements: caterer, speakers, venue, florist.

On the day

- Check the venue; look out for lighting, heating, presentable toilet facilities. Make sure that there is someone on the door to take tickets (if necessary) and to direct guests to the function room. Check that the cloakroom is attended.
- Discuss any problems with the caterer. Check that your instructions have been carried out.
- Be prepared to meet the guest speaker and to show him or her to the function room. If necessary, you should also have arranged a microphone, and checked that it is working. Any professional speaker will tell you in advance what facilities he or she requires.
- After the function is over, supervise the cleaning up. Make sure that straggling guests are able to find taxis or other transport (you may need to persuade those who have drunk too much to leave their cars behind). Check for personal property that may have been left behind.
- Remember to pay the outside contractors promptly.

GREEN NOTE: RECYCLE GLASS

Corporate functions usually leave in their wake a mountain of empty bottles. Ensure that somebody is detailed to take them to a local bottle-bank for recycling (you cannot rely on a catering firm to do this).

11.3 Invitations

Invitations and replies are always worded in the third person (*Mr and Mrs J Bloggs are invited to...* rather than *You are invited...*). An invitation should give the following information:

- name of host
- date, time and place of function.
- dress code
- replies information
- time the function is expected to end (usually indicated as 'Carriages XX pm')

The Directors of
Office Management Consultants Ltd
request the pleasure of the company of

Mr J Fielding and Guest

at

Hollyfield Hotel
26 Hollyfield Lane, Hoxton

on

Saturday 15th June 1998
at 7.30pm

Black Tie
Carriages 11pm   *RSVP*

The following is typical:
Some invitations give details of the event. For example: 'To cele-brate the launch of project x'. You may also like to give a tele-phone number or address to which replies should be sent, and it could be handy to give the name and extension number of the person co-ordinating the event.

If you are unsure what wording or layout to use for your invita-tion, try a stationers or a local printing firm for ideas.

Dress codes

Dress codes appear in a number of forms:

Black tie = dinner jacket and bow tie for men; evening wear (long or short, trousers are nowadays often acceptable) for women.

White tie = full evening dress – white tie, tails, wing collar, etc. for men; ball gowns and jewels for women.

Lounge suit = smart business suit for men; business suits or cocktail dresses for women.

Replying to an invitation

Reply as promptly as possible, in writing, using the following form or something similar:

> *Mr J Fielding accepts with great pleasure the kind invitation of The Directors of Office Management Consultants Ltd for Saturday 15th June*

11.4 Speech-making

It may be that it is appropriate to have someone make a speech at the function you are planning. It is often a good idea to engage the services of a professional after-dinner speaker for large events such as dinner-dances. Alternatively, you may wish to ask the company chairperson or a senior member of staff to say a few words appropriate to the occasion.

Engaging a professional speaker

● Contact possible speakers in good time and explain the type of function you are planning. Give some thought to the type of subjects you would like the speaker to talk about, and how long you would like the speech to go on (after a large dinner and much drinking, 15 or 20 minutes is usually quite adequate). A general, wide-ranging speech may be enough, or you may wish a more specific topic to be discussed. Make sure the speaker understands what the occasion is about and what you expect him or her to say.

- Try to attend a prior occasion on which the speaker is 'performing', to gauge the kind of speech he or she normally gives. Alternatively, try to get details of recent engagements and call the organizers for an appraisal.
- Make a firm booking and discuss a fee and expenses.
- In the week of the event, confirm the booking, and ask what facilities the speaker will require. Often this only amounts to a microphone and a lectern. Send the speaker details of travel to the venue, parking facilities, etc. Be prepared also to arrange overnight accommodation if the speaker has to travel a distance to the venue.
- You will also need someone to introduce the speaker, and this is usually someone from the host company. When you have found a suitable candidate, you will need to supply him or her with details of the speaker's career (which can be had from the horse's mouth). Some speakers like to write their own introductions, and this only makes life easier for you.
- On the day, greet the speaker and show him or her around the venue. At dinners and luncheons, it is usual to treat a professional speaker as an honoured guest. Don't ply the speaker with drinks – he or she will not thank you!
- After the event, make sure that you pay the speaker promptly.

Also recommended, for detailed information on all aspects of speaking in public is *Collins Pocket Reference Speaking in Public.*

12
Hands Across the Sea
DOING BUSINESS ABROAD

12
Hands Across the Sea
DOING BUSINESS ABROAD

Dealing with companies and governments in foreign countries has never been more important to British business. The restructuring of the former USSR, along with the consolidation of the common market in the EU (European Union), and new opportunities to trade with the countries of Southeast Asia and the Pacific Rim, along with faster and more reliable communications technology have all led to the rise in contact with foreign colleagues.

This means that not only will office workers begin to communicate with foreign businesses on a more regular basis, but that executives will be asked to travel more frequently (even if it is only a day trip to Paris).

This section covers foreign travel and communications, giving advice for those planning trips, for those actually doing the travelling, and for those who have to remain in the office, but who are in touch through a variety of means.

The key to a successful trip is to start planning early. Much of the documentation required could take months to arrange, and health aspects such as vaccinations must be dealt with as soon as possible. However, we do not live in an ideal business world, and it often happens that people are asked to travel at short notice, and so this section also includes information about how you can get together the necessary documentation quickly.

12.1 Planning a trip

Business travel is an expensive business, and so good planning is necessary to ensure that the person travelling is able to give value for money, spending the minimum amount of time organizing and the maximum amount of time and energy transacting business.

Checklist

When planning a trip, you will need to make some or all of the following arrangements:

● Passport and visas if travelling outside the EU.
● Vaccinations and other healthcare arrangements.
● Travel: car hire, air tickets, rail tickets, etc.
● Insurance
● Accommodation
● Foreign currency and other methods of payment.
● Back-up information/briefing, maps.
● Appointments and events (attendance at functions, for instance).
● Arrangements for contacting the office while abroad (by telephone, for example).
● A typed itinerary, with confirmed meetings and travel schedules.
● If you have a mobile telephone on which you plan to be contacted, ensure that it will work abroad. You may need to arrange special coverage for areas outside the normal range.

Planning an itinerary

An itinerary is a list of the places a person is due to visit on a trip, along with details of flights (or other transport schedules), meetings, etc. It should be written in chronological order from the moment the traveller leaves for the point of departure. The layout on the following page (p.288) could be used as a template.

When drawing up an itinerary and arranging meetings don't forget to take the following into account:

● Leave time for delays and unforeseen circumstances, such as being held up in customs. Flights that stop over for fuelling may be subject to local delays, and flights to certain countries, especially Africa, South America and parts of Asia like India, are notoriously unreliable.
● Leave time for the traveller to recover from a long flight, especially when travelling east, or when flying overnight.
● Leave time between meetings for the traveller to reach the next port of call in good time. (Get a map of the area so that you can plan meetings in a logical sequence that reduces travelling time.)
● Take the international dateline into account.

NAME OF TRAVELLER:

_____

TITLE OF TRIP AND INCLUSIVE DATES:

_____

DAY AND DATE:

_____

TIME: _____
Starting point (home, office)
Give method of transport (taxi, hire car, etc.).
Give name and telephone of car hire or taxi service.

TIME: _____
Arrival at point of departure (say, an airport).
Give details of terminal, flight number and destination, time and latest check-in time.

TIME: _____
Arrival at destination country.
Give the time as local time and details of time difference.

TRANSFER: _____
Give details of transfer to city, hotel, etc., with directions or car hire firm name and telephone number if appropriate.

TIME: _____
Arrival at hotel.
Give name of hotel, full address, telephone and fax number.

TIME: _____
Meeting details.
Give name of contact, name of company, full address, with telephone and fax numbers.
Give details of matters to be discussed and cross-reference to briefing documents if necessary.
Give a deadline for the end of the meeting if that would be helpful.

TIME: _____
Return to hotel.
It may also be useful to make a note of telephone calls that need to be made in-country, e.g. for meetings that have not been confirmed.

TIME: _____
Evening function.
Give details of address, dress requirements, host, etc.

Remember to make a copy of the itinerary for reference in the home office while the traveller is away, and file a copy for future reference. The traveller's husband or wife may also appreciate a copy of the itinerary.

Checklist – Choosing a hotel

Hotels are best chosen by recommendation, but if booking an unknown hotel, check for the following:

- Security (especially if the woman is travelling on her own);
- Are business services (typing, fax, etc.) offered? Will you be able to hook up the modem from your laptop computer, or recharge your mobile telephone battery?
- Is IDD available in the room?
- Are bathrooms en suite?
- Is dinner as well as breakfast provided?
- Location – is it close to places to be visited?

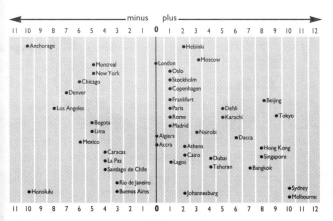

12.1-1 World time zones.

Watch out for the UK time change to British Summer Time in the spring, which moves the clocks forward by one hour.

● Is garage parking available?
● Is there a television in the room, if you want one?

World time zones

The international date line runs through Greenwich, near London. It marks the centre of the world (at least as far as setting your clock is concerned). To the west of the date line, hours are added to Greenwich Mean Time. To the east of the date line, hours are subtracted from Greenwich Mean Time. See 12.1-1.

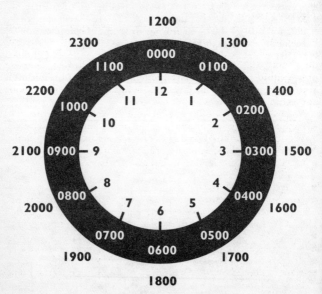

12.1-2 The 24-hour clock – conversion chart.

The numbers listed on the inside of the circle represent the 12-hour clock. In the middle ring, the 24-hour clock names for the hours of the morning are given, and the 24-hour clock hours of the afternoon and evening are given in the outer circle.

The 24-hour clock

The 24-hour system is used to give times in transport schedules so that there is no confusion about morning or afternoon. In the 24-hour system, the hours are named using four digits. The first two digits relate to the hour, and the second two relate to the minutes. To convert from the 12-hour system to the 24-hour system, simply add 12 hours. For example, 3pm in the 12-hour system is 1500 hours in the 24-hours system. See 12.1-2 for a quick-reference guide.

Things to take with you

If you are flying to your destination(s), decide whether you need to take hold luggage (which is stowed in the hold, and so you will need to wait for it to be retrieved at the other end), or whether, on a short trip, you may be able to get away with hand luggage only (within certain standard limits – check with the airline). Your flight ticket should give you details of weight restrictions and excess baggage fees.

You will probably need some or all of the following items:

● Passport, tickets and other travel documentation (e.g., driver's licence and car-hire bookings, copies of invitations extended by host companies, insurance documentation, etc.).
● Certificates of vaccination if required by the destination country.
● Copy of the itinerary.
● Foreign currency, traveller's cheques, credit or debit cards, or other methods of payment, along with lists of serial numbers and emergency phone numbers in the event of losses.
● Lined note pad and pens.
● A few sheets of the company stationery and some envelopes.
● Address book (preferably pocket-sized).
● Maps of the region to be visited, including underground maps, timetables, etc.
● Separate files containing documentation and briefings for each meeting scheduled.
● Travel health kit, preventative medicines (e.g., for malaria), and supplies of other medication.
● Any portable office equipment, such as mobile telephones, laptop computers or portable facsimile machines, as well as the appropriate means to charge them.

Sources of travel information

Details of international and domestic flights are available on Prestel, Oracle and Ceefax, as well as on the Internet. The *ABC World Airways Guide* lists international flights.

The *ABC Rail Guide* gives rail schedules for the UK and some European destinations. It also includes information on ferry and hovercraft services across the Channel. The central number for the National Railways provide telephone information services for inland and international services. For train times and fares information, ring 0345 484950. Check the *Business Directory* for local details. 'Talking timetables' are available for both local and international travel.

If you are planning a trip into Europe by rail, another useful publication is *Cook's Continental Timetable*, and for eastern Europe and the Middle East, get a copy of the *ABC Air/Rail Europe and Middle East Guide*. Eurostar can provide you with details of their services on 0345 303030.

Economist Publications publishes a series of excellent travel books geared specifically towards business people. They cover a wide range of countries and include background briefings on industry, commerce, economics and etiquette, as well as the usual information on places to stay, eat and enjoy yourself.

12.2 Documents for foreign travel

It can take an age to have passports and visas issued, so the key advice is to get started early.

Passports

If you are a British citizen, you will need a passport to travel to almost all countries except the Republic of Ireland (there is no passport control between the UK and the Republic, but you are advised to ensure you have identification (e.g., a driver's licence) with you when you travel.

If you are travelling to an EU country, you need only obtain a visitor's passport. If travelling to France for no longer than 60 hours, a British Excursion Document is acceptable in place of a passport. Forms, visitor's passports and excursion documents are all available from the Post Office. Visitor's passports are only issued if you take the form to the Post Office in person.

However, if you are travelling to any other country, you will require a full British passport that is currently valid.

Passports by post

Pick up an application form from the Post Office, and send it to the Glasgow Passport Office (the address is on the form). It takes about three weeks to issue a passport by this method, and during holidays seasons, it can take several months.

Passports in person

If you are travelling at short notice, fill in the passport application form and take it to your nearest passport office. Be prepared for a long wait before your application is dealt with. Avoid the lunchtime rush. The London office is at the following address:

> Clive House
> 70–78 Petty France
> LONDON
> SW1H 9HD
> Open Mon–Fri: 9am–4pm

There are regional passport offices in Glasgow, Belfast, Liverpool, Newport and Peterborough.

Passports applied for in person at a passport office take about 10 days to arrive. Only in extreme circumstances does the passport office issue passports in 24 hours, and you will need to show a valid travel ticket.

Visas

Most countries outside the EU, including the Commonwealth countries, require that you have a visa before you travel. In many cases, you will not be allowed onto a plane to that destination without a visa. The length of time it takes to have a visa issued depends upon the issuing Embassy or Consulate, but it can take a while, so start planning well in advance, and take holidays (including the issuing country's public holidays) into account.

Requirements for visas differ from country to country and they can change from time to time depending on the political climate. Check by telephone with the visa section of the Embassy or Consulate concerned for specific regulations, instructions and restrictions.

As with passports, it is possible to apply for a visa by post, but this can take a long time. Some travel agencies also run visa services. Alternatively, go to the visa section of the relevant Embassy or Consulate and be prepared for a long wait. If you need to travel at a moment's notice, Thomas Cook runs an emergency visa service.

12.3 Methods of payment abroad

There are several ways to pay for goods and services while abroad.

Foreign currency

Foreign currency for the major countries is available from the foreign exchange departments of banks, bureaux de change and some travel agents. Small amounts in the major currencies (including US dollars and European currencies) are available on request. However, larger amounts must be ordered, and you should do so several days before travelling. It is possible to pay for foreign currency by cheque (drawn on a British bank), credit card, payment card or in cash. You will be asked to pay a percentage commission.

For countries that do not have a 'hard' currency (one that is readily traded) you may have to wait until you arrive to change your money into currency. In many of these cases, you may only be able to change currency at recognized outlets such as banks, and you will need to keep your receipts. Commissions and exchange rates in such countries are often high, and although it is usually illegal, you may be able to change currency at a better rate 'on the street' or purchase goods and services in US dollars or sterling.

In most countries, you will be able to use your Visa card or bank card in bank machines, which will dispense local currency and debit your bank account at home with the appropriate amount, usually at that day's exchange rate. Check with your bank to see which countries allow you to use your normal cash withdrawal cards. You will be charged a commission for withdrawing cash on a credit card.

Traveller's cheques

Essentially, traveller's cheques are equivalent to cash and can be bought in the foreign currency (or a favoured currency such as US dollars) or in your own for conversion overseas. Sign each one of your traveller's cheques as soon as you receive them – you will be asked to counter-sign them in the appropriate place when you wish to cash them, and to produce your passport as identification.

In the event of loss, most companies will replace traveller's cheques within a few days (on the same day with some companies), and you should keep a separate record of serial numbers and encashments, to be produced when claiming new cheques.

You can buy traveller's cheques from banks, travel agents and other agents such as American Express. Issuing agents will provide you with an emergency telephone number to call in the event of loss.

Credit cards

Many credit cards, including Mastercard, Visa, Diner's Club and American Express can provide you with goods and services abroad. In some countries, you will also be able to use your card in cash dispensers in the usual way (see above). In some countries it is not a good idea to use credit cards, because the information can be stolen and used by unauthorized people. Always ensure that all backing carbons associated with receipts are destroyed (these can be used to 'steal' your credit card information). Credit card companies provide an emergency service. Remember to take that telephone number with you.

Eurocheques

Cheques that can be made out in any European currency and used to draw cash or to purchase goods and services when backed up by a Eurocheque card. The payment is then made directly from your bank account. Fees may be charged, including handling fees paid to the foreign bank and a possible standing charge at your home branch.

Open credit

An option that enables you to use a single branch of a foreign bank in the same way as you would use your own account back home. Your local branch can organize this for you, and it becomes useful when you are going to be in one particular place for any length of time.

12.4 Car hire and driving abroad

Hiring a car is normally a simple matter provided the driver is above a certain minimum age and has held a driver's licence for a minimum period of time (usually one year).

Insurance

Most car-hire firms provide minimum insurance, but check cover. In some European countries you may need an International Motor Insurance Certificate (commonly known as the green card). Details are available from the AA or the RAC. If you travel regularly by car, in the UK or abroad, membership of one of these organizations gives access to a number of useful services. You may have to supplement any car insurance with special health insurance.

Picking up the car

Many car-hire services offer several pick-up services. You may be able to arrange to have the hire-car brought to your point of departure (say, the office), or you may find it convenient to pick up the car yourself. Alternatively, arrangements can be made to have a car waiting for you when you touch down in the foreign country (known as fly–drive), or at the destination rail station (known as rail–drive).

It is also possible, if you only need the car for a one-way trip, to drop the car off at a designated point, rather than returning it to the place where you picked it up.

Car-hire firms and travel agents will have details of all services available.

Driving licence

Always take your driving licence with you if travelling by road. It may also be necessary to acquire an international driver's licence. Information is available from travel agents and motoring organizations.

WARNING

The vast majority of road accidents involving foreign drivers take place within a short distance of the port of entry. It will take a British driver a long time to get used to driving on the Continent, and you must be fully alert when doing so. Drive carefully, take frequent breaks and never drink and drive.

12.5 Health notes for travellers

What precautions you take to guard your health when abroad depends largely on the area to which you are travelling and the activities you will be involved in once you arrive. Start thinking about health planning at least six weeks in advance of your trip. This will give you time to arrange vaccinations (some of which need to be administered a certain time before you travel), health insurance and other precautions.

Vaccinations

Depending on which region you are travelling to and to a certain extent the time of year you are going, you may need to arrange to be vaccinated against a number of diseases, including:

> Tetanus – recommended for travellers to all countries
> Diphtheria – recommended for travellers to all countries
> Poliomyelitis
> Typhoid
> Hepatitis A and B
> Yellow fever
> Tuberculosis
> Cholera
> Rabies
> Japanese encephalitis
> Tick-encephalitis
> Meningitis
> Measles

Some vaccinations are free under the NHS, but you will need to discuss them with your GP before you start. GPs rarely keep stocks of all the vaccines required (and some are not always up to date with constantly changing requirements). Therefore check with the Embassy or High Commission of the country concerned for advice, and ask especially if there are any vaccinations for which you will need an official certificate to show at the border (yellow fever and cholera, for example).

If you are not able to get to your GP, there are a number of private clinics specializing in vaccinations, who will keep a central record of your vaccinations, and provide you with treatment immediately. They will also give you extra up-to-the-minute advice on health precautions when abroad. Thomas Cook, for example, have a number of such clinics. Here is the address of the clinic in central London (open daily; appointment only necessary on Saturdays).

> Thomas Cook Vaccination Centre
> 45–50 Berkeley Street
> LONDON
> W1A 1EB   Tel: (071) 499-4000

British Airways Travel Clinics
British Airways has clinics throughout the UK including Heathrow Airport. Details of regional clinics available on 01276 685040 (24-hour recorded listing).

Health insurance

Travellers to EU countries may benefit from reciprocal health agreements, provided they have filled in and had stamped form E111, available from the Post Office, or with the leaflet *Health Advice for Travellers* (see publisher's address below). Remember to take the form E111 with you when you travel.

However, many services (including emergency repatriation and payments for drugs) are not covered by reciprocal health agreements, and so you should also look into the possibility of private medical insurance. Read the small print carefully, especially that regarding 'dangerous activities' (sometimes including driving a car!) and instructions for documentation of claims.

Detailed lists of what services are available in EC countries, instructions for filling in and using form E111, and details of state benefits for those who contract an illness abroad, are given in the leaflet *P5 Traveller's Guide to Health*, available from:

Health Literature Line 0800 555 777 (free of charge, 24 hours). They will send out up to 10 copies to individuals, and up to 30, if you are calling on behalf of a corporation.

Precautions while abroad

Again, the type of precautions you take depend on where you are going and the kind of accommodation you will be using. Here are some guidelines:

- Don't drink water unless it has been boiled or treated. Equally, always refuse ice cubes, regardless of how hot it is. You may also need to use treated water for cleaning your teeth.
- In hot countries, protect your skin from the sun, using creams with a high SPF factor, adequate clothing and a hat.
- In hot countries, follow the local habit of not doing strenuous work during the heat of the day. Be sure to drink more (non-alcoholic) liquids than usual to replace water lost in sweating. You may also need to replace lost salt.
- Pay special attention to personal hygiene. Always wash your hands before eating and after going to the lavatory.
- Protect yourself from insect and animal bites. Avoid all animals (even pets) and use suitable clothing, insect repellents and netting to prevent bites.
- Avoid cold or reheated food, which could be contaminated. Be wary of the following foods: unpasteurized milk and milk products, raw vegetables and unpeeled fruits, undercooked meat or fish, shellfish.

Special warnings

AIDS and Hepatitis B

Both contracted through blood and blood products, usually through sexual intercourse or use of hypodermic syringes.

- Do not engage in sexual intercourse with anyone but your regular partner. In some countries, a large proportion of prostitutes are HIV positive.
- Follow the guidelines for safe sex, use a condom and avoid high-risk practices.
- Do not allow your skin to be pierced unless you are sure the instruments used have been sterilized or that they are new. This includes: ear-piercing, tatooing, acupuncture.

- Do not allow the administering of any blood product unless you know that it has been screened. (Gamma Globulin, the vaccination against hepatitis, for example, is made from blood products.) If you require a blood transfusion or any other blood product, have somebody contact your Embassy or Consulate in-country for advice.
- Carry your own needles and other instruments. However, it is unwise to carry loose syringes (from a customs point of view). Look into the purchase of a sealed emergency first aid kit, which includes the required needles.

Malaria

There is no vaccination against malaria. You will need to take two sets of tablets, and the course must be started one week before entering an infected area. However, the preventative tablets are only about 70% effective, so the emphasis should be on preventing bites.

If malaria is not recognized and treated promptly, it will kill. If you are in a region affected by malaria and you become ill, whatever the symptoms, get a malaria test. This is because malaria can imitate the symptoms of many diseases, including jaundice, influenza, diarrhoea, among many others, and fatalities sometimes occur because malaria was not diagnosed at an early enough stage.

Other medical conditions

If you suffer from significant medical conditions, such as diabetes, haemophilia or angina, keep a note of the proper name of the condition on your person, along with the generic names of any medication that you are taking. This will enable emergency medical staff to take your condition into account when treating you.

If you take regular medication, keep it in the container in which it was prescribed, with the official label intact. This should reduce any drugs problems when passing through customs.

Planning checklist

- Vaccinations; check for certificate requirements
- Insurance
- Dental check-up

- Preventive medicines (e.g. for malaria)
- Insect repellants
- Sun screens
- First aid kit, including needles if necessary
- Notes of ongoing medical conditions and needs

On your return

If you have been prescribed any medicines while abroad, it may be that they are illegal in this country. If in any doubt, declare your medicines at customs.

If, after your return, you develop any kind of illness, consult your GP and tell him or her where you have been. This should alert the GP to the possibility of diseases not found in the UK. If your GP does not give satisfactory treatment, contact a specialist hospital for Tropical Diseases.

If you have been taking malaria tablets while you were abroad, continue to do so for a whole month after you return.

Further information on health aspects of travel can be obtained from the Medical Advisory Service for Travellers Abroad (MASTA) at the following address:

MASTA
London School of Hygiene and Tropical Medicine
Keppel Street
LONDON
WC1E 7HT
Tel: (0171) 631-4408
Traveller's Helpline: 0891 224 100

12.6 Business etiquette abroad

Ways of doing business vary from culture to culture, and knowing how to avoid offending or embarrassing a foreign host can mean the difference between making or breaking the deal. On the whole, the European and American countries operate roughly along the lines of the British, but customs change when entering the Arab and Islamic world and when dealing with the Chinese, the Japanese and Southeast Asian countries.

The main rule, therefore, is to prepare yourself. Learning even a smattering of the host language will show that you have made an effort, and even pronunciation and grammar mistakes will be forgiven. Equally, make an effort to find out about the host company, so that you appear knowledgeable, but it is best not to discuss religion, politics or sex.

The intricacies of business etiquette in foreign countries are as complicated as some foreign languages. You may find it useful to find an agent in-country who can act as guide, interpreter and cultural adviser.

The following is only a miscellaneous guide to some of the more important differences between the customs of Europe and other cultures.

Japan

- The key is showing respect, both for one's host and for one's own organization. Never express dissatisfaction with your own company, and never criticize the host company or individuals within it.

- Business cards are a major business tool in these areas. You should have your details printed in English and in Japanese (usually on the other side). It is a good idea to do the same in other countries where the script is not Roman (e.g. China, Hong Kong, Thailand, etc.). You will need a very large number – cards are passed out to absolutely everyone. Never write on a person's business card. When presenting business cards, do so with both hands, with the Japanese writing uppermost. When accepting business cards, do so with both hands and take time to read them carefully (this signifies your full attention and due respect). Place the card in front of you so that you can see it during the meeting.

- In Japanese names, the surname is given first, followed by the personal name. The suffix -san is attached to the end of the surname and means the same as Mr. You can choose whether to call your host Mr Chan or Chan-san, but take your cue from your host. The same goes for personal names. Never assume that you are on first-name terms until your host indicates this is the case. However, the development of long-term personal relationships is vital if your are to be successful in doing business with Japan.

- The bowing ritual is an integral part of daily life, and the level of the bow changes with the relationship of the people greeting each other. In general, a subordinate will bow lower than his superior. Take your lead from your host, and if you are in the selling position, always aim to bow slightly lower than your host. The Japanese do not, on the whole, like to be touched, so be wary of shaking hands.

● Business in Japan is shot through with caution. It is a mark of respect that the Japanese will take time to consider your proposals fully. Never show impatience. Meetings can be long and pauses for thought are frequent. Don't be rattled by this – it is after all, simply a sign of respect.

● The hierarchy is very important in Japanese business life, and so it is important to match people with the same status in negotiations. You may well have to prove your status and authority. Large delegations are an indication of the Japanese company's serious interest in your proposals. You should try to match them by bumping up the size of your own team.

● Women doing business in Japan are regarded with unease by most older business people. A woman will impress if she has a good knowledge of Japanese language and customs. Above all, never appear loud and aggressive. (The same advice goes for men too.)

● The Japanese rely heavily on paperwork for information. You will impress if you write good meeting reports, and provide a good solid company profile (in Japanese and English).

Arab and Islamic countries

By comparison with the stand-offish and quiet Japanese, the peoples of the Arabic and Islamic countries are generally more demonstrative. However, transacting business can be a very slow process.

● Men should wear business suits – shirtsleeves are permissible in many instances. Women should never wear trousers. Skirts should be at least knee-length (in some countries, skirts must cover the ankles), and sleeves should fall to below the elbow. Women should also carry something with which to cover their heads if necessary.

● In many Muslim countries, alcohol is banned. Even if your hotel serves alcohol, you should not be seen drinking in public. In other countries, however, this rule is more flexible – alcohol is available and many Muslims do drink, but only in private. To avoid compromising your host's religious integrity, don't offer him or her a drink in public, even if you both got drunk together the night before.

- Never touch food, drink or cigarettes with your left hand.
- An Arab or Muslim woman should never be touched by a man who is not her husband. Never speak to a woman unless you have been formally introduced. You may find that you can only speak to women through their husbands. Equally, it is considered impolite to ask after your host's wife (or wives).
- You may be expected to remove your shoes when entering certain buildings.
- Punctuality is not vital, and you may be kept waiting, sometimes for a long time. Never lose your patience, it may lose you the contract.
- If you show too much interest in one of your host's possessions, he may feel forced to make a gift of it to you.
- Gift-giving is appreciated, as is gratitude for hospitality.
- Muslims take Friday as their day of rest. Saturday is a normal working day, and Sunday may sometimes also be taken as a non-work day.
- Show respect for Muslim law and religious practices. Some Muslim and Arab countries have extremely harsh penalties (including flogging and the death penalty) for certain kinds of behaviour, including drinking alcohol, taking drugs and swearing.
- The Arab and Muslim countries are still unused to women in business. Some business women therefore find it invaluable to engage an agent to act as interpreter and guide. Women, should, like men, show respect and be polite.
- As with the Japanese, doing business is for the Arabs and Muslims, a personal matter. Aim to make warm long-term friendships, and you stand a better chance of succeeding.

12.7 Communications

Phoning home

BT and most of the competitive telephone services offer a chargecard service, which enables callers to make calls from any telephone, both in the UK and abroad. The caller contacts the international operator or the UK Direct operator (see below), and asks to make a BT Chargecard call. Calls are then billed to the card, and itemized bills are submitted. The advantage of issuing BT chargecards to staff are that they do not have to carry large amounts of change (especially foreign currency), and need not risk offending hosts by making international calls from their telephone. Also, itemized bills enable the company's accountant to keep track of expenses.

Alternatively, BT also operates a service known as UK Direct, which enables reverse charge (collect) calls to be made. The call is connected through an English-speaking UK Direct operator. The same service is available in the UK, providing foreign visitors with own-language operators to help with international calls.

If you need to make a phone call while on a flight, BT also offers a service called SkyPhone, which enables you to call while still in the air. Calls are paid for by major credit cards or on account.

Details of all BT business services are available in their booklet *Phoning Abroad: the business handbook* along with regular supplements to the IDD information given in *The Code Book*. Contact BT on 0800 800 856 (freephone) for free copies. If you subscribe do a different telephone service, contact your main information number for details of what they offer.

Addressing a letter abroad

When corresponding with European clients or trading partners, use the following forms of address:

English	Mr	Mrs	Miss	Messrs	c/o
German	Herr	Frau	Fräulein	Firma	bei
Spanish	Sñr	Sñra	Sñrta	Sres	supplicada en casa de
French	M	Mme	Mlle	MM	chez
Italian	Sr	Sra	Srina	Spett.	presso Ditta

The following are European translations for Ltd:

German	GmbH
Spanish	S.A.
French	S.A.
Italian	Società anonima

For other foreign words and phrases, see Foreign words and phrases, p.50.

International Direct Dialling (IDD) codes

The following list gives IDD codes and instructions for selected countries. The country code is given for all countries, then + AC is written if a local area or city code is required before dialling the specific number you want. For city code information for the western European countries see the tables in section 12.8. For other codes see BT's *The Code Book*.

Alternatively, contact International Directory Enquiries (dial 153). If no direct dialling number is listed for a country, you will need to be connected through the appropriate International Operator (dial 155).

COUNTRY	Code + Instructions
Algeria	00-213 + AC + no.
Angola	00-244 + AC + no.
Argentina	00-54 + AC + no.
Australia	00-61 + AC + no.
Austria	00-43 + AC + no.
Bahrain	00-973 + no.
Bangladesh	00-880 + AC + no.
Belgium	00-32 + AC + no.
Belize	00-501 + AC + no.
Benin	00-229 + no.
Bermuda	00-1-441 + no.
Bolivia	00-591 + AC + no.
Bosnia-Hercegovina	00-387+AC + no.
Botswana	00-267 + no.
Brazil	00-55 + AC + no.
Brunei	00-673 + AC + no.
Bulgaria	00-359 + AC + no.
Burkina	00-226 + no.
Burundi	00-257 + AC + no.
Cameroon	00-237 + no.
Canada	00-1 + AC + no.
Canary Islands	00-34 + AC + no.
Central African Republic	00-236 + no.
Chad	00-235 + no.
Chile	00-56 + AC + no.
China	00-86 + AC + no.
Colombia	00-57 + AC + no.
Congo	00-242 + no.
Costa Rica	00-506 + no.
Côte d'Ivoire	00-225 + no.
Croatia	00-385 + AC + no.
Cuba	00-53 + AC + no.

COUNTRY	Code + Instructions	COUNTRY	Code + Instructions
Cyprus	00-357 + AC + no.	Jordan	00-962 + AC + no.
Czech	00-420 + AC + no.	Kenya	00-254 + AC + no.
Denmark	00-45 + no.	Kuwait	00-965 + no.
Djibouti	00-253 + no.	Latvia	00-371+ AC + no.
Ecuador	00-593 + AC + no.	Lebanon	00-961 + AC + no.
Egypt	00-20 + AC + no.	Lesotho	00-266 + no.
El Salvador	00-503 + no.	Liberia	00-231 + no.
Estonia	00-372 + AC + no.	Libya	00-218 + AC + no.
Ethiopia	00-251 + AC + no.	Liechtenstein	00-41-75 + no.
Falkland Islands	00-500 + no.	Luxembourg	00-352 + no.
Fiji	00-679 + no.	Macao	00-853 + no.
Finland	00-358 + AC + no.	Madagascar	00-261 + AC + no.
France	00-33 + no.	Madeira	00-351-91 + no.
Gambia	00-220 + no.	Malawi	00-265 + no.
Germany	00-49 + AC + no.	Malaysia	00-60 + AC + no.
Ghana	00-233 + AC + no.	Mali	00-223 + AC + no.
Gibraltar	00-350 + no.	Malta	00-356 + no.
Greece	00-30 + AC + no.	Mauritania	00-222 + no.
Greenland	00-299 + no.	Mauritius	00-230 + no.
Guadeloupe	00-590 + no.	Mexico	00-52 + AC + no.
Guatemala	00-502 + AC + no.	Morocco	00-212 + AC + no.
Guyana	00-592 + AC + no.	Mozambique	00-258 + no.
Haiti	00-509 + AC + no.	Namibia	00-264 + AC + no.
Honduras	00-504 + no.	Nepal	00-977 + AC + no.
Hong Kong	00-852 + no.	Netherlands	00-31 + AC + no.
Hungary	00-36 + AC + no.	New Zealand	00-64 + AC + no.
Iceland	00-354 + AC + no.	Nicaragua	00-505 + AC + no.
India	00-91 + AC + no.	Niger	00-227 + no.
Indonesia	00-62 + AC + no.	Nigeria	00-234 + AC + no.
Iran	00-98 + AC + no.	Norway	00-47 + AC + no.
Iraq	00-964 + AC + no.	Oman	00-968 + no.
Irish Republic:	00-353 + AC + no.	Pakistan	00-92 + AC + no.
Israel	00-972 + AC + no.	Panama	00-507 + no.
Italy	00-39 + AC + no.	Paraguay	00-595 + AC + no.
Jamaica	00-809 + no.	Peru	00-51 + AC + no.
Japan	00-81 + AC + no.	Philippines	00-63 + AC + no.
		Poland	00-48 + AC + no.

COUNTRY	Code + Instructions
Portugal	00-351 + AC + no.
Puerto Rico	00-1-787 + no.
Qatar	00-974 + no.
Romania	00-40 + AC + no.
Russian Federation	00-7 + AC + no.
Rwanda	00-250 + no.
Saudi Arabia	00-966 + AC + no.
Seychelles	00-248 + no.
Sierra Leone	00-232 + AC + no.
Singapore	00-65 + no.
Slovakia	00-421 + AC + no.
Slovenia	00-386 + AC + no.
Somalia	00-252 + AC + no.
South Africa	00-27 + AC + no.
Spain	00-34 + AC + no.
Sri Lanka	00-94 + AC + no.
Sudan	00-249 + AC + no.
Swaziland	00-268 + no.
Sweden	00-46 + AC + no.
Switzerland	00-41 + AC + no.

COUNTRY	Code + Instructions
Syria	00-963 + AC + no.
Taiwan	00-886 + AC + no.
Tanzania	00-255 + AC + no.
Thailand	00-66 + AC + no.
Tunisia	00-216 + AC + no.
Turkey	00-90 + AC + no.
Uganda	00-256 + AC + no.
United Arab Emirates	00-971 + AC + no.
Uruguay	00-598 + AC + no.
USA	00-1 + AC + no.
Venezuela	00-58 + AC + no.
Yemen Arab Republic	00-967 + AC + no.
Yemen (PDR)	00-967 + no.
Yugoslavia	00-381 + AC + no.
Zaire	00-243 + AC + no.
Zambia	00-260 + AC + no.
Zimbabwe	00-263 + AC + no.

Using translators and interpreters

In these days of European economic union, and the prospect of entering monetary union at some stage, there is more and more need for being able to communicate in the language of a company's clients and trading partners. If a company trades regularly with a foreign country in western Europe, then they should employ at least one person who can speak the language. Some companies go to the extent of finding fluent speakers and set up direct telephone lines, answered by a person speaking the relevant foreign language.

However, if your company trades only intermittently with Europe, or with countries in eastern Europe, or the Middle or Far East, it may be necessary to engage the services of a translator to translate incoming and outgoing documents. It may also be necessary to hire an interpreter to accompany you if you are travelling abroad.

Translators for most languages are fairly easy to come by. *The Yellow Pages* or local *Business Directory* will give contact numbers for local agencies specializing in translation services. British Telecom also offers a comprehensive translation service, including on-line simultaneous interpreting. Contact the operator for details.

For translation services, ask about fees, normally quoted in a price per 1000 words. Make sure that the price quoted is for the wordage of the document in the original language. Also, make sure that the agent understands the nature of the document to be translated and recommends somebody who can deal with any technicalities.

Interpreters for foreign trips are usually engaged on the ground in the destination country. A client firm or agent may be able to recommend somebody (you may have to pay travel and food expenses as well as a daily fee). Alternatively, contact the foreign country's Consulate or Embassy in the UK, or the Chamber of Commerce in-country, for advice. If the city you are travelling to has a university that teaches an English course, you may be able to hire a student on the spot (and often at a cheap rate) to act as your interpreter.

When using an interpreter, make sure that you speak slowly and that you pause at a logical moment so that the interpreter has time to relay your words to the listener.

Even if you are using an interpreter, it is courteous to be able to say a few words in the foreign language yourself, even if it is simply to say hello and apologize for not speaking the language.

12.8 European countries – basic facts

The following tables give information for the major western European countries outside the UK. It is designed to help plan a trip abroad or to aid communications between your office in the UK and one or more of these countries.

Notes

- Holders of valid UK passports do not require visas for the countries listed below. However, political circumstances change, so if unsure, check with the relevant consulate or embassy. If you are making arrangements for nationals of other countries (especially from Turkey or South Africa), it is vital to check visa requirements).
- There is no passport control between the UK and the Republic of Ireland, but travellers should carry some form of identification, such as a driver's licence or passport.
- Official languages are given first in the list, followed by other languages that are widely spoken, especially in a business context.
- Public holidays given are national holidays. If making appointments, check with your contact that the date is not a local holiday.
- Working hours vary from company to company. The times given are a rough guide only.

AUSTRIA

Capital city	Vienna
Other major cities	Innsbruck, Graz, Linz, Salzburg
IDD code(s)	00-43: Vienna – 1, Innsbruck – 512, Graz – 316, Linz – 732, Salzburg – 662
Language(s)	German; English and sometimes French
Time zone	GMT + 1; daylight saving April–Sept
Office hours	Mon.–Fri. 8am–5pm. Lunch breaks: noon-1pm or 1–2pm. Government offices vary

Public holidays

Jan 1	New Year's Day
Jan 6	Epiphany
May 1	Labour Day
Aug 15	Assumption
Oct 26	National Day
Nov 1	All Saints Day
Dec 8	Immaculate Conception
Dec 25	Christmas Day
Dec 26	St Stephen's Day

Variable:	Easter Monday, Ascension, Whit Monday, Corpus Christi
Currency	Schilling (S) = 100 Groschen
International airports	Graz: Thalerhof Airport
	Klagenfurt: Flagenhof Airport
	Innsbruck: Kranebitter Airport
	Linz: Hörsching Airport
	Salzburg Airport
	Vienna: Schewechat Airport
Electricity supply	220 V, 50 Hz, AC

BELGIUM

Capital city	Brussels
Other major cities	Antwerp, Ghent, Liège
IDD code(s)	00-32: Brussels – 2, Antwerp – 3, Ghent – 91, Liège – 41
Language(s)	Dutch/French/German; English widely spoken
Time zone	GMT + 1; daylight saving April–Sept
Office hours	Mon.–Fri.8.30am–noon; 1–5pm

Public holidays	Jan 1	New Year's Day
	May 1	Labour Day
	July 21	National Day
	Aug 15	Assumption
	Nov 1	All Saints Day
	Nov 11	Armistice Day
	Dec 25	Christmas Day
Variable:	Easter Monday, Ascension, Whit Monday	
	If the holiday is a Sunday, Monday is taken as well	
Currency	Belgian franc (F) = 100 centimes	
International airports	Antwerp: Deurne Airport	
	Brussels Airport	
Electricity supply	220 V, 50 Hz, AC; 110 V some areas	

DENMARK

Capital city	Copenhagen
Other major cities	Aalborg, Aarhus, Odense
IDD code(s)	00-45: No area code required
Language(s)	Danish; German, English widely spoken
Time zone	GMT + 1; daylight saving April–Sept
Office hours	Mon.–Fri.8.30am or 9am–4pm, 4.30pm or 5pm

Public holidays	Jan 1	New Year's Day
	May 1	Labour Day (pm only)
	June 5	Constitution Day (pm only)
	Dec 25/26	Christmas
Variable:	Maundy Thursday, Good Friday, Easter Monday, Ascension Day, General Prayer Day (4th Fri. before Easter), Whit Monday	
Currency	Danish krone (kr) = 100 ore	
International airports	Copenhagen: Kastrup Airport	
Electricity supply	220 V, 50 Hz, AC	

FINLAND

Capital city	Helsinki
Other major cities	Tampere, Turku-Abo
IDD code(s)	00-358: Helsinki – 0, Tampere – 31, Turku-Abo – 21

Language(s)	Finnish/Swedish, English common, German
Time zone	GMT + 2; daylight saving April–Sept
Office hours	Mon.–Fri.8 or 8.30am–4 or 4.30pm;
	lunch ½ hour between 11.30am and 1pm
	Government offices close earlier

Public holidays	Jan 1	New Year's Day
	May 1	Labour Day
	Dec 6	Independence Day
	Dec 25/26	Christmas
Variable:	Epiphany (Sat. nearest Jan 6), Good Friday,	
	Easter Monday, Saturday after Ascension Day,	
	Whitsun Eve, Midsummer (Sat. nearest June 24),	
	All Saints Day (Sat. nearest Nov 1)	
Currency	Finnish markka (mk) = 100 penni	
International airports	Helsinki: Vantaa Airport	
Electricity supply	220 V, 50 Hz, AC	

FRANCE

Capital city	Paris	
Other major cities	Bordeaux, Lille, Lyons, Marseilles, Nantes, Nice,	
	Strasbourg, Toulouse	
IDD code(s)	00-33 Greater Paris – 1 + 8 digits	
	The rest of France has no area codes	
Language(s)	French; English	
Time zone	GMT + 1; daylight saving April–Sept	
Office hours	Mon.–Fri. 9am–12.30pm, 3.30pm–6.30pm	
Public holidays	Jan 1	New Year's Day
	May 1	Labour Day
	May 8	Victory Day
	July 14	Bastille Day
	Aug 15	Assumption
	Nov 1	All Saints Day
	Nov 11	Armistice Day
	Dec 25	Christmas Day
Variable:	Easter Monday, Ascension Day,	
	Whit Monday	
Currency	French Franc (F) = 100 centimes	

International airports	Bordeaux: Mérignac Airport
	Lyons: Satolas Airport
	Marseilles: Mérignane/Marseille-Provence Airport
	Mulhouse: Basel-Mulhouse Airport
	Nice: Côte d'Azur Airport
	Paris: Charles de Gaulle Airport
	Paris: Orly Airport
	Strasbourg: Strasbourg-Entzheim Airport
	Toulouse: Blagnac Airport
Electricity supply	220 V, 50 Hz, AC. 110 V in some areas

GERMANY

Capital city	Bonn
Other major cities	Berlin, Köln, Düsseldorf, Frankfurt (am Main), Hamburg, Munich, Stuttgart
IDD code(s)	00-49: Berlin – 30, Bonn – 228; Köln – 221, Düsseldorf – 211, Frankfurt (am Main) – 69, Hamburg – 40, Munich – 89 Stuttgart – 711
Language(s)	German; English widely spoken
Time zone	GMT + 1
Office hours	Mon.–Fri. 8.30am or 9am–4.30pm or 5pm.
Public holidays	Jan 1 New Year's Day
	April 17
	April 20
	May 1 Labour Day
	May 28
	June 8
	Oct 3
	Nov 19
	Dec 25 Christmas Day
	Dec 26 St Stephen's Day
Variable:	Epiphany, Assumption
Currency	Deutschmark (DM) = 100 pfennige
International airports	Berlin: Schonefeld Airport
	Berlin: Tegel Airport
	Bremen: Bremen-Neuenland Airport
	Dresden: Klotzsche Airport
	Düsseldorf: Lohausen Airport

	Frankfurt Airport
	Hamburg: Fuhlsbuttel Airport
	Hanover: Langenhagen Airport
	Köln: Köln-Bonn (Wann) Airport
	Leipzig Airport
	Munich: Riem Airport
	Nürnberg Airport
	Stuttgart: Echterdingen Airport
Electricity supply	220 V AC

GREECE

Capital city	Athens
Other major cities	Heraklion, Larissa, Patras, Salonica
IDD code(s)	00-30: Athens – 1, Heraklion – 81 Larissa – 41, Patras – 61 Salonica – 31
Language(s)	Greek; English, German, French, Italian
Time zone	GMT + 2; daylight saving April–Sept
Office hours	Mon.–Fri. 8am–2/3pm, 5pm–7.30/8pm
	Government offices: 8am–3pm
Public holidays	Jan 1 New Year's Day
	Jan 6 Epiphany
	March 25 Independence Day
	May 1 Labour Day
	Aug 15 Assumption
	Oct 26 St Dimitrius Day (Salonica)
	Oct 28 'No' Day
	Dec 25 Christmas Day
	Dec 26 St Stephen's Day
Variable:	1st day of Lent, Good Friday, Easter Monday, Ascension Day, Whit Monday
Currency	Drachma (Dr)
International airports	Athens: Hellinikon Airport
	Corfu: Kerkyra Airport
	Heraklion Airport
	Rhodes: Maritsa Airport
	Salonica: Mikra Airport
Electricity supply	220 V, 50 Hz, AC

IRELAND, REPUBLIC OF (EIRE)

Capital city	Dublin
Other major cities	Cork, Galway, Limerick, Waterford
IDD code(s)	Dublin: 0001 (no other code required)
	Other parts: 00-35 Cork – 21, Galway – 91,
	Limerick – 61 Waterford – 51
Language(s)	English; Irish Gaelic
Time zone	GMT; daylight saving March–October
Office hours	Mon.–Fri. 9am–5.30pm
Public holidays	Jan 1 New Year's Day
	March 17 St Patrick's Day
	Dec 25 Christmas Day
	Dec 26 Boxing Day
Variable:	Good Friday, Easter Monday, 1st Monday in June,
	1st Monday in August, Last Monday in October
Currency	Irish punt (I£) = 100 pence
International airports	Cork Airport
	Dublin Airport
	Shannon Airport
Electricity supply	220 V, 50 Hz, AC

ITALY

Capital city	Rome
Other major cities	Bologna, Florence, Genoa, Milan, Naples,
	Palermo, Turin, Venice
IDD code(s)	00-39: Rome – 6, Bologna – 51, Florence – 55,
	Genoa – 10, Milan – 2, Naples – 81,
	Palermo – 91, Turin – 11 Venice – 41
Language(s)	Italian; English, French, German, Spanish
Time zone	GMT + 1; daylight saving April–Sept
Office hours	Mon.–Sat. 8/9am–1/1.30pm, 4/4.30/5pm–7pm
	Government offices: 8.30am–2pm
Public holidays	Jan 1 New Year's Day
	April 25 Liberation Day
	May 1 Labour Day
	Aug 15 Assumption
	Nov 1 All Saints Day
	Dec 8 Immaculate Conception

	Dec 25 Christmas Day
	Dec 26 St Stephen's Day
Variable:	Easter Monday
Currency	Lira (L)
International airports	Bologna Airport
	Florence: Pisa-Galileo Galilei Airport
	Genoa: Cristoforo Colombo Airport
	Milan: Forlanini-Linate Airport
	Milan: Malpensa Airport
	Naples: Capodichino Airport
	Rome: Ciampino Airport
	Rome: Leonardo da Vinci (Fiumicino)
	Sicily: Catania-Fontarossa Airport
	Turin: Casselle Airport
	Venice: Marco Polo-Tessera Airport
Electricity supply	220 V, 50 Hz, AC. 110 V in some areas

LIECHTENSTEIN

Capital city	Vaduz
IDD code(s)	00-41-75 no other code required
Language(s)	German; English
Time zone	GMT + 1; daylight saving April–Sept
Office hours	Mon.–Fri. 8am–noon, 2–5pm
Public holidays	Jan 1 New Year's Day
	Jan 6 Epiphany
	Feb 2 Candlemass
	Mar 19 St Joseph's Day
	Mar 25 Annunciation
	May 1 Labour Day
	Aug 15 Assumption
	Nov 1 All Saints Day
	Dec 8 Immaculate Conception
	Dec 25 Christmas Day
	Dec 26 St Stephen's Day
Variable:	Good Friday, Easter Monday, Ascension Day
	Whit Monday, Corpus Christi
Currency	Swiss Franc (Fr) = 100 Rappen
International airports	None: Travel from Zurich Airport, Switzerland
Electricity supply	220 V, 50 Hz, AC

LUXEMBOURG

Capital city	Luxembourg
IDD code(s)	00-352 No other code required
Language(s)	French, German; English
Time zone	GMT + 1; daylight saving April–Sept
Office hours	Mon.–Fri. 8.30am–noon, 2–4.30pm
Public holidays	Jan 1 New Year's Day
	May 1 Labour Day
	June 23 National Day
	Aug 15 Assumption
	Nov 1 All Saints Day
	Nov 2 All Souls Day
	Dec 25/26 Christmas
Variable:	1st Monday in Lent, Easter Monday, Ascension Day, Whit Monday
Currency	Luxembourg Franc (F) = 100 centimes
	Belgian Franc also used
International airports	Luxembourg: Findel Airport
Electricity supply	220 V, 50 Hz, AC

NETHERLANDS

Capital city	The Hague, Amsterdam (commercial capital)
Other major cities	Eindhoven, Groningen, Haarlem, Rotterdam, Utrecht
IDD code(s) 00-31:	Amsterdam – 20, Eindhoven – 40
	Groningen – 50, Haarlem – 23,
	The Hague – 70,
	Rotterdam – 10, Utrecht – 30
Language(s)	Dutch; English, German, French
Time zone	GMT + 1; daylight saving April–Sept
Office hours	Mon.–Fri. 9am–5pm
Public holidays	Jan 1 New Year's Day
	April 30 Queen's Birthday
	Dec 25/26 Christmas
Variable:	Good Friday, Easter Monday, Ascension Day, Whit Monday
Currency	Gulder (f, fl or gld) = 100 cents

International airports	Amsterdam: Schiphol Airport
	Maastricht Airport
	Rotterdam: Zestienhoven Airport
	The Hague: Amsterdam or Rotterdam airports
Electricity supply	220 V, 50 Hz, AC

NORWAY

Capital city	Oslo
Other major cities	Bergen, Drammen, Kristiansand, Stavanger, Tromsø, Trondheim
IDD code(s)	00-47: Oslo – 2, Bergen – 5, Drammen – 3, Kristiansand N. – 73, Kristiansand S. – 42, Stavanger – 4 Tromso – 83, Trondheim – 7
Language(s)	Norwegian; English, German
Time zone	GMT + 1; daylight saving April–Sept
Office hours	Summer: Mon.–Fri. 8am–3pm
	Winter: Mon.–Fri. 9am–4pm
Public holidays	Jan 1 New Year's Day
	May 1 May Day
	May 17 Constitution Day
	Dec 25/26 Christmas
Variable:	Maundy Thursday, Good Friday, Easter Monday, Ascension Day Whit Monday
Currency	Krone (kr) = 100 ore
International airports	Bergen: Flesland Airport
	Oslo: Fornebu Airport
	Stavanger: Sola Airport
Electricity supply	220 V, 50 Hz, AC

PORTUGAL

Capital city	Lisbon
Other major cities	Barreiro, Coimbra, Oporto, Setubal,
IDD code(s)	00-351: Lisbon – 1, Barreiro – 1 Coimbra – 39, Oporto – 2, Setubal – 65
Language(s)	Portuguese; Spanish, French, English

Time zone	GMT; daylight saving April–Sept
Office hours	Mon.-Fri. 9am–noon, 2–7pm.
	Government offices close at 5pm
Public holidays	Jan 1 New Year's Day
	April 25 Liberty Day
	May 1 Labour Day
	June 10 National Day
	Aug 15 Assumption
	Oct 5 Republic Day
	Nov 1 All Saints Day
	Dec 1 Independence Day
	Dec 8 Immaculate Conception
	Dec 25 Christmas Day
Variable:	Carnival, Good Friday, Corpus Christi
Currency	Escudo (esc) = 100 centavos
International airports	Faro Airport
	Lisbon: Portela Airport
	Madeira: Madeira-Funchal Airport
	Oporto: Pedras Rubras Airport
Electricity supply	220 V, 50 Hz, AC. 110 V in some regions

SPAIN

Capital city	Madrid
Other major cities	Barcelona, Bilbao, Seville, Valencia Zaragoza
IDD code(s)	00-34: Madrid – 1, Barcelona – 3, Bilbao – 4,
	Seville – 54, Valencia – 6. Zaragoza – 76
Language(s)	Spanish (Castilian); French, English, Catalan
Time zone	GMT + 1; daylight saving April–Sept
Office hours	Summer: Mon.–Fri., 8.30am–3pm
	Winter: Mon.–Fri., 9am–2pm, 4.30–7pm
Public holidays	Jan 1 New Year's Day
	Jan 6 Epiphany
	March 19 St Joseph's Day
	May 1 Labour Day
	July 25 St James's Day
	Aug 15 Assumption
	Oct 12 National Holiday
	Nov 1 All Saints Day
	Dec 6 Constitution Day

	Dec 8	Immaculate Conception
	Dec 25	Christmas
Variable:	Maundy Thursday, Good Friday, Easter Monday, Corpus Christi	
Currency	Peseta (pta)	
International airports	Alicante Airport	
	Barcelona: Muntadas Airport	
	Bilbao: Sondica Airport	
	Canary Islands: Las Palmas Airport	
	Ibiza Airport	
	Madrid: Barajas Airport	
	Malorca: Palma Airport	
	Malaga Airport	
	Santiago: Santiago Compostela Airport	
	Valencia Airport	
Electricity supply	220 V, 50 Hz, AC. 125 V in some areas – it is advisable to check	

SWEDEN

Capital city	Stockholm
Other major cities	Gothenburg, Malmo, Norrkoping, Uppsala, Vasteras
IDD code(s)	00-46: Stockholm – 8, Gothenburg – 31, Malmo – 40, Norrkoping – 11, Uppsala – 18, Vasteras – 21
Language(s)	Swedish; Finnish, English, German
Time zone	GMT + 1; daylight saving April–Sept
Office hours	Mon.–Fri. 8.30am–3/4/5.30pm
Public holidays	Jan 1 New Year's Day
	Jan 6 Epiphany
	May 1 Labour Day
	Dec 25/26 Christmas
Variable:	Good Friday, Easter Monday, Ascension Day, Whit Monday, Sat closest to Midsummer Day
Currency	Krona (kr) = 100 ore
International airports	Gothenburg: Landvetter Airport
	Malmo: Sturup Airport
	Stockholm: Arlanda Airport
Electricity supply	220 V, 50 Hz, AC.

SWITZERLAND

Capital city	Berne
Other major cities	Basle, Geneva, Lausanne, Zurich
IDD code(s)	00-41: Berne – 31, Basle – 61, Geneva – 22, Lausanne – 21, Zurich – 1
Language(s)	German, French; Italian, English
Time zone	GMT + 1; daylight saving April–Sept
Office hours	Mon.–Fri. 7.30am–5.30pm. Closed for 1–2 hours over lunchtime
Public holidays	Jan 1 New Year's Day
	Dec 25 Christmas Day
	Dec 26 St Stephen's Day
Variable:	Good Friday, Easter Monday, Ascension Day, Whit Monday
Currency	Swiss franc (Fr or F) = 100 centimes
International airports	Basle: Basle/Mulhouse Airport
	Berne: Belpmoos Airport
	Geneva: Cointrin Airport
	Zurich: Kloten Airport
Electricity supply	220 V, 50 Hz, AC.